# AMERICA'S
# COUNTRY SCHOOLS

# AMERICA'S
# COUNTRY SCHOOLS

Andrew Gulliford

THE PRESERVATION PRESS

The Preservation Press
National Trust for Historic Preservation
1785 Massachusetts Avenue, N.W.
Washington, D.C. 20036

The National Trust for Historic Preservation in the United States is the only private, nonprofit national organization chartered by Congress to encourage public participation in the preservation of sites, buildings and objects significant in American history and culture. Support is provided by membership dues, endowment funds, contributions and grants from federal agencies, including the U.S. Department of the Interior, under provisions of the National Historic Preservation Act of 1966. For information about membership, write to the Trust at the above address.

*Dedicated to all those pioneer schoolteachers*
*who taught in one-room schools*
*and made do with so little,*
*to Esma Lewis,*
*who came into the West when the country was young*
*and taught three generations of Colorado children,*
*and to Jesse Stuart (1906–84),*
*who believed in the spirit of the one-room schoolhouse*

Printed in the United States of America
88  87  86  85  84      5  4  3  2  1

Library of Congress Cataloging in Publication Data

Gulliford, Andrew.
  America's country schools.

  Bibliography: p.
  Includes index.
  1. Rural schools—United States—History.  2. School buildings—United States—History.  I. Title.
LB1567.G88  1984      371'.01'0973      84-17776
ISBN 0-89133-112-3

Andrew Gulliford taught elementary school for six years in rural western Colorado. From 1980 to 1982, he served as director of "Country School Legacy: Humanities on the Frontier," a project funded by the National Endowment for the Humanities on which *America's Country Schools* is based. He is currently a teaching fellow in the School of Journalism and a doctoral student in American culture at Bowling Green State University, Bowling Green, Ohio.

Edited by Diane Maddex, editor, The Preservation Press, and Gretchen Smith, associate editor.
Designed by Marc Alain Meadows and Robert Wiser, Meadows & Wiser, Washington, D.C.
Composed in Bembo by Monotype Composition Company, Inc., Baltimore, Md.
Printed on 70# Warren Patina by Collins Lithographing and Printing Company, Inc., Baltimore, Md.

Endleaves: *Snap the Whip* (1873), by Winslow Homer. (*Harper's Weekly*, Library of Congress)

# Contents

## Country School Legacy

## Country School Architecture

## Country School Preservation

# Foreword

Nostalgia always seems to figure in Americans' contemplations of the country school, even for those who know the reality behind the myth. I started my teaching career in a Wisconsin country school and remember well the low pay, lack of status, isolation, rigorous teaching duties and pervasive odors of oiled mops, soft coal, drying mittens, sweaty young bodies and the lean-to privy. Like Andrew Gulliford, I have studied the history of these buildings and rural education, and I know the hard realities behind them—realities that have contributed to modern social problems such as teenage violence, sexual harrassment, underfunding and budget cutting, teacher burn-out, poor teacher training, ethnic prejudice and the never-ending controversies between local control and centralized authority and between traditional pedagogy and informed professionalism.

Yet, I still regard country schools with affection, as do many Americans. Despite the realities mentioned, these schools seem to represent simpler times, surer values, clearer dedication and homely virtue. Many of these feelings derive from the buildings themselves: small, isolated in natural settings, they weather harmoniously with the environment, even when they have been abandoned to neglect. Because they are house-sized, they also lend themselves to preservation and adaptive use. It is entirely appropriate that rural schoolhouses be adapted to a wide variety of uses, because during their active lives these buildings doubled (and tripled) as dance halls, community centers, theaters and city halls and were now and then pressed into service as forts, courtrooms and hospitals. Some still find educational uses as part of a larger school system or, more frequently, as museums of early education, while many continue to function as community centers for day care, senior citizen services and meetings of 4–H clubs, Future Farmers of America, gun clubs and other recreational groups. Artists' studios, antiques shops and real estate offices are common commercial uses, and many schools are now charming homes.

The simple architectural unity of these structures disguised the remarkable complexity of the activities they contained, just as the presence of a single teacher disguised the versatility that rural school teaching required and as the isolated settings masked the interrelationships with local, regional and national concerns. The complexities and interrelationships emerge in this book in very human terms, for much of the story is told in the words of the participants themselves—teachers, students, neighbors. This approach is, in other words, a contextual approach to understanding historic structures, something that might well be emulated in other historic preservation projects that often seem limited to bricks and mortar. Regardless of how schoolhouses are adapted to new uses, each contains a rich heritage of memories that transcend the mundane, for unlike many commercial and industrial buildings, country schools were designed for the development of moral, spiritual and aesthetic values along with the practical skills of the three Rs.

The cradle of the country school was New England; the integration of the school into the political fabric of the nation occurred in the Northwest Territory. This book has a preponderance of material from the prairies and mountains of the West. This emphasis stems from the fact that the western region has the largest assemblage of documentary evidence about rural school buildings, education and life. How this came about is worth understanding, because it may point the way for projects in other regions and locales.

In several respects *America's Country Schools* is the final way station in an odyssey whose goal was to reassess the significance of the country school in American life and history. As Andrew recounts in the preface, in 1977 he and I attempted to win the support of the National Endowment for the Humanities for a nationwide survey of rural education, using the district school as a focus for the identification and cataloging of buildings, photographs, local documentary resources, oral histories, textbooks and teaching materials along with treatises on school design, teacher training, state and local curriculums and legislation, all to be encoded for computer coordination with U.S. Census tracts. Ultimately, this survey was to be a model that might be followed using other structures such as county courthouses and churches as focal points. It was indeed an ambitious idea that, if carried to fruition, would have created a data bank with the potential to unlock a network of documentary and artifactual materials touching the social, economic and spiritual lives of most Americans throughout our history. The program officers at the Endowment were not encouraging, however, partly because of the cost—our proposed budget was well over a million dollars—but also because the proposed project overlapped the purviews of a half dozen agencies. Both objections had practical validity, yet a stronger reason seemed to be that the subject was not important enough to pursue. Urban, not rural, was the watchword for historical investigations of the 1970s. I abandoned my efforts and turned over my materials to Andrew.

A little more than a year later, my telephone rang and Andrew announced that he had just been notified that the NEH had awarded the Mountain Plains Library Association a grant of $275,000 for a similar project that he had proposed, "Country School Legacy: Humanities on the Frontier." The main differences from the earlier application were that the project had been scaled down to eight predominantly rural western states and that it included a public program element, bringing discussions about education values into libraries and refurbished schoolhouses in cities, towns and hamlets throughout the West. Despite a tight schedule, all elements were completed, depository libraries were designated in each state and, to a large extent, a model for other such projects was established. The public programs, incidentally, generated additional documentary and factual information as well as encouraged a number of local movements for preservation of schoolhouses.

I was pleased to be invited to serve on the executive committee administering the project, along with Gail Parks, then education program director of the National Rural Center; Frank Fuller, a specialist in continuing education; Brenda G. Hawley of the Pikes Peak Library District in Colorado Springs and Joseph Anderson of the Nevada State Library, both librarians; and three officials of state humanities committees, Pat Marchese of Nevada, Delmont Oswald of Utah and Everett Albers of North Dakota, all of whom did important work to move the project along smoothly. I also finally met Andrew (our collaboration up to this time had been by telephone and letter). Andrew had been a fourth-grade teacher in Silt, Colo., but was already widely experienced both as a successful professional photographer who taught photography in the regional community college and as an oral historian and writer on state bicentennial projects. He had had no administrative experience, but from June 1980 to January 1982 he ably administered a quarter-million dollar budget and a part-time staff of researchers, writers, archivists, lecturers, media producers and community contacts in eight states. "Country School Legacy" was featured in numerous newspaper articles, in *American Heritage* and *History News* magazines and in the NEH's presentations to Congress and to Presidents Carter and Reagan. In 1982 the project was given an award of merit by the American Association for State and Local History.

This book, thus, is a final way station because it is constructed in large part from materials and knowledge generated by the Country School Legacy project, but it goes beyond that in widening the context to include the entire United States. The book can be used in many ways. First, I recommend it for browsing: In addition to the striking photographs and drawings, it has engaging anecdotes and excerpted passages full of harrowing adventures, humor, pathos and tragedy. Second, it is a comprehensive history of rural education. Third, it is a valuable resource for preservation and museum interpretation, providing comparisons of architectural types, accounts of school furnishings, curriculums and practices and lists of schoolhouses to observe and study. My only caution in using this as a resource and reference work is a happy one: Country schools were under local control, so your own school, if you are lucky enough to have one, is likely to embody highly individual departures from the descriptions. Getting to know your school is a personal thing, requiring much digging into school records, state curriculums, textbooks, local histories, photographs and reminiscences, not to mention real archeological digging. Such research leads to a fourth use of the book—as a spur to additional research efforts. Both Andrew and I have noticed in our travels the paucity of rural schools in the southeastern states, underscored by the list of preserved schools. Wisconsin has as many preserved schools as all the Southeast, Iowa twice the number. Extant country schools are scarce in Alabama, Louisiana, Mississippi, Missouri, North Carolina and Virginia. The lack of country schools in these states, of course, reflects the unique culture of the South. Elementary schooling in the home (sometimes in plantation schools such as at Stratford, the Lee home) or in private academies is part of the South's education legacy, as is illiteracy among many poor whites and blacks. However, photographs from the 1930s indicate the existence of many folk vernacular schoolhouses that should be sought out and preserved, for they are a vital part of the southern heritage that is missing.

The book can be used in one more way: It is an aid in looking to the future in American education. The 1980 census demonstrated that for the first time since Washington's era, the demographic movement has changed from urbanization to a return to country and town. Furthermore, school consolidation, professional specialization and busing have not proved to be the unalloyed blessings they were promised to be. Rightly or wrongly, parents are finding ways to circumvent state and federal regulations and reexert local control. As Andrew writes of an earlier time, "Rural people knew, however instinctively, that to lose their school meant to lose the focus of their community." Reviving the old country school as a panacea would, of course, be reactionary madness, for it would certainly reproduce the shortcomings that I noted earlier. Yet, country schools have virtues to be studied and considered with care. As I wrote once before, in "Educational Legacy: Rural One-Room Schoolhouses" (*Historic Preservation*, July-September 1977), about my own odyssey from teacher at the little Sunny Crest School to university professor: "The farther I travel from that quaint and fragrant beginning, the closer is my affinity to the goals of the resourceful and idealistic rural teacher, for whom no subject, course or age was separated from its neighbors, and with whom the school day became an invitation to circles of experience, widening outward from the common room so that child, community, nature, books and imagination were unified in an adventure of growing and learning."

We can still learn from the country school.

Fred E. H. Schroeder
*University of Minnesota—Duluth*

# Preface

Authors recognize when a book is finished, but they often wonder when it truly began. I started photographing and researching country schools after reading an article entitled "Educational Legacy: Rural One-Room Schoolhouses" in the July-September 1977 issue of *Historic Preservation*, the magazine of the National Trust for Historic Preservation, but I also grew up a mile from a one-room red-brick schoolhouse surrounded by large cottonwood trees on the high plains of Colorado. I enjoyed riding horseback to that schoolhouse, and I often wondered what it would have been like to attend school there.

Years later, after I began my first teaching job in Silt, Colo., my wife and I visited an abandoned one-room school in the Rocky Mountains late one fall afternoon when the aspen leaves were turning bright gold. Sitting cross-legged on the dusty, hardwood floor, we fantasized about what a marvelous summer home the white, weatherboard school could become. During those teaching years, I spent my spare hours photographing and interviewing old-timers in the rugged northwest corner of Colorado. Time and again the people I interviewed spoke about country schools. A one-room school education was a common thread that ran throughout their lives.

So this book began for a number of reasons, and because I am from the West it focuses primarily on the mountains and plains, although I have done research from coast to coast. This book is by no means comprehensive—the complete story of American country schools would fill several bookshelves. Rather, this book is an attempt to describe an icon and a building type unique to American education, culture and history.

Other authors have also found the topic fertile and fascinating. Excellent recent publications include *Education in Rural America: A Reassessment of Conventional Wisdom* (1977), edited by Jonathan P. Sher, *The Old Country School* (1982), by Wayne E. Fuller, *Pillars of the Republic: Common Schools and American Society, 1780–1860* (1983), by Carl F. Kaestle, and *Women Teachers on the Frontier* (1984), by Polly Welts Kaufman.

These books all help place the country school experience in its proper regional and national contexts, but they do not focus on the architectural and photographic dimensions featured in *America's Country Schools*. The photographs included here speak for themselves. A single image of a young woman schoolteacher standing with her pupils lined up beside her in front of a sod schoolhouse tells us a great deal about the cultural context of rural education. Some children are barefoot, while others wear sturdy new boots, knickers and bow ties. The teachers pictured are young and old, married and single, men and women, with an air about them that is both earnest and steadfast. The rural school buildings vary from crude dugouts and frame shacks to scaled-down examples of major architectural styles.

These photographs present the country school, primarily one room, in all its facets. Some of these photographs come from the Library of Congress, specifically the Farm Security Administration and Historic American Buildings Survey collections, as well as numerous state and local historical societies and private donors throughout the United States. Some of the finest documentary photographers who worked in rural America in the 1930s and 1940s have photographs featured in these pages. Country schools and country children were photographed by Lewis Hine, Dorothea Lange, Russell Lee, Arthur Rothstein, John Vachon and Marion Post Wolcott. The following photograph collections have been abbreviated in the credits: Farm Security Administration (FSA), Office of War Information (OWI) and Historic American Buildings Survey (HABS). I enjoyed taking some of the photographs myself, and these have been placed in the Country School Legacy collection (CSL), portions of which are deposited in university libraries throughout the Midwest. In the summer of 1978, my wife and I drove the length of the West Coast, and I stopped repeatedly to record on film what was obviously an integral part of the rural American landscape. One-room schools stood everywhere. I continued to photograph them across the United States.

In the preface to his book *Alistair Cooke's America* (1973), Cooke writes: "The exciting way to learn about the history of this country, and the experience of settling it, is to dig it out of the landscape." I agree. From my journal I find this entry: "We rolled into Shawnee, Wyo., last night with an orange and purple sun setting behind us and dozens of antelope on either side of the road. The last of the sun's rays reflected a rich amber in the school's western windows, and the bell tower with its four-cornered roof and large iron bell stood silhouetted in the twilight. The school stands on a slight knoll, and is a landmark visible for miles. . . ." And this entry from Spearfish Creek, Black Hills, S.D.: "The Centennial School is carefully boarded up and sits proudly on its little acre. The front part is fenced, but to the south a hillside makes a natural boundary and to the east runs a creek—dry now in the last days of August. A magnificent oak tree casts its morning shadow on the school. Children must have played in and up and around that tree every recess for years."

More than anything else, the isolation of rural schools appealed to me. Tucked away in forgotten canyons and mountain hollows or out on vast stretches of the Great Plains, the schools are often the only physical proof of communities and settlements that have withered and died because families have moved on. As a fourth-grade teacher who taught in a small mountain town, I know what it is like to be welcomed into a close-knit community. Yet, I could only theorize about those days when young and inexperienced schoolteachers taught 30 or 40 children in remote log cabin schools where the ink froze during the night and mountain lions drank from nearby springs.

I was convinced that the topic of country schools would make an excellent research project and that rural people of all ages would welcome the opportunity to talk about their schooling. I knew that in the West, where settlement had occurred later than anywhere else in the continental United States, it would be possible to interview both teachers and students who had been educated in one-room schools. At an oral history workshop I learned about the Mountain Plains Library Association, with member libraries and librarians in Colorado, Kansas, Nebraska, Nevada, North Dakota, South Dakota, Utah and Wyoming (recently Montana has also joined the association). I approached the MPLA executive board about sponsoring a public program grant from the National Endowment for the Humanities through the Division of Public Programs and the Library Program. The MPLA board gave its unanimous consent, and I spent six months writing the grant proposal. In 1980 the NEH provided a $275,000, two-year grant, and "Country School Legacy: Humanities on the Frontier," under my direction, was off and running with a research team of 24 librarians and humanities scholars in the eight states served by the MPLA. At that time no one could conceive of the magnitude of the project or the tremendous amount of public support we would generate. The original proposal called for 160 seminars; instead, we held more than 300 in libraries, museums, historical societies, nursing homes, public schools, colleges and universities. In addition to the primary research and oral history interviews, the project produced a 26–minute color film and two traveling exhibits tailor-made for each of the eight MPLA states.

Fiscal requirements of the grant called for voluntary donations of research time and use of facilities to approximate 50 percent of the cash award, or $138,000, but we generated $375,000 in in-kind donations because the project excited senior citizens, retired teachers, rural librarians, country school graduates, historians and architects from around the United States. Consequently, almost all of the interviews used in *America's Country Schools* were conducted for the project.

Thomas J. Schlereth writes in *Artifacts and the American Past* (1980), "The myths and icons that Americans have often made of their history are usually rooted in a nostalgic wish for a previous golden age that in reality never existed." The idealized icon of the one-room schoolhouse is certainly false. Many children suffered under short-tempered, ill-trained teachers forced to teach in buildings in which no self-respecting farmer would have kept his cows. Yet, other communities took pride in their schools and hired competent teachers at competitive wages.

In *America's Country Schools* selected aspects of the country school legacy are examined to help explain the all-pervasive myth of "the little red schoolhouse." School records, teachers' grade books and the schoolhouses all provide a marvelous mirror for gaining insight into rural areas. Studying country schools requires an in-depth analysis of local history materials because a complete set of state education reports does not exist for the period before 1900. Documentation does exist for one-room schools, however, in public records such as early newspaper files, real estate transfers, school board minutes, teachers' attendance records and private documents such as journals, photographs and unpublished manuscripts. Historic one-room schools can be easily identified on early county atlases and on updated quadrant maps. Because country schools were being used in substantial numbers as late as the 1940s, a wealth of information can be gleaned from oral history interviews.

For additional historical research or as an exercise in studying material culture, the buildings themselves are the most important document. Each mark on the floor and on the desks tells a story. Why do some schools have bell towers while others do not? Why are there no windows on certain school walls? Where was the stove, and what was used for fuel? Is that a bullet hole above the door? Has the school ever been moved? What artifacts can be found inside? Near Pleasant Lake, N.D., the Grand Harbor School still had an original bookcase well stocked with many early edition textbooks in August 1980. On the blackboard were the dates of every precinct election and the number of votes cast since June 1960. In 20 years no one had smudged or erased the chalk.

*America's Country Schools* begins with an attempt to place country schools in the larger social and historical framework of American education. As with all overviews, it is admittedly brief and necessarily incomplete. Chapter 2 describes the country school curriculum and provides a historical perspective for the current interest in the back-to-basics movement. Chapter 3 presents anecdotes and memoirs to describe teachers' lives on the western frontier at the close of the 19th century and the beginning of the 20th century. Chapter 4 features oral history material on the role country schools played as rural community centers. Chapter 5 was read under a different title at the 22nd annual meeting of the Western History Association; the material has been revised and expanded for inclusion here. Little else has been written about the assimilation of immigrants and minorities through rural schools. Chapter 6 looks at country schools still in operation in remote areas of the United States.

Part II features an examination of country school architecture. The last part describes efforts to preserve the heritage of country schools by individuals, local and county historical societies, state organizations and the National Park Service. Many schools are prime candidates for preservation. Others have been restored and are now successful museums visited by children eager to experience living history programs.

I hope that this book will be read by people concerned with American education, its past and its future, and by all the preservationists who have worked so hard to save one-room schoolhouses throughout the United States. I also hope that anyone who has ever seen a country school, taught in one, learned in one or wondered what went on inside those four unadorned walls will read this book and come away with a better understanding of a significant part of our American life and landscape.

Andrew Gulliford

# Acknowledgments

I find it impossible to acknowledge individually the hundreds of individuals who assisted in researching the Country School Legacy project during the two-year period of the National Endowment for the Humanities grant (1980–82), sponsored by the Mountain Plains Library Association.

Dozens of country school graduates and former one-room school teachers consented to be interviewed by Country School Legacy staff members and me. Publicity in the *National Retired Teachers Association Newsletter* resulted in correspondence with retired teachers from all over the United States who sent manuscripts describing their years teaching in one-room rural schools.

Information and photographs that appear in this book were previously published in *American Heritage, Annals of Wyoming, Christian Science Monitor, Education Times, Education Week, History News, Humanities, People and Policy: A Journal of Humanistic Perspectives on Colorado Issues* and *Utah Preservation/Restoration.* I thank the editors for their willingness to use my material and to allow me to reprint it.

Special thanks go to historical society staff members in the departments of historical research and historic preservation and in photographic archives in Colorado, Kansas, Nebraska, Nevada, North Dakota, South Dakota, Utah and Wyoming. In addition, each state historic preservation office and department of education was contacted by letter. Thank you for your cooperation and the country school material that you forwarded to me.

I am indebted to Dr. Fred E. H. Schroeder, professor of humanities, University of Minnesota–Duluth, for his willingness to work with a young, unknown historian-photographer, for his guidance and enthusiastic support of the Country School Legacy project and this book, which we first conceptualized in 1978, and for his scholarship, to which this book owes a great debt; to Randall Teeuwen, for his consistent encouragement, companionship and photographic expertise; to Brenda G. Hawley, associate director in charge of technical services for the Pikes Peak Library District, Colorado Springs, Colo., because she believes in documenting local history; to Joseph Edelen, executive secretary, Mountain Plains Library Association, I. D. Weeks Library, University of South Dakota, for his prudent management of the NEH grant funds; to Berkeley Lobanov, who designed the traveling exhibits, and to Country School Legacy staff members who helped with the research: in Colorado, Charles H. Johnson, Edwin and Joanne Dodds and Pat O'Neill; Kansas, Dr. Paul A. Haack, Donna R. Jones and Sarah E. Judge; Nebraska, Dr. Ernest Grundy, Jim Dertien, Sandra Scofield and J. V. Brummels; Nevada, Nancy Cummings, Hazel Potter and Dorothy Ritenour; North Dakota, Dr. Warren Henke, Mary and Robert Carlson and Daniel Rylance; South Dakota, Herbert Blakely, Philip Brown and Caroline Hatton; Utah, Jessie Embry and Scott Birkinshaw; and Wyoming, Robert J. Barthell, Ruby Preuit and

Milton Riske.

I also wish to express gratitude to Thomas Phelps, National Endowment for the Humanities; Mary M. Ison, Prints and Photographs Division, Library of Congress; Renzo Riddo, Heather Huyck and Thomas Solon, National Park Service; Barbara Sudler, Colorado Historical Society; James Schott, education and media consultant; Dr. Maxine Benson, Kansas State Historical Society; William Barton, Wyoming State Museum; Billie Gammon, Washburn-Norlands Foundation, Livermore, Maine; Carrie Papa, Monroe Schoolhouse Museum, and Hardyston Heritage Society, Hamburg, N.J.; Betty Ward, Silt Library, Silt, Colo.; the Interlibrary Loan Department, Colorado Reference Center, Denver Public Library; Dr. Leslie H. Fishel, Jr., director, Hayes Presidential Center, Fremont, Ohio; David L. Parke, Jr., associate director, The Farmers' Museum, Inc., Cooperstown, N.Y.; Dr. Kristine Fredriksson, curator of history, The Museum, Texas Tech University, Lubbock, Tex.; and Kathleen M. Olson, curator, Fort Missoula Historical Museum, Missoula, Mont.

I also wish to express gratitude to Thomas Phelps, National Endowment for the Humanities; Mary M. Ison, Prints and Photographs Division, Library of Congress; Renzo Riddo, Heather Huyck and Thomas Solon, National Park Service; Barbara Sudler, Colorado Historical Society; James Schott, education and media consultant; Dr. Maxine Benson, Kansas State Historical Society; William Barton, Wyoming State Museum; Billie Gammon, Washburn-Norlands Foundation, Livermore Falls, Maine; Carrie Papa, Monroe Schoolhouse Museum, and Hardyston Heritage Society, Hamburg, N.J.; Betty Ward, Silt Library, Silt, Colo.; the Interlibrary Loan Department, Colorado Reference Center, Denver Public Library; Dr. Leslie H. Fishel, Jr., director, Hayes Presidential Center, Fremont, Ohio; David L. Parke, Jr., associate director, The Farmers' Museum, Inc., Cooperstown, N.Y.; Dr. Kristine Fredriksson, curator of history, The Museum, Texas Tech University, Lubbock, Tex.; and Kathleen M. Olson, curator, Fort Missoula Historical Museum, Missoula, Mont.

I gratefully acknowledge permission to reprint quoted material from the following publishers and authors: American Association for State and Local History—"Schoolhouse Reading: What You Can Learn from Your Rural School," by Fred E. H. Schroeder. *History News*, April 1981; Kearney State College Press—"Poet in Residence at a Country School," by Donovan Welch. From *The Rarer Game*, copyright 1980; Nora Mohberg—*A Home for Agate*, by Nora Mohberg; John G. Neihardt Trust—*All Is But a Beginning*, by John G. Neihardt. Copyright 1972 John G. Neihardt. Permission courtesy of John G. Neihardt Trust, Hilda N. Petri, trustee; Popular Press—"The Little Red Schoolhouse," by Fred E. H. Schroeder. From *Icons of America*, 1978; *Psychology Today*—"Our Children Are Treated Like Idiots," by Bruno Bettelheim and Elizabeth Hall. From *Psychology Today*, July 1981; Viking Penguin—*East of Eden*, by John Steinbeck. Copyright 1952 by John Steinbeck. Copyright renewed 1980 by Elaine Steinbeck, John Steinbeck IV and Thomas Steinbeck. Reprinted by permission of Viking Penguin Inc.; Westminster Press—*Winter Thunder*, by Mari Sandoz. Copyright MCMLI by The Curtis Publishing Company. Copyright MCMLIV by Mari Sandoz. Used by permission of The Westminster Press, Philadelphia, Pa.; World Publishing— *To Teach, To Love,* by Jesse Stuart. Copyright 1970. Reprinted by permission of the Jesse Stuart Foundation; Houghton Mifflin Company—*Let Us Now Praise Famous Men,* by James Agee and Walker Evans. Copyright 1939 and 1940 by James Agee. Copyright © renewed 1969 by Mia Fritsch Agee. Reprinted by permission of Houghton Mifflin Company; Houghton Mifflin Company—*My Antonia,* by Willa Cather. Copyright 1918, 1926, 1946 by Willa Sibert Cather. Copyright 1954 by Edith Lewis. Copyright © renewed 1977 by Walter Havighurst. Reprinted by permission of Houghton Mifflin Company; Karl S. Rolvaag—*Peder Victorious,* by O. E. Rolvaag. Copyright 1929. Doubleday—*The Little Red Schoolhouse,* by Eric Sloane. Copyright 1972; James Rooney—quoted material from *Journey from Ignorant Ridge*; Raymond's Printing—*Early McCoy,* by Clark C. and Margaret Ewing.

Thanks are due Eugenia Marchello and typists Mary Ellison, Debbie Fritzlan, Pat Havens and Clara Straight. I am also indebted to my loving wife, Stephanie Moran, for her patience, understanding and eagerness to travel throughout remote areas of the United States while I photographed and researched country schools.

A last acknowledgment is due Diane Maddex, editor, and Gretchen Smith, associate editor, of the Preservation Press. I am deeply grateful for their professional guidance and their belief that a book was indeed hidden within the voluminous material of my manuscript and photographs. *America's Country Schools* has taken its final shape because of their skillful editing. Betsy K. Eisendrath assisted with copyediting, and Denise McHugh, Helen Cook and Becky Evans helped with production of this book.

It seemed, as I recall it, a lonely little house of scholarship, with its playground worn so bare, that even the months of sun and idleness failed to bring forth any grass. But that humble little school had a dignity of a fixed and far off purpose. . . . It was the outpost of civilization. It was the advance guard of the pioneer, driving the wilderness farther into the west. It was life preparing wistfully for the future.

James Rooney, in *Journey from Ignorant Ridge,* 1976

Still sits the school-house by the road,
A ragged beggar sunning;
Around it still the sumachs grow,
And blackberry-vines are running.

John Greenleaf Whittier, "In School-Days," 1869

*opposite*
East Lansing School, near Groton, N.Y., 1907. Teacher and students watch as the flag is raised at the start of the school day. (Verne Morton, permission of Verne Morton Collection, DeWitt Historical Society)

*above*
African School (c. 1825), Nantucket, Mass., built for blacks and later used as the African Baptist Society Church. (Jack E. Boucher, HABS)

*left*
Ledyard, Conn., school (c. 1910) designed according to an architectural plan book, 1940. (Jack Delano, FSA)

*below*
A little red schoolhouse (1813), Prescott, Mass. (HABS)

*top*
Forestdale School (1877), North Smithfield, R.I. (Walter Nebiker, Rhode Island Historic Preservation Commission)

*above*
Paradise School (1875), Middletown, R.I. (Jim Gibbs, Rhode Island Historic Preservation Commission)

*above*
Center Sandwich School (c. 1840), Center Sandwich, N.H., 1940. (Marion Post Wolcott, FSA)

*left*
Clapboard school (c. 1820), Gloucester, Mass. (HABS)

*right*
Hexagonal stone school (c. 1800), Darlington, Md. (HABS)

*above*
Frame school (c. 1840), North Branch, N.Y. (C. Beck, Library of Congress)

*right*
Schoolchildren at District No. 1 school (c. 1920), Troy, N.Y. (HABS)

*left*
Whigs Corners School (c. 1875), Whigs
Corners, N.Y., during a May Day celebration, 1913. (New York State Historical Association, Cooperstown)

*below*
Queen Anne–style school (c. 1880), East
Marion, Long Island, N.Y. (Library of
Congress)

*right*
School (c. 1870) for blacks, Gee's Bend, Ala., 1937. (Arthur Rothstein, FSA)

*below*
Greek Revival–style school (c. 1840), the first built in Pike County, Ala., 1939. (Marion Post Wolcott, FSA)

*right*
Interior of a black school (c. 1875), Anthoston, Ky., 1916. (Lewis W. Hine, Library of Congress)

*below*
Austere frame school (c. 1900), near Morehead, Ky., 1940. (Marion Post Wolcott, FSA)

*above*
Williamson School (c. 1900), Blanch, N.C., 1940. (Marion Post Wolcott, FSA)

*right*
Fugate School (c. 1900), Breathitt County, Ky., 1940. (Marion Post Wolcott, FSA)

*above*
Clapboard school (c. 1870), Minnesota, 1926. (John Runk, Minnesota Historical Society)

*left*
Bear Creek School (c. 1870), Iowa. (Iowa State Historical Department)

*below*
Bungalow-style school (c. 1915), Grundy County, Iowa, 1939. (Arthur Rothstein, FSA)

*right*
District school interior, Iowa, 1893.
(Iowa State Historical Department)

*below*
Eagle Harbor Schoolhouse (c. 1858),
Eagle Harbor, Mich., 1902. (James F.
O'Loughlin, Library of Congress)

*left*
Stonefield School (c. 1890), now restored at Nelson Dewey State Park,
Cassville, Wis. (National Trust for Historic Preservation collection)

*above*
Teacher and children outside a Wiscon-
sin school (c. 1880), 1939. (John
Vachon, FSA)

27

*right*
Salina School (c. 1890), Salina, Colo.
(James V. Sturtevant, Colorado Historical Society)

*right, middle*
Centennial School, District No. 9,
Montgomery County, Kans., 1892.
(Kansas State Historical Society)

*above*
Two-story clapboard school (c. 1890),
Barnes County, N.D. (State Historical
Society of North Dakota)

*right*
Sod school (c. 1890), Woods County,
Okla. (National Archives)

*left*
Log school (c. 1880), near Rushville, Neb., with teacher Phoebe Churchill and students. (Nebraska State Historical Society)

*below*
Board-and-batten school, Hecla, Mont., with teacher Blanche Lamont and pupils, 1893. (Henry W. Brown, Library of Congress)

*right*
Bishop School, near Wells, Nev.,
c. 1896. (Northeastern Nevada Museum)

*far right*
Pleasant Valley School (c. 1880), Oregon. (Oregon Historical Society)

*below*
Ophir School (c. 1890), Tooele County,
Utah. (Utah State Historical Society)

*right*
Adobe school (c. 1900), Taos County,
N.M., 1930s. (National Archives)

*below*
Picket-style log school (c. 1890), Berlin,
Nev., 1902. (Nevada Historical Society)

# COUNTRY SCHOOL LEGACY

# Country Schools in American Education

For almost 250 years the country school was the backbone of American education. As late as 1913, one-half of the schoolchildren in the United States were enrolled in the country's 212,000 one-room schools. Although only about 835 of these one-teacher, one-room schools, or .05 percent of all public school buildings, remain in use today, the country school continues to be a powerful cultural symbol to many Americans.

Perceptions of American country schools are clouded by two contradictory myths. One is that country schools are the poor stepchildren of American education—primitive buildings where, under intolerable conditions, young, inexperienced teachers try to instill in their students a modicum of knowledge. Another is the myth of the little red schoolhouse pleasantly situated beneath shade trees and full of bright, young students eager to learn their lessons and please their teacher. Neither view is wholly true nor wholly false. In some country schools, discipline was lax and learning incidental, but other schools were orderly, efficient and staunchly supported by the community, offering children an opportunity for education that few of their parents had enjoyed. Adults, too, were served by the local school. They came together at the school to hold meetings, cast ballots and participate in fund raisers and celebrations: The school housed the activities that joined people into a community, and the identity of rural communities became inextricably linked with their schools.

The building names reflected important beliefs and the values of the community as well as the names of states, generals, presidents, animals, cities and descriptions of locales. In Douglas County, Kans., parents named schools Harmony, Apple Pie and Good Intent. Near Eagle, Colo., one school was called the Bellyache School because of a cold mountain stream from which children drank. An Iowa school was named Puckerbrush and a Wyoming school Poison Spider. Other schools had names such as Brush Creek, Broken Bone, Windy Point, Dunkley, Fly Gulch, Moon Hill, Elk Head and even Barefoot Nation. Hundreds of schools were named Fairview and Prairie Rose. Schools were named for settlers who had donated the land (Mohler, Mercer, Hansen), families who had the most children in attendance (Ise, Petersen, Stumpf) and the dreams of settlers (Beulah, Excelsior, Victor and Enterprise). In Kansas, animal names for schools included Buzzard Roost, Wildcat, Oriole, White Eagle, Possum Hollow, Poor Puss and Snake Den. The names of faith included Mt. Carmel, Mt. Hope, Church and St. John. Names from locales included Rose Valley, Frog Pond, Flint Rock, Dry Creek, Elm Slough, Cottonwood and Grove Center. School boards frequently used the word "pleasant," as in Pleasant Hill, Pleasant Valley, Pleasant Ridge and Pleasant View. Schools were named after communities, and communities were named after schools. The Battlement School was located on Battlement Mesa in Parachute, Colo., in the Colorado River Valley; schools also were

*opposite*
*The District School* (1900), by William Ladd Taylor. In this early 19th-century schoolhouse, the schoolmaster dictates spelling words to his pupils, who are "toeing the line." (Library of Congress)

found on Mamm Creek, Divide Creek, Dry Hollow Creek and in Peach Valley.

From the beginning of the 18th century to the middle of the 20th century, schools in rural America were invariably one-room schools. If the farm population expanded, two one-room buildings could be joined together to form a larger school. If the population decreased, the building could be moved to another part of the school district or sold to another school board. The buildings were seldom larger than one room because they served an exclusive clientele, the children of families who lived in the immediate vicinity of the schoolhouse.

A one-room schoolhouse was a heavy responsibility for a single teacher who may have had 30 children in eight grades. The teacher's voice could not carry beyond the single classroom, and discipline proved difficult enough; there was no practical reason to add extra rooms or dividing walls. A one-room school may have had a small cloakroom to act as a buffer against frigid winter winds, but all instruction took place in one room. Larger country schools with a basement or an additional room were not built in rural areas until after the turn of the 20th century and then only in small numbers.

Country schools were predominantly one-room schools, and in this book the terms "one-room school," "country school" and "rural school" are considered synonymous unless otherwise indicated. In current education terminology, the phrase "one-teacher school" is used instead of "one-room school." But, historically, one-room schools often had more than one teacher. Only one person may have been on the school board payroll, although older pupils regularly helped younger pupils, and occasionally younger pupils helped adults as immigrant parents attended class to learn English and the American monetary system.

## Colonial Schooling

The history of country schools began in the colonial period with the evolution of a unique American concept—free, nonsectarian public education. In the New England colonies, education was an important issue. In 1647 the government of Massachusetts Bay enacted the first statute in America providing for the establishment of a school system. The preamble reflects anxious citizens' concern "that learning may not be buried in the graves of our fathers." Moreover, in Puritan New England, learning was considered a necessary part of preparation for salvation. Church and state were not separate. As Clifton Johnson noted in *Old-Time Schools and Schoolbooks* (1904), church elders formed schools so that students could learn to read the Bible.

The 1647 law provided for the establishment of petty schools, which became the forerunners of grammar schools. The law specified that "scholars"—i.e., children and apprentices—gain the "ability to read and understand the principles of religion and the capital laws of the country." The General Court of Massachusetts, "taking into consideration the great neglect of many parents and guardians in training up their children," required that the selectmen in each township make provision for building schools. Schoolhouses were constructed by parents in the district, and town committeemen met in the summer to consider repairs; usually, the repairs were never completed. Students endured broken windows and leaky ceilings, at least until cold weather set in.

Gradually, as the population increased in the colonies, subscription schools evolved, supported generally by well-to-do parents who could spend a few pennies a week on their children's education and spare their children between seasons on the farm. Financial support for these schools came from subscriptions, tuition, land rental fees and taxes. Rarely was the schoolteacher paid more than a subsistence wage, and payments frequently took the form of gifts of barley, grain and Indian corn. In 1644 a Massachusetts teacher was voted "six pounds toward the schoole & to tacke [tax] the benefet of the scollers provided that he teach six months in the yeare together."

Home schooling figured prominently in colonial America as did informal education. One type of informal school that evolved was the dame school. Unmarried or widowed older women often held classes in their own homes, where they knitted and sewed while encouraging children to learn to read and write—if only their names and a few popular lines from the Bible. Girls also learned household skills such as needlework that they would use in later life as wives and mothers; boys learned to help around the farm or at the forge and by the age of 12 were frequently apprenticed to a tradesman. Wealthy parents hired tutors to instruct their sons in the classics.

Formal education in a classroom was a luxury enjoyed primarily by white middle- and upper-class children whose schooling was not a drain on their parents' financial resources. Boys destined for the ministry, their father's firm or a clerk's office stayed in school longer and learned academic and business skills. Although education was far from standardized and teaching methods differed widely, the consensus was that teachers who spared the rod would spoil the child. Children from poor families, on the other hand, were encouraged from an early age to make their own way in life. Opportunities for them to learn to read or write were haphazard or nonexistent.

Teachers in colonial schools taught reading, writing and arithmetic only as secondary elements; the primary focus was on Scripture, biblical teachings and rudimentary Latin. Texts varied widely in quality and moral content. Most books, such as *The Universalist Spelling Book* and *The New England Primer,* had fables and woodcuts demonstrating the consequences of any wrongdoing and serious injury that would befall a student who lied, cheated or stole. A homily included in many texts of the period admonished:

Good children must

| | |
|---|---|
| Fear God all day, | Love Christ alway, |
| Parents obey, | In secret pray, |
| No false things say, | Mind little play, |
| By no sin stray, | Make no delay |

In loving good.

In the 17th and 18th centuries, parents believed that their children were born into sin. By the beginning of the 19th century, the influence of philosophers of the Age of Enlightenment, particularly John Locke, had stimulated a profound change in beliefs about children and education. In the 17th century children were considered inherently evil, but by the 19th century parents believed their children were inherently good. Children were then considered to have minds like blank slates; they were encouraged to learn a variety of skills and subjects in addition to biblical injunctions.

*Educating an Electorate*

Thomas Jefferson, believing that the people are the safest depositories of government, thought free public education imperative for a strong democracy. Only educated citizens would be able to substantiate his belief that "the government that governs least, governs best." His concept of allocating land in the Northwest Territory for public education purposes became the basis of the Land Ordinance of 1784, which the Confederation of States passed as the Northwest Ordinances of 1785 and 1787. These laws provided a legal framework for education that was adopted throughout the Northwest Territory (which would become the states of Ohio, Illinois, Indiana, Wisconsin and Michigan) and, later, by all the western states. Education provisions in the Northwest Ordinances allowed public lands to be leased to benefit local schools. As new states were formed, the federal government allotted one section in every township of 36 sections for support of common schools, a term used until 1875 to describe one-room country schools. Because of the abundance of free land, however, revenues from land leases proved an ineffective source of funding for education. As a result, in the mid-1820s Congress approved the sale of public lands and states were to establish permanent funds to endow public schools. However, much of the land was sold to settlers and speculators at ridiculously low prices, even for the frontier, and officials neglected, diverted or fraudulently spent the proceeds. As a result, in many communities the only reliable source of funding for schools came from the parents themselves.

Because land-holding patterns varied greatly throughout the country, schools were not established in the same manner. The New England township model, which was adopted in the Northwest Territory, was not used in the South, where, because of the lack of available public lands to assist in school funding, private schools and home tutoring flourished in place of common schools. As a result, public schools were never as prominent in the South as they were in other parts of the United States.

In the 19th century, free public education was still more a goal than an actuality. By the 1830s private and subscription schools in the East had been replaced by public schools. As the frontier moved westward, each new settlement, once it had provided for its first winter's needs, turned its attention to education. School terms varied from a few weeks to a few months. Usually a traveling schoolteacher made an appearance or a widow or single young woman took charge of teaching children their letters. Land grant monies to support education remained sequestered by state treasurers and rarely trickled down to help fund local schools, so parents themselves provided for their children's

Country school students in a mining district in the Colorado Rockies. (Pike's Peak Library District, Colorado Springs, Colo.)

Frame school (c. 1900), Amherst, Neb. The bell tower is a notable embellishment on this vernacular school. (Solomon D. Butcher Collection, Nebraska State Historical Society)

Barefoot students in front of their board-and-batten school (c. 1870) in the North Carolina mountains. (Margaret W. Morley, North Carolina Division of Archives and History)

education. Teachers' salaries reflected the relative wealth and stability of the families that supported local schools.

Because rural one-room schools were often isolated, better teachers frequently sought jobs in town schools; there they received higher pay and were not under the thumb of rural school trustees, who often had limited schooling and a shortsighted view of education. Thus, many rural schools were forced to accept teachers of lesser credentials and limited ability. In some cases, teachers simply perpetuated the narrow beliefs and ignorance of the community.

Rural schools were frequently overcrowded, materials were hard to obtain, and repairs and improvements were subject to the financial whims of parsimonious school boards hesitant even to replace dog-eared textbooks. The standard teaching tool was *McGuffey's Eclectic Readers*, and the standard teaching methods were rote memorization and recitation. Carl F. Kaestle has noted in *Pillars of the Republic* (1983) that "from transient teachers, crowded rooms and stiffled toddlers to community spelling bees and delightful sleigh rides, the rural schools of the early nineteenth century reflected the close local control, the broad parental discipline, the parsimony and the limited educational needs of rural communities in the early American republic." Kaestle concludes, "Rural district schools were much the same in 1830 as they had been in 1780." However, sex-role stereotyping diminished somewhat by the mid-19th century, when girls began to attend public schools regularly.

By the mid-19th century, important educators such as Horace Mann in Massachusetts, John Pierce in Michigan, Samuel Lewis in Ohio and

Henry Barnard in Connecticut had come to view education as a public enterprise, as did Emma Willard, Catharine Beecher and Mary Lyon, who urged women to become teachers. Education reformers argued that only an educated electorate could make reasonable choices at the ballot box, but the concept of "taxing one man's property to educate another man's child" created opposition to public education. In *The Transformation of the School* (1964), Lawrence A. Cremin notes, "The fight for free schools was a bitter one and for 25 years the outcome was uncertain. Local elections were fought, won and lost on the school issue. . . . The tide of educational reform flowed in one state only to ebb in another. Legislation passed one year was sometimes repealed the next." The struggle for tax-supported public education has been described as second only to the abolition of slavery in the intensity of emotions it aroused, but Horace Mann offered an ingenious solution—place control of local schools in the hands of the public. Antagonism towards taxation, offered as an alternative to the ineffectual establishment of interest-bearing permanent school funds, diminished with the rising idealism that combined education and national progress. Over-zealous reformers also believed that "every schoolhouse opened closes a jail." By 1860 the question of free public education had been largely settled, and the concept became firmly established as an American ideal.

Interior, Comanche County School, near Protection, Kans., 1901. (CSL)

## Education Reforms

Before the Civil War, the American education system, if it could be called that, suffered from a lack of standardization and direction. In 1840 one-fourth of the adult population was illiterate. Progressivism did not affect American education until the 1890s and did not take hold in rural areas until after the turn of the century. As urban schools began to improve and provide a curriculum relevant to the needs of their students, country schools began to decline in the opinions of American educators. Caught up in the new spirit of progressivism, educators sought to standardize textbooks and learning skills. The McGuffey readers, which had served country schools faithfully for 50 years, fell into disrepute. Rote memorization and recitation seemed trite. The new curriculum emphasis was on manual training or woodworking for boys and home economics for girls. Sexual stereotyping was reinforced: Girls were to study domestic science, and boys were to learn a trade.

These reforms were intended primarily to aid urban students in their adjustment to an industrial society and to instill a sense of teamwork in the replication of manual tasks, similar to chores that farm children completed daily. Educator John Dewey believed that rural students learned more from doing household chores and farm work than they learned in school. The new education, advocated by Dewey and his followers, stressed an awareness of culture and art, which did not exist in most country school curriculums. Dewey also thought it imperative to teach the spirit of cooperation, an idea that had always been integral to country school education. School administrators introduced manual training in imitation of farm chores, and they encouraged classroom teamwork with the project method, in which several students worked together to complete a common assignment. Yet, the administrators criticized country schools as being out of step with the 20th century.

Educators emphasized the need to assimilate the thousands of immigrant children jammed into schools in New York, Pittsburgh, Cleveland and Chicago. Today, revisionist historians believe that many of the altruistic motives of early 20th-century school reformers served only to strip immigrants of their culture. Similarly, the standardization of country schools destroyed local community autonomy and students' understanding of their own indigenous regional backgrounds.

Country schools, however isolated, felt pressures to reform. States passed legislation requiring that all instruction be in English, so children of immigrants were forced to learn the language quickly. County superintendents began to use standardized tests for eighth-grade graduates. New stress was placed on penmanship, particularly the Palmer Method, and teachers and superintendents sought to uplift and enlighten their charges. While America was coming to terms with child labor problems and Jane Addams was beginning her work in the tenements, country school administrators were heeding the call to reform education, a major component of which was consolidation. Most educators sought not to improve the quality of country schools but rather to eliminate them entirely in favor of more "progressive" consolidated schools with more rooms, more teachers and more students in one place.

### School Consolidation

Part of the impetus for school consolidation came from the federal government. In 1908 President Theodore Roosevelt formed the National Commission on Country Life to find solutions for rural problems, not the least of which was "the rural school problem." The country life movement, whose slogan was "Better farming, better business, better living," introduced new farming and soil conservation techniques and demonstrated the more efficient use of mechanized agricultural equipment. Its advocates, often at odds with country residents themselves, believed that country schools should be consolidated. Paved roads and the advent of automobiles and school buses eliminated the need to have country schools within walking distance of pupils. A half dozen one-room ungraded schools could be consolidated into one larger school with separate grades in separate classrooms. In the interest of efficiency, education became compartmentalized.

Throughout the United States, civic leaders and educators jumped on the bandwagon to save rural students from their own schools. State school superintendents provided architectural plans for the "model" rural schools, but the real goal was to make them miniature duplicates of their urban counterparts. One of the best spokesmen for the consolidation movement was N. C. MacDonald, a rural school specialist and state school superintendent for North Dakota. The following remarks, from his address entitled "A Square Deal for the Country Boy," given in 1911 before the North Dakota Educational Association, set forth his reasons for consolidation and professionalization in education (although he neglected to cite the condition of country school girl students).

> The title . . . implies that [the country boy] has not been treated fairly. And such is the case. . . . . he has been overworked, deprived of rest, play and school on the farm . . . he has been driven, bribed, jeered, flattered, hounded, goaded, ridiculed into leaving the farm home poorly equipped for the town and city. At any rate, to the city he has come in ever increasing hundreds in the last decade, there to eke out a precarious existence or to fall prey to designing and unscrupulous money-mad men, or to add to the great army of the city unemployed. . . .
>
> For the past two months some 5,000 rural and small town schools have been in session, but with less than 10 percent of those boys in the upper grades that ought to be there. Where are they? . . . They are out doing the work of full grown men, threshing, plowing and marketing grain. . . .
>
> All this physical hardship has nearly made a physical wreck of the country boy as a class. He should stand upright as an arrow, full of chest, square of shoulder, strong of limb, and clear of eye. But, look at him, the product—or rather, the by-product of our boasted twentieth century civilization. He is 16, but his body is nearly wrecked; for, is he not stooped, hollow-chested, round-shouldered, shambling in his walk, produced by overwork and poor school teaching. . . .

Other state school superintendents also exerted pressure on rural schools to consolidate by linking state financial support for one-room schools to compulsory attendance laws. School superintendents advised state legislatures to provide additional funding for consolidated schools. Mabel Carney, in *Country Life and the Country School* (1912), stated that by September 1909, 1,402 one-room schools in Indiana had been abandoned; in 1911 Indiana reported 13 consolidated schools; Minnesota, 60; Kansas, 75; Washington, 120; Idaho, 20; Oklahoma, 86; Virginia, 100; Louisiana, 210; and Iowa, 60. In 1913 the Iowa legislature

Boys wait for the school bus in the morning, Malhour County, Ore., 1939. (Dorothea Lange, FSA)

Federal-style clapboard school (c. 1840), Catskill Mountains, N.Y., 1949. This school was one of 28 in the area that had recently been consolidated. (National Archives)

Slater School (1918), Slater, Wyo. In use until 1944, this was a standard school meeting state design and construction requirements initiated during the early 1900s. (Andrew Gulliford)

passed a bill providing state aid for consolidated schools offering instruction in agriculture, domestic science and manual training.

The issue of rural school consolidation created bitter debate throughout the United States. A spate of books published between 1908 and 1925 advocated rural school consolidation, often in glowing terms. Carney acknowledged that "the one-teacher school system, as frequently maintained, has served humanity long and well. . . . But it has served its day. . . . It has no place in the highly complicated social life of today, in which competition is the keynote of the age. . ." (*Country Life and the Country School*). In his influential book, *Rural Life and Education* (1914), Ellwood P. Cubberly, professor of education at Stanford University, viewed consolidation as a way to "redirect and revitalize" country schools and "a system better adapted to the needs of rural people."

At the beginning of the 19th century, some rural Americans had questioned the value of public education in small district schools, but by the beginning of the 20th century, those same schools had become an integral part of country life. As professional educators and school administrators pushed for consolidation, country schools were gradually abandoned. The buildings fell into disrepair or were scavenged for available lumber. Windows were broken, roofs collapsed, and schools were left to deteriorate.

Rural people knew, however instinctively, that to lose their school meant to lose the focus of their community. Boards and trustees of one-room schools went to great lengths to try to keep their schools open; they specifically hired teachers with children of their own who would attend the school and augment declining enrollment. The loss of a one-room school symbolized an abrupt entry into the 20th century and a shattering of the community spirit of the original settlers. Parents feared that if their children left the community to attend school elsewhere, they might one day leave permanently. And as country schools consolidated, the exodus from the farms increased.

School consolidation bitterly polarized rural communities and set neighbor against neighbor. The issues were not as simple as increased taxes and better schooling for children. Parents realized that the centralization of rural schools meant the beginning of the end for rural farm life as they had known it. C. G. Sargent wrote in his introduction to *The Rural and Village Schools of Colorado* (1914), "When a movement was started to reorganize some of the districts where conditions were not favorable, bitter and determined opposition arose." Sargent commented on the situation in a Colorado county west of the Continental Divide: "Few movements within the history of the county have aroused more interest or provoked more discussion." He was describing rural Colorado, but he could have been describing the consolidation controversy in any state in the nation.

The federal government's view of rural schools in 1919 was set forth by H. W. Foght in the Bureau of Education's bulletin "Rural Education." This study was a general overview of rural education with information on the typical rural school problems of inadequate supervision, desperate financial needs and below-standard curriculums. The report indicates that approximately 200,000 one-teacher schools were still in use in rural communities and that these provided the only means of education for the large majority of rural children. Foght noted that 19 states had reorganized their schools along county lines but suggested that "in broken mountain districts or in sections of the country cut by streams and ragged coast lines, or in sparsely settled regions, such reorganization is seldom feasible and should not be urged."

The traditional myth of the little red schoolhouse as a citadel for learning has been seriously exaggerated, and yet the problem of undereducated rural children could not be solved simply by eliminating one-room schools. In *Let Us Now Praise Famous Men* (1941), James Agee wrote of the plight of rural children attending a consolidated school in Cookstown, Ala., in 1936: "For they would be at a disadvantage if they had more of it, and at a disadvantage if they had none, and they are at a disadvantage in the little they have; and it would be hard and perhaps impossible to say in which way their disadvantage would be greatest." The school building he described as "a recently built windowy 'healthful' red brick and white-trimmed structure which perfectly exemplifies the American genius for sterility, unimagination and general gutlessness in meeting any opportunity for 'reform' or 'improvement.' "

During the school year 1934–35, California operated 1,360 one-room schools, and in 32 California counties one-room schools represented more than 50 percent of the school buildings; across the nation, however, one-room schools continued to close. By 1938 more than 19,000 one-room schools had been abandoned near urban areas and throughout the Midwest. The closing of one-room country schools forever changed the rural American landscape and diminished close community ties and a sense of social cohesion among rural Americans. Historian Wayne E. Fuller in *The Old Country School* (1982) acknowledges, "In all America there was, perhaps, no better symbol of the shared community life people remembered than the one-room schoolhouse standing in the center of an independent school district. . . . The people of the district had voted for its construction, picked the place where it would stand and controlled its use when it was completed." He concludes: "At one stage or another of this process, they had, in most cases, even fought over it as families fight; yet it belonged to all the district's families, and because it was their own, most people in the community were interested in what took place there."

Educators had thought that if school plans included full basements that could be used for community purposes, districts would vote for new school construction. Many districts did go along with consolidation plans, but not without a long backward glance at the utilitarian buildings they were abandoning. Plans for South Dakota standardized schools called for full basements that would provide a community room with an arched stage and gasoline generators to make electricity; a few of those schools were built in the 1920s, and they remain standing.

The American Association of School Administrators, which had always favored consolidation, made this prophetic statement in 1939 in *Schools in Small Communities*:

> Keep the schools and the government of the schools close to the people, so that the citizens generally, including the parents and taxpayers, may know what their schools

are doing, and may have an effective voice in the school program. . . . The relationship of the schools to the natural community and the closeness of the school to the people are of first-rate educational significance and are not to be sacrificed in the interest of "efficiency." If such a sacrifice is made to establish economical districts, we will find in a generation that something of deep significance which money cannot buy has been destroyed.

School consolidation increased after World War II and continued rapidly for 20 years until the early 1960s. In a 1950 federal report entitled "The One-Teacher School: Its Midcentury Status," Walter H. Gaumnitz and David T. Blose confirmed the downward trend in the nation's one-teacher schools as farms grew larger and more mechanized and the population shifted from rural areas to cities and from rural states to urban states. The report pointed out that only the north central prairie region, characterized by "rigorous winters, sparse population, wide open spaces, and undeveloped year-round roads," continued to have two-thirds or more of its schools as one-teacher schools. Although by 1947 one-teacher schools still served one and a half million students, half of the one-teacher schools in the nation had closed since 1917.

In consolidating schools, reformers not only sent children out of their communities to school, they also instituted a set of values alien to those of rural students. Writing about rural communities and school consolidation, sociologist Robert Coles states in his foreword to *Education in Rural America*, edited by Jonathan P. Sher (1977), "A people possessed of its own intelligence and sensibility is given credit for neither, made the subject of all sorts of manipulative schemes, sometimes rather costly, in the name of 'modernization' or progress. . . . No one is urging that the past be romanticized. The·point is not to call for a self-indulgent nostalgia." Coles goes on to describe how rural communities do need outside assistance but also "how very much they have to offer us, to teach us, even at times to help us out."

Out of necessity country schools have been practicing for more than a century what the most sophisticated education systems now encourage—smaller classrooms, programs that allow students to progress at their own rate and students who help each other learn. We seem to have come full circle in our appreciation of the community values inherent in the one-room school, where the teacher taught students of various ages and abilities in a familylike atmosphere. Small private, parochial and alternative schools based on the one-room school model have begun to flourish. Many former country school teachers and students share the belief of Ellis Ford Hartford, who wrote in *The Little White Schoolhouse* (1977), "It may be found that there was more to the little white schoolhouse and the neighborhood surrounding it than is suggested by mere nostalgic recollection and remembrances of former pupils. . . . Perhaps it is pertinent to suggest that Americans might well seek some of the same strengths and values in their diverse patterns of communities. . . ."

Country schools have always been important in the rural areas of this nation, as a symbol both of cultural continuity and of the opportunities to be gained from education. The role of country schools in America is not over.

Brush College, Iowa's smallest "college," in 1966, its final year of operation. (Leslie C. Swanson)

# The Four Rs:
# Reading, Writing, Arithmetic, Recitation

The teaching and learning that took place in country schools was, at best, a fulfillment of Thomas Jefferson's vision of public education and, at worst, a haphazard process. In all cases, the quality of education was determined by the teacher's abilities, the local community's resources and the students themselves.

In the mid-19th century, the school year was divided into two terms. The typical summer term extended over five months, from May to August or September. The winter term varied from state to state, depending on local planting and harvesting times; it generally began after harvest in November and continued until just before spring plowing, usually around early April. After 1900 the school year was standardized into one nine-month term, beginning in September and ending in May.

The ages of the students varied considerably. Before the Civil War, children in rural areas were sent to school at the age of three or four, partly to get them out of the house and partly because parents believed that the school was an extension of the family and, therefore, the proper place for children. In Ohio between 1845 and 1864, children of three or four began learning how to spell. Older girls and boys would watch over their younger brothers and sisters. By observing the other students in the classroom, the four-year-olds learned basic skills. Although by 1860 schools in eastern towns and cities were discouraging children from entering school before the age of six, country schools did not raise the minimum age until a decade later.

Husky farm boys as old as 17 and 18 also attended country schools. Before the advent of the mechanical reaper and other labor-saving farm machinery, older children were expected to work in the fields. Consequently, many farm boys could complete their education only during the winter terms, when farm work was slack. For this reason, most districts preferred to hire a man teacher for the winter months. During the winter, all subjects were taught, even algebra. Frequently, adult farmhands and immigrants who had little education also would attend.

Students were organized not by grade but according to general level of ability. They often sat two to a desk and shared the same books. Impaired students had to get by as best they could without the benefit of eyeglasses or hearing aids. Because country schools functioned as ungraded classrooms, teachers had to prepare lessons to accommodate the learning ability and progress of each child. With a school full of pupils who ranged in age from six to 16, a teacher giving instruction in reading, writing, arithmetic and health had to prepare a variety of individualized lessons. The teacher could prepare similar assignments and drills for the nine-year-olds, but students who were 14 required different lessons, as did those children who were six or 12. A teacher with 20 students of varying ages and skills had to prepare as many as 40 daily lessons.

Children were exposed to every lesson many times; they heard it

*opposite*
Rosebud Agency School (c. 1895), Nebraska. Teacher Ella J. Bruner instructed white children in this school held in a doctor's house on the reservation. (Nebraska State Historical Society)

time after time as older students recited for the teacher in front of the room and then, later, read it themselves from their texts. Each child worked at his or her own pace and was promoted from reader to reader when the teacher believed that each was ready. Former country school student Bill May from the S Bar S Ranch near Steamboat Springs, Colo., reports that one-room schools provided "the almost unlimited opportunity for the 'gifted' pupil to advance. By having the chance to hear older students recite (after their own assignment was completed), it was not uncommon for children in the fifth or sixth grade (and sometimes even younger) to have mastered practically everything presented to the seventh and eighth grades."

A busy teacher often encouraged assistance from older pupils. Older students helped younger ones with their work and carried out classroom duties such as firing the stove, filling the water buckets and heating lunches. In *Memoirs of South Dakota Retired Teachers* (1976), edited by Ruth Morgan, Floyd Cocking vividly recalls his first year at the Pringle School in Custer County:

> One of my seventh grade girls was pretty sharp, and I had to hustle to keep her busy and challenged. And then I found the solution. Two of my fifth graders seemed to need more personal help than I had time to give, so I had Anne start helping them. Within a week, she was my full-fledged teacher aide during parts of the day. She loved it. So did I. And everyone profited from it. Of course, she did not get paid. But she got a better education.

Strict discipline prevailed in most country schools. During the colonial period, schoolmasters assumed their charges to be "morally deficient" and stressed the hellfire-and-brimstone philosophy of the Puritans. Teachers demanded immediate obedience and, for the most part, they got it. Spontaneity was not allowed in the classroom until the latter part of the 19th century. In urban schools the regimentation was almost militaristic, but in the country, smaller classes and individualized instruction contributed to a more relaxed environment.

Classroom conditions, too, were a factor in the education process. Teachers and students were forced to endure cramped classrooms and overcrowding. In winter there were additional hardships. The smells of wet wool clothes and bags of asafetida, an offensive-smelling resinous material hung around children's necks as health amulets, drove many teachers to open the windows, only to be met by a blast of icy wind. As soon as the window was closed, the air again became stuffy. Students alternately froze and roasted, depending on their proximity to the potbellied stove. The corners of the room could be almost as cold as the out-of-doors. The constant freezing and thawing of the children's feet often gave them chilblains, which made their feet itch intensely as they warmed up, so that throughout the day the room resounded with the constant noise of boots shuffling under desks.

## The Framework of the Day

The framework of a school day varied from region to region and from period to period. The following description of the school day is drawn from 1842 records of the Norlands School, District No. 7, Livermore Falls, Maine, but is representative of country schools during the mid-

Morton School, District No. 4, near Groton, N.Y., 1907. Students practiced their arithmetic skills at the blackboard. (Verne Morton, permission of Verne Morton Collection, Dewitt Historical Society)

19th century. Generally, school was in session from 8:00 a.m. to 4:00 p.m. When the teacher rang the bell—the bell in the bell tower, if the school had one, or a hand bell—to signal the beginning of the school day, the students formed two lines outside the school, one for the girls and one for the boys. The girls entered first and stood by their desks or benches as the boys entered. The teacher greeted the students, the students were seated, and the morning exercises began. These exercises could be religious, consisting of Bible readings or moral instruction.

No time was wasted in getting to work. The teacher explained the assignments, making sure that all students had textbooks, slates and slate pencils. The students were divided into groups, according to the books they read. The groups alternated their tasks: The younger students were called to the front of the room first to recite their lessons, while the older students worked on other assignments. Then, the older students recited their lessons, while the younger ones worked on their assignments. Recitation, memorization, copying and reading went on simultaneously. As the students worked on their assignments, the teacher walked up and down the aisles, checking each student's work.

Jones School, near Groton, N.Y., 1907. Students play drop-the-handkerchief. (Verne Morton, permission of Verne Morton Collection, DeWitt Historical Society)

At midmorning, the students were allowed to "turn out" briefly for privy privileges, the girls first and then the boys, and then followed a short recess. After doing farm chores before dawn and sitting in a stuffy classroom for a few hours, the children could hardly wait for recess. Running, jumping, leaping, ducking, pushing the smaller children—all were standard recess activities. Wise teachers stayed inside, where their territory was well defined.

When everyone was back in the classroom, arithmetic assignments were made. When the youngest children completed their slate work, the teacher checked it and sent them to the back of the room to work on other assignments, while the older students were called to the front of the room to be quizzed on their grasp of mathematics. Next followed the writing lesson. The teacher passed out the copybooks, in which students copied maxims written on the blackboard, pondering the meaning of the maxims as they worked. The younger students practiced writing their names by making the letters with a dry quill pen before actually using ink. At the close of the writing lesson, the class discussed the meaning of the maxims.

At noon, classes were interrupted for an hour for lunch. The students cleared their desks and sat at attention, hands folded on their desks. Each row of students, in turn, went to the entry to get their lunch pails and tin dippers of water. In warm weather, many teachers allowed the students to eat their lunches outside. After lunch, the students helped with the chores of carrying in firewood and fetching pails of water. In the time remaining, the children were free to play.

Most schools had no designated playgrounds or fences. Children could wander as far as they wished as long as they still could hear the bell. Besides the typical games of andy-over, snap-the-whip, dare base, steal-the-bacon and kick-the-can, children in western schools enjoyed the lively sport of gopher branding, imitating their fathers who branded calves.

At the end of the hour, the teacher rang the bell, and the students again lined up to enter the schoolhouse. The afternoon session often began with the reading of a moralistic story and a discussion of the moral. The afternoon assignments included grammar, geography and history. Again, the younger students recited first and the older students last. The last lesson—spelling—was the most eagerly anticipated. Once a week there was a spelldown. All the students lined up across the front of the schoolroom, and the teacher gave each a word to spell, keeping in mind each person's capability. The words became increasingly complex until one person remained standing. After the spelling lesson, the students helped clean slates, put away books, sweep the schoolroom floor and gather up the tin dippers. Then, row by row, the students retrieved their wraps and lunch pails and stood by their desks until dismissed.

### Reading, Grammar and Spelling

Reading, grammar and spelling were the most important components of the country school curriculum. The standard teaching tool was the primer, a small book that combined all three subjects in one volume. Colonial primers contained little interesting reading material; most were reading and word-lesson books with a few rhymes, verses and woodcuts. Almost all of them, beginning with the *New England Primer* (1760), had illustrated alphabets at the start of the text.

District school, Waynesville, Ind., 1941. Students concentrate on their reading lessons. (National Archives)

Primers were designed to teach children the rudiments of reading. Samuel Worcester's *Primer of the English Language for the Use of Families and Schools* (1826) first introduced the method of reading by breaking words into sounds. Previously, children learned to read only by adding letters onto vowels—"O" became "on," "on" became "one" and so forth—not by forming words through sounds (thus realizing that the same letters have different sounds depending on their placement in a word). Through constant drill and great familiarity with specific books, children haltingly learned to read.

Students advanced from primers to readers. Because there were few books and no standardized tests for reading comprehension, teachers judged students on their performance in reading aloud; literacy criteria of the 19th century were not related to comprehension. Nineteenth-century readers are fascinating because of their content and their illustrations. Through them, farm children received a classical and moral education. Before 1870 children who attended school regularly in the primary grades achieved the reading level of *McGuffey's Third Eclectic Reader*. After the 1870s education standards were raised throughout the United States, and a system of eight grade levels was instituted. Eighth-grade country school graduates were expected to complete McGuffey's fourth or fifth reader or a book of similar difficulty. Even for high school graduates today, mastering *McGuffey's Sixth Eclectic Reader* would be a formidable task. Selections included short essays, poems and stories by some of the most significant figures in English literature; one volume contained selections from Joseph Addison, Francis Bacon, Robert Browning, Elizabeth Barrett Browning, Richard Henry Dana, Charles Dickens, Ralph Waldo Emerson, Benjamin Franklin, Thomas Gray, Oliver Wendell Holmes, Thomas Jefferson, Henry Wadsworth Longfellow, Francis Parkman, Edgar Allan Poe and William Shakespeare.

Rural school, Williams County, N.D., 1937. Working with flash cards required a close relationship between teacher and students. (Russell Lee, FSA)

Despite the poverty of their surroundings and the subsistence level of most small 19th-century farms, country school students were exposed through literature to a broad vision of life. They stood with Horatio at the bridge, were snowbound with Whittier, learned political tolerance from Jefferson and sought the soldier's rest with Sir Walter Scott. During the 1890s and early 1900s, standard literature collections used in conjunction with traditional readers included the Riverside Literature Series, the Canterbury Classics, Macmillan Pocket Classics and the Laurel English Classics. Third-grade books included an adapted version of Daniel Defoe's *Robinson Crusoe.* Fourth-grade selections were Washington Irving's "Rip Van Winkle" and Johann Wyss's *Swiss Family Robinson,* while fifth graders wrestled with William Cullen Bryant's "Thanatopsis" and Nathaniel Hawthorne's "The Great Stone Face." Seventh graders read Oliver Goldsmith's *Deserted Village,* Samuel Coleridge's "Rime of the Ancient Mariner" and Alfred Lord Tennyson's *Enoch Arden.* It is unlikely that all students read these books and poems, yet they were all expected to make the attempt. Many of these volumes are still tucked away in closets and on book shelves of deserted country schools.

One former pupil from Utah recalls:

> We were drilled in phonics more vigorously than is required of students today. Instead of rushing over from 20 to 40 pages of a reading assignment, we were given from five to 10 with this injunction: "Take your reader home, go into a room by yourself—stand, take a position as if facing a class and read the lesson five times aloud." We were required to learn the hard words in the lesson. From the drilling, a pride was conceived in learning to read well.

Grammar was taught by exercises in parsing, or diagramming. Later, grammar books derived from primers focused solely on such exercises. Proper sentence structure and the correct use of adverbs, adjectives and prepositional phrases were implicit in the diagramming, but few explanations were ever offered as to how grammar and syntax worked. Rules were to be memorized and exceptions noted, but a thorough understanding of written grammatical usage was never stressed, although teachers were quick to criticize oral errors, specifically, the use of "ain't."

In *The Hoosier Schoolmaster* (1871) by Edward Eggleston, the character Squire Hawkins declares, " 'Spelling is the corner-stone, the grand, underlying subterfuge, of a good eddication. . . .' " Spelling featured long, almost unpronounceable words. Spelling recitations were daily rituals in most country schools. Monthly spelldowns between rival districts drew large audiences of adults and children. Yet, most of the students had no idea of the meaning of the words. The most famous of all country school spelling books was Noah Webster's *The Elementary Spelling Book* (1855), commonly known as the Blue-Back Speller. Webster, a former country school teacher, wrote such a successful spelling book that 35 million copies were produced between 1855 and 1890. Historian Henry Steele Commager called the Blue-Back Speller as essential a tool of civilization in frontier America as the Kentucky rifle. The 1866 edition alone sold 1.5 million copies, even though not a single definition was given for any of the words listed in its 174 pages. Although good spelling and correct pronunciation were almost a fetish, there was no concern for the correct use of words.

At end-of-school exercises, local ministers would often be called on

Composition and spelling books were some of the standardized supplies available for schools after the turn of the century. (Centennial School Supply Company, Denver)

to evaluate the success of the school term. One minister, in a story from Warren Burton's *The District School As It Was by One Who Went to It* (1833), asked the pupils to stand and spell a few words:

> They expect words as long as their finger, from the widest columns of the spelling-book, or perhaps such as are found only in the dictionary. "Spell wrist," says he to the little speller at the head. "O, what an easy word! R-i-s-t. Wrist." It is not right. "Spell gown, Anna." "G-o-u-n-d." "O, no, it is gown, not gound. The next try." None of them can spell this. . . . The teacher is disconcerted and mortified. It dawns on him, that while he has been following the order of the book, and priding himself that young scholars can spell such monstrous words—words which, perhaps, they will never use, they cannot spell the names of the most familiar objects. The minister has taught him a lesson.

Today, no teacher would teach students to spell words without teaching them also the meaning of the words. A century ago, the ability to spell words was a mark of erudition and a sign of status in small rural communities. Few people hearing someone pronounce a long, multisyllabic word ever considered whether the speaker used it correctly.

## Writing and Penmanship

In the early years of American education, only cursive writing was taught; no printing was allowed. Today, children begin with hand lettering and then progress to cursive writing. Printing takes longer because each letter is individually formed. Cursive writing is a faster process because the letters flow together and unite to make separate words. The famous Spencerian copybook, *The Spencerian Key to Practical Penmanship* (1866), developed by Platt Rogers Spencer, featured elaborate flourishes and intricate designs within the enclosed spaces of capital letters such as *P* and *S*. Spencer even suggested using a metronome during penmanship exercises to aid in establishing consistency in the up-and-down strokes. Despite the book's title, Spencer's handwriting style had little practical application because his style required a great deal of time and concentration to ensure the correct number of flourishes and filigrees for words that began and ended sentences and paragraphs. The style was delicate and beautiful but hardly suited to an America that increasingly saw itself as more businesslike and efficient, even in rural schools.

By the end of the 19th century, American handwriting had changed. The fancy script of Spencer was replaced by "vertical" writing, a cross between cursive and printing. In 1894 A. N. Palmer introduced the Palmer Method of penmanship in his book *Palmer's Guide to Business Writing*. The Palmer Method successfully combined the clarity of manuscript letters with the ease of cursive writing. His long, continuous writing strokes of circles and ovals and pushes and pulls came to dominate American penmanship exercises. Palmer changed the way Americans wrote by combining speed with legibility and producing a handwriting style easy to teach, learn and read. Teachers were required to drill their students in "writing a good hand," and thousands of country school pupils practiced until their penmanship became neat, clean and—most important—legible.

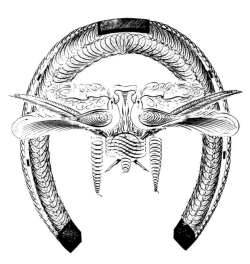

Artistic design created by repetition of the various strokes used for penmanship exercises. From "Real Pen Work, Self-Instructor in Penmanship." (Lone Star School, Centennial Village, Greeley, Colo.)

## *Arithmetic*

Of all the subjects taught in country schools, mathematics was the most practical. Students and their parents were interested in numbers not for numbers' sake—they wanted to solve problems on the farm. They wanted to know, for example, how many bushels of wheat could be expected from a 20-acre parcel if the wheat threshed 30 bushels to the acre? What would it be worth at 75 cents a bushel? The sixth-grade written work in the 1933 South Dakota Course of Study included these practical math problems:

Etching from McGuffey's *Third Eclectic Reader* illustrating a short story with a moral about a found pocketknife.

> If the gross income tax in South Dakota is one percent on salaries below $2,000 a year, what will a teacher pay as gross income tax if she received $75 a month for nine months?

> The window pane area of a schoolroom should be 20 percent of the floor area. Find how many square feet of window pane area your schoolroom should have. (First measure length and width of floor and find its area.)

> There are 96 senators in the U.S. Senate. It takes 66⅔ percent vote to approve a treaty. If all senators are present, how many must vote for a treaty to have it pass?

> For a long time, passenger railroad fare was thirty-six cents per mile: now it is only two cents a mile in many places. What percent reduction was given by the railroads?

Arithmetic in country schools was serious business. Country school teachers learned to expect farmers in overalls to appear at the door wanting to know the answer to such mathematical questions as what the tonnage of hay in a haystack was, given the rough dimensions of the stack. Students had to figure percentages, interest rates, square roots, cube roots and times tables. According to Almira Martin in her article in the *Utah Educational Review* (1903), everyone "learned the tables from the 2s to the 12s, and learned them backward and forward. All who could recite them both ways sure made a hit."

Like many subjects in rural schools at that time, arithmetic was to be memorized. Children were not taught arithmetic until they were nine years old, but from that point on they were drilled continually. The most proficient students could figure huge sums in their heads. The students knew the rules and could work problems with a proficiency all but unknown in the current world of hand-held calculators, but they had no understanding of the concepts that made the rules work.

The first American arithmetic textbook was Isaac Greenwood's *Arithmetic, Vulgar and Decimal* (1729). Nicholas Pike's *New and Complete System of Arithmetic,* first published in 1788, included a six-page table of contents; the subjects covered ranged from interest, compound interest, pensions, annuities and weight systems to foot measurement and explanations of barter. There was even a rule for determining the date of Easter for any year from 1753 to 4199. Arithmetic textbooks written especially for children evolved little by little from standard reference books used by schoolteachers and tradesmen. The English edition of the *Schoolmaster's Assistant* (1743), "being a plain arithmetic adapted to the United States," went through 68 editions between 1800 and 1843. A large measure of the book's success can be traced to its use of the new American currency, the base 10 system, which facilitated calculations. The most influential arithmetic textbook throughout the

19th century was Warren Colburn's *Intellectual Arithmetic* (1863). Generations of textbook publishers, inspired by this book, brought out other works on mental arithmetic featuring simple problems that could be done easily without blackboard or paper. Some arithmetic textbooks reflected religious preoccupations. The *Franklin Arithmetic* (1832) included the following problems:

> Four rivers ran through the garden of Eden, and one through Babylon; how many more ran through Eden than Babylon?
>
> Judas, one of the 12 apostles, hung himself; how many were there left?
>
> Adam was 930 years old when he died, and 130 when Seth was born; how old was Seth when Adam died?

## Recitation and Elocution

Both recitation and elocution played prominent roles in the country school curriculum. Recitation was stressed, not only because of the lack of textbooks and paper but also because the prevailing education belief during the 19th century was that the mind was like a muscle: If not continually flexed, it might atrophy or lose all its knowledge. Consequently, students memorized many works, including such lengthy poems as William Cullen Bryant's "Ode to a Waterfowl" and Thomas Gray's "Elegy Written in a Country Churchyard" as well as speeches, proclamations and witty verses.

Having read Henry Clay's orations and Daniel Webster's speeches, country school students also practiced public speaking. They learned to enunciate, pronouncing each word with care and precision. (Naturally, they did this without losing much of the local pronunciation and intonation.) Of course, merely speaking a piece was not enough; one had to gesticulate properly, too. Perhaps the best descriptions of the gestures that elocutionists thought appropriate come from William Scott's *Lessons in Elocution,* originally published in England and published in this country in 1785:

> Rage expresses itself with rapidity, interruption, noise, harshness and trepidation. The neck stretched out; the head forward, often nodding and shaking in a menacing manner, against the object of the passion. The eyes staring, rolling and sparkling; the eyebrows drawn down over them; and the forehead wrinkled into clouds. The nostrils stretched wide; every vein swelled; every muscle strained; the breast heaving and the breath fetched hard. The mouth open, and drawn on each side toward the ears, showing the teeth in a gnashing posture.

If anger was expressed by the gnashing of teeth, love was expressed by peaceful smiles.

> Light up the countenance with smiles. The forehead is smoothed and enlarged; the eyebrows are arched; the mouth a little opened and smiling; the eyes languishing and half shut, doat [sic] upon the beloved object. The countenance assumes the eager and wistful look of desire; (see Desire) but mixed with an air of satisfaction and repose. The accents are soft and winning; the tone of the voice persuasive, flattering, pathetic, various, musical, rapturous.

For isolated, unlettered rural children, who usually had only their family and pet farm animals to talk to, public speaking was both a terrifying challenge and an exhilarating opportunity to soar above the

Etchings from *Elementary Geography* (E. P. Dodds, 1902) provided a lesson in how to tell time; clues were given by the clock on the wall and the direction of the sunlight.

mundane. Trapped in specific family roles and obligated to perform the same dreary farm chores day in and day out, country school students, by declaiming the words of a Roman senator or the captain of a sinking ship, could become those heroes. Many youthful politicians gave their first impassioned speeches in one-room schools.

## History and Geography

History was rarely taught in country schools until after the 1870s, and then it was often combined with civics. However, state histories were popular, as were folio page geographies, which were elaborately illustrated, oversized books. Students had always been called on to describe where the boundaries of the states lay, but not until the mid-19th century were printing techniques advanced enough that mass reproduction of maps, charts and illustrations was possible.

The first geography book printed in America was Samuel Goodrich's *Tales of Peter Parley About America* (1828), which was immensely popular. Given the lavishness of the geographies and the belligerent patriotism of the time, the popularity of these books is easily understandable. For the first time, the course of empire and the thrust of civilization seemed as clearly understandable as the new railhead out on the prairie. Geography books were proof of human progress. The inaccuracies and misrepresentations were ignored—the gross errors in mapmaking (for example, the depiction of railroads that never existed) and the underlying premises that all Indians were savages and the white race was supreme. Most geography books were partly fiction, yet they were accepted as doctrine by country school teachers and students who shared the narrow social views of their generation.

## Physiology and Hygiene

In the late 1880s, a push was started to make physiology and hygiene required subjects. Most counties had official courses of study or books and outlines that were set forth by the county superintendent of schools; for example, the 1890 South Dakota legislature specified that physiology textbooks must devote "at least one-fourth of their space to the consideration of the nature and effects of alcoholic drinks and narcotics" and that health was to be taught "as thoroughly as arithmetic and geography." Physiology texts appear to have been a concession by public schools to the growing temperance movement, although many also stressed the evils of tobacco. This concern is in marked contrast to Pike's *New and Complete System of Arithmetic,* which included problems on measuring beer and gauging a mash tub.

Also included in the physiology texts were references to the dangers of overstudy. In the mid-19th century, Dr. Calvin Cutter and his son wrote several popular texts on physiology and hygiene; one of them, *Anatomy, Physiology and Hygiene* (1853), advanced a notion that became quite popular:

> In youth, much mischief is done by the long period of attendance at school, and the continued application of the mind which the ordinary system of education requires. . . . In early and middle life . . . an unusual degree of cerebral disorder is

a common consequence of this excessive and continued excitement of the brain. This unhappy result is brought on by severe study.

Most country school pupils did not have the chance to be exposed to such dangers.

## Moral Instruction

Instruction in values and ethics was part of the daily class schedule. A 1907 South Dakota law reads:

> Moral instruction intended to impress upon the minds of pupils the importance of truthfulness, temperance, purity, public spirit, patriotism and respect for honest labor, obedience to parents and due deference for old age, shall be given by every teacher in the public service of the state.

At that time, most of South Dakota's schools were one-room country schools. The 1914 South Dakota course of study shows that ethics was not to be treated as a separate subject but incorporated into the opening exercises and into reading and language instruction.

Other states also echoed South Dakota's concern for moral and religious instruction. Such instruction included deportment, character building, patriotism and larger concepts of ethical behavior taught by means of fables, moral stories, inspiring biographical examples, biblical stories and even biblical passages.

## Books

Many schools had only a half dozen books for all the students. Before the Civil War, a school of between 20 and 30 pupils would struggle along with fewer than a dozen books, and often the students themselves brought whatever books they could from home. Most schools had a dictionary; some districts preferred Webster's and others used Worcester's. Most schools had Bibles and perhaps a hymnal or two for the Sunday services. The result of this lack of books was that rote memorization became a standard teaching technique.

Primers such as *The New England Primer,* published in at least 400 printings and several editions between 1760 and 1843, were descended from hornbooks. A hornbook was a wooden tablet covered with a thin sheet of horn to protect the surface; paddlelike in shape, it narrowed to a handle at the bottom. On the surface of the tablet were displayed the alphabet and religious aphorisms, such as "In Adam's fall we sinned all."

The content of early textbooks was almost entirely religious, and there seems to have been a peculiar fascination with death. In *Old-Time Schools and Schoolbooks* (1904), Clifton Johnson cites a primer page with the following lines:

> Foolishness is bound up in the Heart of a Child, but the Rod of correction shall drive it from him.

> Liars shall have their Part in the Lake which burns with Fire and Brimstone.

> Upon the Wicked God shall rain an Horrible Tempest.

A verse from *The New England Primer* describes Death greeting a

A page from *Watson's Elementary Speller.* Words introduced in this lesson are spelled out at the top of the page.

boy who has sinned:

> Youth, I am come to fetch thy breath,
> And carry thee to th' shades of death,
> No pity on thee can I show
> Thou hast thy God offended so.
> Thy soul and body I'll divide,
> Thy body in the grave I'll hide,
> And thy dear soul in hell must lie
> With Devils to eternity.

By the 1840s, books with strict moral and religious overtones gave way to secular texts.

American publishers did not begin systematically printing textbooks until the first quarter of the 19th century. The books that were published usually served all grade levels, and a wide variety of texts found their way into the common schools. As the country expanded, more children began attending one-room schools. Academies and colleges opened their doors, and a market for textbooks developed; professors were encouraged to write the definitive American arithmetic or a well-illustrated American geography text.

Around 1830, with the advent of better printing methods and the introduction of woodcuts and illustrations into children's textbooks, a new curriculum began to appear. For the first time, publishers seriously sought to make books interesting for children. Gone were the heavy moral overtones of the colonial primers. In their place were engravings of cats and dogs, children in pony carts and even flowers and gardens.

In 1838 New York began to establish a library in each school district, and many states followed suit. Texts were chosen for both adult and student use, and by 1841 Gov. William H. Seward could report that of the 11,000 common schools in New York, "there are very few which have not complied with the act of providing for the establishment of school district libraries" ("A Digest of the Common School System of the State of New York"). Districts bought a variety of readers and books such as *The Hoosier Schoolmaster* by Edward Eggleston, *Poems Here at Home* by James Whitcomb Riley, *The Vicar of Wakefield* by Oliver Goldsmith, *Robinson Crusoe* by Daniel Defoe and *The Scarlet Letter* by Nathaniel Hawthorne. Literacy was highly valued, but unfortunately most of the books purchased far surpassed the reading skills of the students for whom they were intended.

Even if students could read at a basic level, there was no uniformity from school to school in the textbooks used or even in the subjects taught. As late as 1890, Nebraska had no standardized texts. The curriculum consisted of whatever books the children could bring from home. Until 1907 each county superintendent in Utah could select the textbooks to be used in one-room schools in his area. No state supervision existed. As late as the 1950s, a shortage of books continued to plague one Utah district where the only two teachers' editions of basic readers were copies the teachers themselves had bought.

Book shortages presented problems both for teachers and for students. Margie Hartman attended the Broken Bone School at Pleasant Lake, N.D., from 1957 to 1964. Because of the shortage of books, one teacher recommended that she not read books more difficult than her age level because then she'd have nothing to read the next year. Although the Broken Bone School was generally locked when class was not in session, everyone in the community knew the key was hidden in a large, native oak tree in the front schoolyard. Because their father was a rural mail carrier, the Hartman girls arrived at school early, let themselves in and began to play—and read.

### Teaching Aids

Teachers made learning fun by inventing games involving the memorization of states and capitals, times tables, names of presidents, geography facts and, of course, the alphabet. One readily accessible teaching aid was the Sears, Roebuck catalog, which saw multiple use as a reader, textbook, encyclopedia and source of arithmetic lessons.

A letters and numbers board used in the 1940s to permit younger students to practice skills on their own. (Andrew Gulliford)

A Michigan teacher in Della Lutes's novel *Country Schoolma'am* (1941) devises an exciting teaching aid by having her students draw the outline of the United States on the blackboard. With no maps to guide them, the students outline the country and meticulously place each state boundary, river, stream and mountain. Verbal battles arise over which rivers flow in which direction, and there is some confusion about the difference between the Rocky Mountains and the Sierra Nevada. However, over a period of weeks, to the astonishment of the students and the delight of the teacher, the entire United States begins to take shape on the blackboard in their schoolroom.

Few country schools had aids such as globes, but occasionally a district would purchase a tellurian, or movable model solar system, that demonstrated the rotation and revolution of the earth and sun. In *Mountain Path* (1936), Harriet Simpson Arnow writes of a young woman teaching in an isolated one-room Kentucky school accessible only by mule. The teacher, Louisa, had done a fine job of teaching the products of the state by having her students bring in samples of red and yellow corn, beans, cowpeas, a piece of wool, a fox tail, a strip of groundhog hide, pink and white quartz and tobacco leaves. She tries to instruct the children, who have never been out of their hollow, about the countries in the world, but they have no maps or globes. One of her students, Rie, has a flash of inspiration—she suggests creating their own globe by drawing with colored chalk continents and oceans on the potbelly of the stove. The final touch was a pumpkin. "Puzzled, Louisa watched in silence while Rie put the pumpkin on a vacant desk about 10 feet from the stove. She patted it affectionately. 'This yer, Teacher, is th' sun. She's round an' she's yeller, an' she kin come up an' go down.' " What the student had hit upon in her own way was what educators call manipulatives, physical objects used to teach specific principles of mathematics or science. Country schools had to rely on handmade manipulatives, because of the scarcity of funds.

### Music

Singing played a major role in a country school education, if not as a regular part of the curriculum, certainly as an integral feature of special community programs held in the schoolhouse. Music was often used to open officially the school day or to begin and end evening programs. During the winter, music played an especially important role; children often sang and danced as they marched around the potbellied stove in an effort to keep warm.

Teachers played, sang and taught according to their musical abilities. As early as the 1860s, Kansas teachers institutes encouraged special attention "to the science of music." Singing became a standard part of daily opening exercises, but, beyond that, music instruction varied with the repertoire and inclination of the teacher. Early music instruction centered on vocal and rhythmic activities until the school board could make a major purchase of a piano or organ, usually financed by an elaborately planned box social.

Organs dominated as the major musical instrument in one-room schools until the last quarter of the 19th century, when the popularity of pianos increased. School boards ordered magnificent upright oak pianos whose ivory keys would develop dips and grooves from the many hands that flew across the keyboard.

The teacher would begin music lessons with a few notes from the piano, and then students practiced songs such as "Marching Through Georgia," "Columbia, Gem of the Ocean," "Rally Round the Flag" and "Home Sweet Home." Singing might last 15 minutes daily and include the memorization of patriotic songs, rounds, folk and country tunes as well as "silly songs" and popular ballads. In the mountains and plains states, children learned music with round notes; in the southern states, shape notes dominated. Singing helped acculturate immigrants, and the songs themselves transmitted religious attitudes and beliefs, personal values and feelings for the beauties of the landscape and the wonders of nature.

Rural school, Baker County, Ore., 1939. This pump organ was the pride of the community. (Dorothea Lange, FSA)

## Graduation

In South Dakota in 1922, 40 percent of students taking the all-day comprehensive examination for eighth-grade graduation failed. Some failed because they were poor students, some because they had poor teachers, but most because they had spent more days helping with farm chores rather than attending school.

Verda Arnold, in *Our Yesterdays* (1970), describes taking the eighth-grade examination in western South Dakota:

> A decree went out from somewhere that all seventh and eighth-grade pupils must go to the county seat to write their final examination. There were four of us from Lame Johnny School. Mason Peterson, Peter Sieger, Evelyn Maxon and me. Poor little country kids. We were all afraid of the big city. The idea of a *final* test was bad enough. But to have to write such a test in a strange big building—oh, no! Miss Carter assured us we all knew enough to pass. Then gave us added relief by offering to go along and just be there. We all passed.

The boys and girls who did take the examinations and pass them had every right to be proud. Most of the tests were held at the county seat under the scrutiny of the county superintendent of schools. No more important rite of passage, other than marriage, existed for country school students. The graduation ceremony, held in early June, was

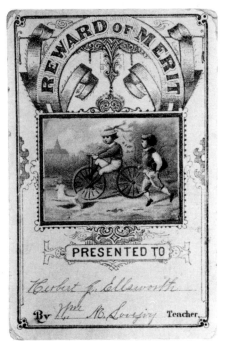

A typical certificate of achievement awarded by teachers in the late 19th and early 20th centuries. (Little Red Schoolhouse Museum, West Farmington, Maine)

Eighth-grade graduates pose for a class portrait, 1905. Their teacher, in the embroidered dress at right, holds the roses they have presented to her. (Wagner, CSL)

usually a formal occasion, attended by the graduates, their parents, other students, members of the community and, even, the county school superintendent.

Despite the inconsistencies and lack of textbooks and a fixed curriculum, country school teachers did an amazing job. In 1900 Iowa, with its white frame schools, and Kansas and Nebraska, with their sod schools, boasted the highest literacy rates in the nation. The one-room school, as in the years before and since, was producing literate graduates—an accomplishment that was due to the teachers and to the four Rs they so faithfully taught.

# Teachers' Lives on the Western Frontier

The building of the school and the arrival of the teacher served as critical turning points in the history of western frontier communities. The labor exerted and time spent in constructing the schoolhouse reflected pioneer parents' commitment to their children's education. Their esteem for education extended to teachers themselves. Young and old alike looked up to the teacher, whether a man or a woman, to fulfill specific community roles, organize social events, plan debates, create special programs and exemplify virtue, temperance and respectability.

Country school teachers had to reflect faithfully the values of the rural communities in which they taught. Yet, in their bearing and in their teaching they were expected to impart a sense of culture and knowledge. As a vital member of the community, the teacher functioned as the social pivot on which all activities turned. If a teacher became too authoritarian or seemed to consider herself or himself socially superior to the community folk, she or he was quickly dismissed. Teachers served as an example and inspiration to the young and a social equal for adults.

One-room school teachers simultaneously performed several exceedingly difficult roles. School boards expected much from them for a very small salary. That country school teachers of both sexes succeeded in providing children with the rudiments of an education and adults with social opportunities is proof of their pluck and perseverance on the frontier.

In "Country Schoolteaching on the Sod-House Frontier" in *Arizona and the West* (1975), Wayne E. Fuller states that "both the Kansas and Nebraska school laws required that teachers be at least sixteen years old before they began to teach, but it was not uncommon for them to begin at 15 or even younger, particularly in the 1870s, when the demand for teachers outran the supply." As late as 1919, a Nebraska study showed that the median age of that state's schoolteachers was only 21.

The "schoolmarm," the single woman teacher, is the stereotype, but in fact men teachers were much preferred, especially for the winter terms, partly because of tradition and partly because it was thought that they alone could control the older farm boys who attended school only during the winter when their time was not completely taken up by farm work. Women were employed to teach primarily in the spring and summer terms, when only younger children were in school. According to Fuller, 52 percent of Nebraska teachers and 47.2 percent of Kansas teachers in 1871 were men.

Within 20 years the statistics changed. In Republic County, Kans., from 1895 to 1976 only 19 percent of the teachers were men. Of the 1,725 one-room schools in operation in Colorado between 1906 and 1913, 84 percent had woman teachers. In Van Buren Township, Renville County, N.D., only eight of the 179 teachers who taught

*opposite*
Sod school (c. 1880), District No. 9, Thomas County, Kans. The teacher, on the far left, hand on hip, had 22 students, ranging from six- and seven-year-olds to the adult male, perhaps an immigrant, in the back row. (Kansas State Historical Society)

between 1902 and 1958 were men. Elk Mountain School District in Carbon County, Wyo., had no men teachers between 1913 and 1936. Although women dominated the education profession on the frontier, men played important roles, especially as disciplinarians.

In *100 Years on the Muddy* (1967), Arabelle Lee Hafner discusses the problems of keeping teachers in Moapa Valley, Nev.:

> There were many teachers brought in at the turn of the century, but their efforts were in vain because of the meanness and trickery played on them by the students. The teachers stayed on the average of two or three months or less until John Crosby came. "Johnny Bull" was a nickname given him by the students. He was a large, athletic, muscular man, and was the only one that was able to control the students or scare them into learning.

Men teachers in Nebraska had to be quick with their fists as well as their wits. Frank Grady, who attended a one-room school in Nebraska in the early 1900s, recalled some features of student discipline:

> The first teacher in Raymond School was run out by the boys, who used stones as weapons of assault. The second met the same gang, but when he had soundly thrashed one boy and the youth's father coming to take up the battle shared the same fate, the reign of terror ended abruptly, and a new respect for the school was established.
>
> The discipline on the whole was pretty good. . . . There were no high-falooting laws, and the teacher could whale the very devil out of you if it would aid in bringing you to time.
>
> [Another teacher] was already in the school on New Year's Day, and [the students] threw brimstone—sulphur, I reckon it's called—down the chimney and smoked him out, getting possession of the premises. . . . Quite a percentage of the big fellows considered the teacher Public Enemy Number One.

In 1875 at the McCarthy School, District No. 29, in Washington County, Neb., the teacher found the students, many of whom were larger boys, difficult to control and was driven out. Jimmy Van Duesen, who took the teacher's place, laid a gun across the top of his desk and said, "Boys, I'm here for business—to teach." He had no trouble.

John G. Neihardt recounts in the first volume of his autobiography, *All Is But a Beginning—Youth Remembered 1881–1901* (1972), his tribulations as a one-room school teacher in Nebraska. As the first day of teaching progressed, Neihardt began the difficult task of assigning his 20 students to desks of the proper size and trying to teach. One of the boys suggested a snowball fight at recess, and the naive Neihardt assented because it would give the students a chance to expend some energy. He did not comprehend their true intentions.

> Bill Kendrick loomed up before me out of the melee. I can see him yet as I saw him then in a vivid, timeless moment—a robust youth, perhaps a trifle overgrown for his years but amply shouldered and chested like a buffalo bull calf. I caught the triumphant grin upon his flushed face as he stooped in front of me, reaching with his right hand for a fistful of snow. I saw and knew and I didn't wait for further information!
>
> In that split second Bill had accidentally placed himself in the best possible position for my trick throw. . . .
>
> It worked. Bill's size and weight were greatly in my favor now. He came down like a wagonload of brick; and it was fun to hear him grunt under the impact of my right shoulder landing in the midst of him!
>
> When I leaped to my feet, I became aware that the tumult was dying out over the battlefield. A ring of spectators was forming about us, and others were running up to see Bill and Teacher in a fracas, as they supposed. But what they saw was a

Molen School (c. 1885), Emery County, Utah, 1907. To ensure that parents knew he was doing a good job, this teacher had his students pose with open books for their class picture. (Utah State Historical Society)

crestfallen Bill shaking snow off his back and grinning sheepishly about him.

"Sorry, Bill," I said. "That's a mean throw—hard to control."

Then Bill did something that made all the difference. He slapped his hand on my shoulder and laughed!

Men teachers were not the only ones who were able to deal with problem students, however. South Dakota teacher Eliza St. John Brophy was asked to accept two large boys from a neighboring district who had thrown a man teacher out the window. When they began to chew tobacco, she ignored them for three days; they did not come back. In another school, a problem developed with immigrant children bringing binder twine to play cat's cradle during school hours. The teacher gathered all the string and made a rope of it. She then made a noose and hung it from the strongest peg on the wall. One of the older immigrant boys told the children in their language that the teacher was going to hang them. Brophy did not contradict him and by stern looks gained the upper hand.

## Women Teachers

By the time the plains were open to settlement, the woman teacher had become an established figure in American education. Many country school teachers came west because they believed that it was their Christian duty to help educate children on the frontier.

In 1840, in a speech recorded in the Fourth Annual Report, Massachusetts Board of Education, the progressive educator Horace Mann urged women to become teachers because "females are incomparably better teachers for young children than males. . . . Their manners are more mild and gentle, and hence in consonance with the tenderness of childhood." As early as 1845, Catharine Beecher, daughter of a prominent New England family of educators and clergymen, called for recruitment of women into the teaching profession. Her highly influential pamphlet *The Duty of American Women to Their Country* (1845) decried the shortage of teachers on the frontier and predicted that men would never fill the gap: "It is WOMAN who is to come in at this emergency and meet the demand. Woman, whom experience and testing have shown to be the best, as well as the cheapest, guardian and teacher of childhood."

In "A Wider Field of Usefulness: Pioneer Women Teachers in the West, 1848–1854" (1982), Polly Welts Kaufman explains the unique qualities of pioneer women who traveled to the Midwest to teach. They came from New England and were "driven by economic necessity, a sense of mission, and even a romantic view of the West." Unlike their peers, "the women demonstrated a will to direct their own lives that was unusual for the majority of women of their time." Of the pioneer women in Kaufman's study, more than two-thirds were already self-supporting, primarily because they had lost one or both of their parents. Unlike the younger teachers who taught 30 years later on the Great Plains, three-quarters of the women in Kaufman's study "had struggled to prepare for their careers" and their median age was over 25. Marriage for them seemed unlikely. In contrast to the stereotype of the demure schoolmarm, Kaufman concludes, these pioneer women

Rural school, Candelaria, Nev., 1880s. A man teacher posed with his students in front of their clapboard schoolhouse. (Nevada Historical Society)

Clapboard school (c. 1900), Buffalo County, Neb., 1907. The teacher, Miss Swensen, posed with her pupils on the front steps. (Solomon D. Butcher Collection, Nebraska State Historical Society)

teachers "represented a special group of ante-bellum women whose spirit was rising. By using the teaching profession as their route to a new life, they achieved a significant amount of autonomy." Moreover, she notes, teaching accorded these women social acceptability as well as a "higher level of self-sufficiency than practically any other group of women."

Until a school could be built and a teacher hired, many frontier mothers took on the task of educating their children, as did Mary Luella Nesmith White, who moved to Nebraska in 1887. Because the closest schools were on the other side of the river, too far from their homestead, White recalls, "[I] considered it my duty to teach the children. This I did in accordance with my time and resources. Often I held a school book in one hand and wielded a white-wash brush with the other. At other times I propped a book in front of the wash-tub while I rubbed soiled clothes on the wash-board with both hands" (Joan Swallow Reiter, *The Women*, 1978). In her pamphlet on women's duty, Catharine Beecher proclaimed that "woman, as mother and as teacher, is to form and guide the immortal mind." By the hundreds and later by the thousands, American women, especially those from New England, answered Beecher's call. By the 1900s young girls sought to become teachers also because teaching was one of the few careers open to women in rural areas.

In *The Sway of the School Bell: Schools and Histories of Brown, Keya Paha, and Rock Counties, Nebraska* (1976), memoirs compiled by the Ainsworth Area Retired Teachers Association, Elsie Petsel Hallock of Ainsworth, Neb., recalled:

> In my home town, the only highly respectable jobs for girls after they graduated from high school were nursing, teaching or clerking in a store. Since my dad ran a general store, and since I was somewhat familiar with that, clerking wouldn't be any fun, and by the time I'd completed my normal training in high school I'd still be too young to go into nurse's training. I *was* going to be respectable and *was* going to earn a living. So, I became a teacher.

In 1909, at the age of 19, Esma Lewis left home for the first time, boarding the train in Dongola, Ill., to teach school at the mouth of Divide Creek near Silt, Colo. She stayed with a member of the school board and his family. To this day, Lewis remembers the sharp, lonely coyote howls that rolled across the mesa on moonlit nights. The first time she heard that eerie sound, it chilled her blood; all she was used to was the croak of bullfrogs. On the first day of school, she began with the Pledge of Allegiance and then said the Lord's Prayer, as much for her own benefit as for that of her students. Lewis taught for 60 years in Garfield County. Like countless other country school teachers, she came to a new country and never left.

For Lewis the sound of yapping coyotes was a nuisance, but Hetty Birdick, who taught at the Rowena School near Boulder, Colo., in 1914–15 had more serious problems with animals. She relates one experience:

> [At] that time it [the schoolhouse] could be reached only on horseback most of the year. Men worked at a large mine where burro power pulled ore cars and brought children to school through the snow drifts. The source of water was a spring, which never froze, on a rocky path 200 yards away. The temperature at that altitude was

Celia Lewis, a Michigan schoolteacher in the early 1900s. Like many other women schoolteachers, she tried to dress well to underscore her position in the community. (Courtesy of Mrs. Hugh E. Henshaw, Harbor Springs, Mich.)

School (1880s), near Forestville, Minn. Teacher Myrtle Cummings stood with her students in front of their two-story clapboard school. (Minnesota Historical Society)

often 40 degrees below zero. I became weary competing with wildlife [to get water from the spring] and shot a mountain lion one frosty morning.

In the West, women were at a premium. The arrival of an attractive, unmarried woman in a frontier town populated largely by men was met with enthusiasm. Tales of bashful cowboys courting the new schoolmarm have long been part of the folklore of the West. Marriages between schoolteachers and range riders did occur, often because of the cowboy's persistence. On the other hand, girls came west seeking adventure and, also, matrimony. Some came from poor backgrounds with few social opportunities, but out West they were in charge of their own school and could meet all the eligible bachelors at local pie socials and square dances. School board members often requested photographs from prospective teachers and made their selection on the basis of appearance. In fact, a single man often worked hard to get on the school board just so he could have a say in the selection of the new teacher.

How many young women came west to teach school and stayed to raise families cannot be estimated. Certainly no history of the West would be complete without a chapter on the influence of schoolteachers on isolated ranch communities. In his novel *East of Eden* (1952), John Steinbeck describes country school teacher Olive Hamilton and the difficulties of being a marriageable single woman in the Salinas Valley of California:

> The teacher was not only an intellectual paragon and a social leader, but also the matrimonial catch of the countryside. A family could indeed walk proudly if a son married the schoolteacher. Her children were presumed to have intellectual advantages both inherited and conditioned. . . .
>
> Olive Hamilton had not only to teach everything, but to all ages. Very few youths went past the eighth grade in those days, and what with farm duties some of them took fourteen or fifteen years to do it. Olive also had to practice rudimentary medicine, for there were constant accidents. She sewed up knife cuts after a fight in the schoolyard. When a small bare-footed boy was bitten by a rattlesnake, it was her duty to suck his toe to draw the poison out. . . . It was far from an easy job, and it had duties and obligations beyond belief. The teacher had no private life. She was watched jealously for any weakness of character. She could not board with one family for more than one term, for that would cause jealousy—a family gained social ascendency by boarding the teacher. If a marriageable son belonged to the family where she boarded a proposal was automatic; if there was more than one claimant, vicious fights occurred over her hand. The Aguita boys, three of them, nearly clawed each other to death over Olive Hamilton. Teachers rarely lasted very long in the country schools. The work was so hard and the proposals so constant that they married within a very short time.

Women teachers paid a heavy price for marriage. Only one family member was expected to earn a living; if a woman married, she immediately forfeited her job. Many a love affair and marriage had to be kept secret. In the 1920s, teaching contracts in Utah required that a teacher who married give up her school and her last month's salary. In one year in Piny, Wyo., six out of seven teachers married. Edington School in Albany County, Wyo., was called the mating ground because of the number of teachers who had to give up their jobs because they married.

In the 1920s Esther Cambell taught in an area of Colorado and Utah frequented by outlaws and cattle rustlers. Although she did a fine job of teaching, one year she was not hired back. The school board trumped up an excuse, but the real reason was that she had married. As the summer ended, however, no unmarried teachers had applied for the little one-room school at Elk Springs, Colo., so the school board reluctantly gave "Miss Esther" her job back.

During the Great Depression, when everyone was out of money and it seemed unfair for a family to have more than one wage earner, the number of laws barring married teachers increased. During World War II, however, thousands of young men left for the service, and the lack of teachers in rural areas created a national crisis. Many married women who had not taught for 20 years found themselves teaching again, with emergency certificates.

### Living Conditions

Usually a teacher's pay included room and board; the teacher would shuttle from home to home, sharing a bed with one or more children. He or she stayed longest with families with the greatest number of children and, frequently, the least privacy and provisions. Sometimes the teacher would sleep alone, but seldom in much comfort or privacy. Phoebe Nater wrote of her Nebraska experiences in *Koshapah* (1972):

> The only other possible door was the one in the teacher's bedroom. This door was warped out of shape. It lacked four inches at the top of being closed. The door hung with icicles and heavy frost. . . . Lying in her bed, this country teacher was nearly insane with anger. Shivering under blankets and dressed in a flannel robe and pajamas, a coat and socks, her breath made a thin sheet of ice around the pillow and covers as she kept her head under the covers and tried to sleep. . . . The supreme test came as dawn arrived one morning. Two coyote trappers, relatives of the family, pushed the frosty frozen door open, and smoking corn cob pipes, walked across the bedroom floor with traps slung over their shoulders and dead coyotes resting outside the door.

In *Memoirs of South Dakota Retired Teachers* (1976), edited by Ruth Morgan, Julia Hall recalled:

> My bedroom was an unfinished attic room with an outside stairway which at times was slick with ice and snow . . . the room was heated with a small wood and coal stove; we used a kerosene lamp. I kept my clothes under the covers so they would be warm in the morning; sometimes my bed was covered with snow. I would go downstairs to wash, eat breakfast and take my school bag and pail to start walking one and a half miles to school.

Living in a single room was often an economic necessity and allowed little freedom. A teacher could not entertain friends or engage in any noisy activity in someone else's home. The room was simply a place to retire after a day's work at school.

The parsimony of country school district officers was notorious. Perhaps no other single characteristic did more to give country school education a bad reputation than the deliberate stinginess of local school boards. They would not buy books. They would not hire qualified teachers. Some district boards would not even buy coal for the stove until after the first heavy frosts of winter. And if the stove was a woodburning one, the wood might arrive cut in sled lengths for economy's sake, leaving to the older students the responsibility of

Sod school (c. 1890), Logan County, Neb. Hardly large enough for three students, this sod school was also the teacher's living quarters, housing a bed and cooking utensils. (Nebraska State Historical Society)

cutting and splitting the wood.

These economies certainly included teachers' wages. Martha Washburn, who taught in a village school in Livermore, Maine, in the 1840s, wrote in her diary in 1843: "For aught I know I may as well do nothing the compensation is so meagre." Although rural teachers' salaries improved during the last quarter of the 19th century, school districts with limited tax bases were at the mercy of national recessions and depressions, in which farm products lost value. Anticipating losses in their farm incomes from an economic crisis or crop failures because of droughts or floods, school board members often sought the most inexpensive teacher they could hire. If a board member's niece agreed to work for $5 less a month than the teacher they had hired, the niece received the job.

Men teachers consistently earned higher wages than women teachers for the same work. In the early 1840s, men in Maine could expect $15.50 per month during the winter, while women received only $5.50 per month for the summer term. In 1880 men in Kansas were paid about $6.50 more per month than women; in 1914 men received about $17 more. In Nebraska in 1914, men were paid $21.89 more a month than women. In Utah throughout the period 1900–20, women received on an average only 70 to 80 percent of what men earned. In *The Rural School in the United States* (1908), John Coulter Hockenberry lists salary data from 34 states. Average monthly salaries for teachers in rural schools were $40 for men and $33 for women ($40 in the early 1900s would have a 1980s purchasing power of approximately $500). Not only were the wages abysmally low, but teachers frequently worked terms of only six or seven months. Salaries had risen after World War I to more than $100 per month. Experienced teachers could command as much as $125 to $140 per month, but after the depression caused the farm economy to collapse, teachers felt lucky to get $75.

To avoid unnecessary expense, school boards regularly fired or failed to rehire experienced teachers; in this way, they could keep teacher salaries at a minimum. Such practices were common through the 1930s, when some schools stopped paying their teachers altogether. Salaries had plummeted along with farm prices during the depression, and few local taxes could be collected, so districts had minimal funds. During the depression many teachers were paid in warrants, similar to IOUs, against forthcoming district tax income. Banks always checked the status of the district account before redeeming the warrant, and in the 1930s many of the warrants were not worth the paper they were written on. Teachers then had the option of not getting paid and letting the warrant collect interest at the bank until the district could redeem it or cashing the warrant at a 20 percent loss and letting the bank profit by the difference and the interest. Moreover, many districts required the signatures of school board trustees to make the paychecks valid. Teachers had no choice but to close school early on the last Friday of the month and go find the trustees, who were often off farming remote parts of their land. The first trustee to be visited was the clerk who made out the checks, then the treasurer and, last, the district president.

Ernest Grundy, a former professor at Kearney State College, Kearney,

Neb., who began his teaching career in Kansas schools during the depression, still remembers one school board president who would take an inordinately long time to endorse a check. With one arm wrapped around the leather reins of his plowhorses and his right foot planted firmly in the soil behind his plow, the man would examine the check closely and say, "Sixty dollars. Sixty dollars a month. That's an awful lot of money in these times, wouldn't you say, Ernest?" Grundy would shuffle his feet in the dry earth, waiting for this humiliating ordeal to be over. The president would look at the check, look at the young teacher standing before him and add, "I sure could use a monthly income like this. Kids need shoes." With hat in hand, Ernest would nod his head in agreement. Finally, the weary farmer would say, "Well, let's head on into the house and see if I can find pen and ink." Such experiences pushed many young teachers into getting more education so they could teach in town schools for better pay.

### Teacher Certification

By the 1880s many teachers in country schools in the West came not from the East but were daughters of the first great rush of homesteaders. As soon as the daughters passed the eighth-grade comprehensive tests, they began to teach—often in the same school they had attended. By the 1880s state laws required teacher certification. To become certified, candidates arrived at the county courthouse to take grueling all-day exams on a date and at a time set by the county superintendent. A passing score qualified a person to teach without a single day of supervised practice teaching. Certified young teachers may have known the subject matter, but many found themselves in one-room schools without the slightest idea of how to teach beyond the tutoring they may have given younger classmates.

A teacher's first-grade certificate issued by South Dakota in 1925. (CSL)

In most states, five levels of teaching certification were awarded to candidates "of good moral character" at least 16 years of age. Persons with minimal qualifications who had been graduated from the eighth grade and had passed the third-grade teaching examinations could receive a third-grade certificate, allowing them to teach between six months and a year without reexamination. Persons who held the third-grade certificate, had one year of teaching experience and had passed the second-grade examinations could receive a second-grade certificate, which was valid for one year and could be renewed for up to four years. Persons who had three to four years of teaching experience, had attended summer teachers training institutes and had passed the first-grade examinations could receive a first-grade certificate, which was valid for two years and could be renewed twice or more with special permission of the county superintendent. Persons who had three years of teaching experience were eligible for certificates good for five years and usable in any school in the state. Graduates of the state normal schools, which at that time were post–eighth-grade, two-year programs, could receive the certificate without examination. Persons who had completed a four-year college program could be granted a lifetime diploma.

In South Dakota, candidates for the third-level certificate had to pass only a general teaching examination. Candidates for the second-level certificate had to pass exams in orthography (spelling), reading, writing, geography, English grammar, physiology, hygiene and United States history. Candidates for a first-grade certificate had to pass these tests as well as tests in civil government, didactics, elementary bookkeeping and current events. To earn the highly coveted state certificates, candidates had to pass exams in algebra, geometry, natural philosophy, physiology and hygiene, drawing, civil government, didactics, general history and American literature. The character of the paper submitted in the examination illustrated the candidate's knowledge of English grammar, orthography and penmanship.

Career-minded rural teachers worked hard to earn their certificates, which represented better job and salary opportunities. As late as the 1940s, however, few one-room school teachers had completed a four-year college degree. Some states—for example, Texas and Oklahoma—did not require a college degree for public school teaching until the late 1950s; Colorado did not require a college degree until 1961.

### Teachers Institutes

Before the establishment of state normal schools or colleges, the only place where teachers could go for further training in their subjects were the teachers institutes offered by state school superintendents during the summer months. Such institutes often provided a much-needed opportunity for socializing with other rural school teachers, many of whom were isolated for months when school was in session. The September 7, 1875, issue of the *Cheyenne Daily Sun* described one such institute:

> Socially, the institute was a grand success, as a mutual admiration society, and as a taffy distributing meeting it also prospered, but so far as the accomplishment of the objects for which it met it was a grand and successful failure. The teachers attended numerously, read a few papers upon subjects with which every well-educated person is thoroughly familiar, excurted, sang, danced and had a good time generally ending with a grand banquet at the Pacific Hotel, listened to a few really good speeches that would paralyze an audience of Missouri fire eaters and stayed up all night to take late trains. . . .

The 1877 Wyoming Institute entertained questions from teachers who needed practical advice, but institute directors gave vague, philosophical answers, such as those recorded in Terrence D. Fromong's "The Development of Public Elementary and Secondary Education in Wyoming 1869–1917" (1962):

> What rules should a teacher make at the opening of a term of school? Few rules are best.

> What constitutes good government in the school room and how is it best secured? Force of character in the teacher with the minimum of apparent control is the true principle.

> Shall we resort to corporal punishment in the school and if so, when? Corporal punishment should be used to save the school, just as bullets are used to save nations.

Despite the ruggedness of the frontier in the territory of Wyoming, education expectations ran high. At the teachers institute in 1879, Gov.

John Wesley Hoyt endorsed the teaching of Latin and Greek in Wyoming schools. Kansas confined itself to more realistic goals for its rural school teachers. The motto for the 17th annual session of the Wabunsee County Normal Institute in 1893 was "He that knows little and knows it, knows much." The Russell County Normal Institute for 1908 stressed orthography, physiology and the U.S. Constitution. By 1930 the Grove County Institute held classes in the three Rs as well as in mental hygiene, character training, health habits and current events.

## County Superintendents

Administration of the dozens of rural schools within a county was the responsibility of the county school superintendent. Besides organizing teachers institutes, the county superintendent provided rural school teachers with valuable guidance, emotional support and needed school supplies. Beginning in the 1870s, the position of county school superintendent was made a public office. Voters elected superintendents for two-year terms and frequently reelected the same superintendent year after year; some county school superintendents held the office for 30 years.

Black school, Kentucky, c. 1900. Black families posed proudly in front of a new county school building. The man on the far right is probably the county school superintendent. (Richard McComb, Kentucky Department of Education)

Single women teachers, isolated in their remote one-room rural schools and confused by conflicting family ties, marriage proposals and a vague notion of career goals, looked to the county superintendent as a mentor. In 1893 Laura Eisenhuth was elected North Dakota state superintendent of schools, the first woman in the nation to hold that position; thereafter, women were increasingly elected to the position. Women had voted in school elections as early as 1838 in Kentucky, and by 1890 15 states and territories had granted women similar school election voting rights. In rural areas of the United States, the fledgling suffragist movement gained ground by supporting women as county school superintendents. Rural school teachers, many of whom were women, eagerly endorsed women for the position and saw it as a well-paying, interesting job that might some day be open to them. In Republic County, Kans., from 1913 to 1969, one-third of all county school superintendents were women, beginning with Lucy Howard, who served from 1896 to 1909. Women filled the office in Albany County, Wyo., from 1885 to 1937. In Brown County, Neb., from 1897 to 1975 only one man was elected superintendent.

Rural teachers had to set an example for the students and parents of their community, and county superintendents had to set an example for their rural teachers. Superintendents tried to visit all schools in their district at least three times a year—in the fall, in the spring and, of course, for eighth-grade graduation, where parents (and voters) would compliment the teacher and superintendent on the successful completion of another school year. At graduation, the superintendent called each student by name and handed the pupil a diploma inscribed with the name of the school district, the location, the date and the signatures of both the superintendent and the teacher. By being present at graduation, superintendents endeared themselves to their constituents and generated support for reelection.

The job, however, was not just smiles and handshakes. Getting to

Red Bud School, Rockcastle County, Ky., 1916. The teacher, standing with her 40 students, estimated that 20 more were absent because of work. The county superintendent was in the doorway. (Lewis W. Hine, National Child Labor Committee, Library of Congress)

the rural schools required feats of endurance. Women superintendents were among the first women in rural areas of the United States to use automobiles in fulfilling occupational duties, but they also rode horseback and used buggies. Superintendents had to plan for all contingencies when they visited rural schools. An early winter snowstorm could make travel difficult. Temperatures eased in spring, but roads could become deeply rutted and covered with mud. Many teachers, starved for companionship and news of the outside world, begged them to stay overnight. In other instances, superintendents simply could not return to the county seat and complete their visits in a day's time so they stayed with farm families along their route.

County school superintendents had the difficult task of mediating differences between local one-room school boards resistant to change and the state legislature and state superintendent of schools, who demanded better teacher preparation and improvement of school buildings. Local teachers became certified by passing county exams that the superintendent devised. County superintendents also provided the course of study, the curriculum guidelines for each of the subjects that teachers were required to teach.

## Expectations of Teachers

In "Sand Tables and One-Eyed Cat: Experiences of Two Texas Schoolteachers," in the *West Texas Historical Association Yearbook* (1981), Lou Rodenberger, an English professor and daughter of rural school teachers, recalls, "The country schoolteachers in the first half of this century were the intellectual, social and often spiritual leaders of communities where, until the 1940s, there were no books, few newspapers and fewer radios." People were interested in everything the teacher did or said or wore. Country school teachers who lived in the community came to be well known; they were important to the whole community, not just to the children in school.

Teachers had to be upstanding citizens who set an example not only to their students but also to everyone around them. They had to be well dressed but not overdressed. Nobody wanted the new teacher putting on airs. Because the community expected them to dress and behave in a certain way, young teachers looked on schoolteaching as an honorable profession and tried to instill in their students a sense of the worth of an education.

Citizens kept their country school teachers under close surveillance to ensure that they followed a stern moral code. In the 1890s Lena Harrison, of Junction, Tex., was returning home from obtaining her teaching credentials when she decided to stop by her uncle's saloon to pay him a social call. The community that had so eagerly welcomed her home now became divided about whether she should leave her teaching job because of this transgression. Helen Redd, on her way to Ucola, Utah, where she was going to teach, was warned by the county school superintendent about the young men in the community. He informed her that it would be disastrous to her career if she were seen with any disreputable cowboys and pointed out which ones were "respectable."

In her book *Ranch Schoolteacher* (1974), Eulalia Bourne writes of being dismissed from her teaching position in the one-room school on Beaver Creek near Flagstaff, Ariz. Sixteen-year-old Bourne had outraged a member of the community by dancing to the ragtime hit "Too Much Mustard" and was fired for her audacity. Within the year, however, the song had swept across the country, and she had the pleasure of teaching the new dance step to the same school board member who had withdrawn his children from her class in protest of her conduct, but she was not rehired.

A reference letter for a teacher, written in 1923 by J. A. Sikkink, the clerk of Dempster School, District No. 1, in Hamlin County, S.D., concerns itself entirely with the young woman's morality and does not mention her teaching ability:

> I sincerely recommend Miss Jeanette E. Kones as a successful teacher. While teaching [at] our school, she was a teacher we could be proud of. A girl of splendid character, with name above reproach. She is a faithful member of her church, and is in all her ways a true Christian, her faith in the Bible is very sincere and her whole attitude expresses good morals and a clean upright life. She is also a very sociable person and a leader in any community. I take great pleasure in recommending Miss Kones to any school board.

In addition to moral responsibilities, teachers also had menial chores. Except for community clean-up days in the fall and spring, teachers generally did all the janitorial work, including the sweeping, scrubbing, mopping, dusting and blackboard washing. Because most children walked to school by the shortest route possible, during the rainy season mud was continually tracked into the building, forming little brown rivulets down each aisle. The mud dried during the day, and the floor required a vigorous sweeping in the afternoon. Robert L. Conger, who attended one-room schools in western Nebraska, recalls the many duties of his former teachers:

> The teacher, aside from being teacher, was counselor, mediator, nurse, judge, jury, disciplinarian and jack-of-all-trades. He or she was also the duly elected janitor. [The tasks] included the housekeeping as well as starting and maintaining the fire in the coal stove. On winter mornings, the temperature on the inside was about like that on the outside. The teacher tried to get there early and get the fire going before the pupils arrived. Any teacher worth his or her salt was enterprising enough to incorporate some of the janitor work into his discipline program.

Farm children often came to school with health problems, and teachers had to initiate daily cleaning routines to combat head lice, scabies and impetigo. Children who caught pinkeye from cattle received the same treatment that the livestock received—boric acid. Today, such nursing practices would be considered illegal. Stan Leftwich, a former state supervisor of rural schools in Colorado, says, "We would be put in jail today for the nursing we did in those years, but what were we to do? No organized health service existed."

According to Maude Lindstrom Frandsen, who taught in rural schools near Brighton, Colo., in the 1920s, health problems were the responsibility of the teacher. If a tooth needed to be pulled, a sticker removed, a broken fingernail cut or a stomachache eased, the teacher had to rise to the occasion. Epidemics could be disastrous. Frandsen remembers a student, the daughter of the school board president, who came to school with a rash. Because the child lived nearby, she was sent home with a note. Within the hour, the child and her mother were back, the mother declaring, "If Susie has a disease, she caught it here at school, so she will stay here." The girl was kept as far as possible from the other children for the rest of the day. That evening, the teacher drove to the county seat to report the case to the health officer. The child had scarlet fever; fortunately, however, no other children contracted the disease. Such incidents, however, often created tensions between teachers and parents.

Country school teachers had to be prepared to cope with emergencies, and snakes were one type of emergency. Rattlesnakes posed deadly problems to inexperienced teachers on the high plains. Teachers needed quick judgment and quick reflexes, and under no conditions could they be squeamish. A teacher quickly learned that if a snake appeared in the schoolyard, it had to be attended to immediately. As one parent remarked, "If a teacher hasn't enough sense and know-how to kill a snake, she had better go back where she came from. It is twenty miles to the closest doctor, and death would arrive first."

Prairie rattlers are at their deadliest in late autumn, and they often seek shelter under buildings and in crawl spaces. In western Kansas, a teacher holding class in a sod schoolhouse turned her head just in time to see a huge rattlesnake fall from the roof and land with a sizzle on top of the woodburning stove. In eastern Colorado, older ranch boys enjoyed killing rattlesnakes during their lunch recess; the largest kill was 16 rattlers in one den. In 1915, in her second year of teaching near Wild Horse, Colo., Lois Lucore went out late in the summer to get her school ready for fall. As she opened the outside door, stepped into the anteroom and fumbled with her keys to the main door, she suddenly fely uneasy. She spun quickly around to face a six-foot-long rattlesnake coiled up in a corner. The unmistakable sound of its rattles sent tremors down her spine, and she jumped backwards out the door.

Maud Clark, who taught in the late 1880s in a country school near Platteville, Colo., saw a rattlesnake she thought was dead come to life. A favorite trick of farm boys who wanted to test a new teacher was to put dead snakes in the teacher's desk, coiling them so they looked alive. In this case, the large snake dangled from a slip-noose at the end of a stick, and the boys knew, although the teacher did not, that the snake was only stunned. In an attempt to gain the respect of her class, Clark, thinking the snake was dead, took the snake by the string, coiled it on the top of her desk and went on with class. It was not until she saw the terrified stares of her younger students that she turned and saw the snake had slithered off her desk and had started toward her. To the intense disappointment of the boys who had brought in the reptile, she did not scream; instead, she tightened the noose. The snake went limp again, and she took it outside, where the boys finished it off.

Storms were another emergency that country school teachers often had to cope with. In the plains states, the ever-present threat of tornadoes terrified rural school teachers, particularly those only a few years older than the children they taught. Usually, though, it was possible to see a tornado coming and take shelter in a storm cellar;

everyone knew what to do if a tornado threatened.

Blizzards posed a different problem, because most farm children who walked or rode to school assumed that they could make it home before a storm worsened. In most cases, either the children left school early and found their way home, or, if a really bad storm threatened, their parents came to pick them up. As late as the 1940s, few rural roads had high centers and graded shoulders, so during a blizzard it was easy to miss the road altogether.

Spring storms were the worst. At that time of year, teachers spent many anxious hours scanning the sky when the barometer fell and the wind increased. Spring storms meant frozen mud, because usually there had been a January thaw and excess water had drained into sloughs and ponds. Such was the case on March 15, 1920, when North Dakota had one of the worst blizzards on record. In two tragic instances, four brothers died while trying to return home from school and a country school teacher died while saving her students. Some snow was falling when Adolph, Ernest, Sorn and Herman Wohlk hitched their horses to the sled and drove the team to school near Ryder, N.D. Hazel Miner, 15, a teacher at Center, N.D., got to school early that day with her brother, Emmet, 11, and her sister, Myrdith, 8, in order to have a fire in the stove when the rest of the children arrived. As the day passed, the sky grew dark and temperatures started to drop quickly. In all the western states, country schools closed early that day, and parents came to get their children. The Wohlk brothers were sure that they could get home, as was Hazel with her younger brother and sister. However, the Wohlk brothers lost their sled in thin ice only a mile from home. Adolph, the oldest boy, started home but never made it. When the rest of the family found the sled, the younger brothers had all frozen to death. The Miners' sled, too, fell through the ice, and the children were drenched. To protect them from the biting wind and fierce cold, Hazel took off her coast, wrapped them in it and lay down on top of them. Fortunately, they survived. The citizens of North Dakota remember Hazel's bravery and have placed a statue dedicated to her in front of the state capitol at Bismarck.

In *Winter Thunder* (1954), a story based on an experience of her cousin, Mari Sandoz, also a country school teacher, describes the terrific blizzard that blanketed the Nebraska plains during the winter of 1949. The schoolchildren and their teacher, Lecia, abandon a school bus stuck in deep snow and start out for the nearest ranch but are forced to make a snow shelter to survive the fury of the storm.

> The teacher squinted back along the line, moving like some long snowy winter-logged animal, the segmented back bowed before the sharpening blizzard wind. Just the momentary turn into the storm took her breath and frightened her for these children hunched into themselves, half of them crying softly, hopelessly, as though already lost. They must hurry. With not a rock anywhere and not a tree within miles to show the directions, they had to seek out the landmark of the ranch country—the wire fence. So the girl started downwind again, breaking the new drifts as she searched for valley ground where fences were most likely, barbed-wire fences that might lead to a ranch, or nowhere except around some hay meadow. But it was their only chance, the girl from the sand hills knew. Stumbling, floundering through the snow, she kept the awkward string moving, the eyes of the older ones straining through frozen lashes for even the top of one fence post,

those of the small ones turned in upon their fear as the snow caked on the mufflers over their faces and they stumbled blindly to the pull from ahead.

Finally they find a small hillside and begin to build a brush shelter with bits of willow branches and the blankets they took from the school bus. The children were cold, hungry and terrified by the storm's ferocity.

But as the blankets came down, part of the loose snow wall was blown in by the force of the blizzard, the huddle of children suddenly white again, the fire almost smothered. So the wall had to be rebuilt in discouragement, but with care, using more brush and sticks, more fire-softened snow to freeze in place as soon as it was struck by the storm. . . . The wall must be finished, and when it was solid, Calla came to whisper under the roar of the wind. "Bill's been eating the lunch," she said.

"Oh, Bill! That's not fair to the others, to your own little sister Joanie!" Lecia called. Suddenly not the good teacher, she grabbed up the containers and hung them on high branches in plain sight for watching, for reminders and derision from the other children. "Why, it may be days before we are found!" she scolded, in her exasperation saying what should have been kept hidden in silence.

She was right—the blizzard of 1949 lasted eight days. Only with patience and the frontier spirit of endurance were the children able to survive, spotted at last by a search plane and later picked up by a rescue party.

Inexperienced or not, the teacher was expected to be knowledgeable in all areas, ever-resourceful, sincere and courageous. In 1915 a survey of Wyoming teachers showed that 41 percent had four full years of secondary training, but 54 percent of the 1,077 teachers responding did not report on their professional training or reported that they had received no such training. Probably many of the teachers had not even been to high school, yet they inspired their students and helped them to adjust to a world outside of their remote rural areas. Occasionally, the children endured the tyranny of a poor teacher who was rehired year after year. A teacher who had a bad temper or no ability to keep order could negatively affect a child's attitude toward learning and give the school district a bad name. More often, however, when former country school students are asked whether they received a good education the response is, "The teacher made the school." Learning seems to have taken place in the kind of environment most educators can only theorize about today, one of trust and confidence. The students were eager to learn, and the teachers believed that they had something to give the students. Rhea Paskett Toyn recalled the teachers she had in Grouse Creek, Utah, in the 1920s: "As a child I became attached to school teachers; they were important in my life. I'd shed tears when they'd go. . . ."

Neil Twitchell, who attended rural schools in Nevada in the 1920s, summarizes the feelings of many country school students toward their teachers:

By far, the most important part of my experience was the relationship between the students and the teachers . . . the closeness . . . of the whole community. . . . And I'm sure you'd find that in almost any of the little communities throughout our nation. I'm sure it wasn't materials. . . . I think a lot of it had to do with just plain old human relations. . . .

Cover sheet for "Thirteen Were Saved," a song about the 1888 blizzard, known as the Schoolchildren's Blizzard because of the many schoolchildren throughout the Midwest who were stranded in one-room schools. The song extols Minnie Freeman of the Myra School District, Neb., who led her students to safety. (Nebraska State Historical Society)

# Country Schools as Community Centers

When 15 miles was a long way to travel in one day with a team of horses, the schoolhouse was the social center of the community. The more remote the area, the more important the school. All groups met there—the wheat growers association, 4-H clubs and homemakers, sewing and quilting clubs. County agents gave demonstrations of new farming products or techniques there. Ladies' aid societies met there. After a wedding, friends would hold a shivaree for the newly married couple at the schoolhouse. Baseball games and field days drew people to the school for wheelbarrow races and potato-balancing contests. When rural people thought about gathering with friends and neighbors, airing complaints about crops and the weather, trading recipes and dress patterns and arguing about politics, they thought about the school.

Each community made its own decisions about who could use the school building. Most communities used the school to house entertainment, social services, political meetings and school-related social events in which the entire community participated. When a dance was planned at the Dry Hollow Schoolhouse, everyone knew where it was—and they all came.

"We had to make our own entertainment in those days," recalls Roberta Ogden, a retired teacher who taught in country schools in Utah and Colorado for many years. "We had a party at the drop of a hat, and the main place to gather was at the schoolhouse. After Christmas, when we were snowed in and there was no way to get out and we needed something to do, we would maybe go down to the schoolhouse and play cards until all hours of the morning. Many times, the roads were so bad and people had come in horse-drawn rigs, so we'd put the horses in the barn, stay all night and get home just after sunrise, in time to do the chores."

Practical frontier communities used the schools for all occasions. The buildings were never locked (most still are not), and newly arrived settlers could always open their bedrolls on the hardwood floors. Margaret Darien, of Basalt, Colo., remembers that "the country school was the heart of the community. People liked to go there and visit friends from up and down the valley."

The school cemented a sense of place for students and parents, bachelors and widows and anyone else within walking or riding distance. In some communities the men maintained the exterior of the building, and the women did their best to keep the interior clean, usually giving it a thorough cleaning before school began in the fall. In a country school, people of all ages came together to learn, to sing and worship, to get married and be buried.

## School Programs

People from miles around came to country schools to attend school programs throughout the school year—at Halloween, Thanksgiving,

*opposite*
Blue School, near Rifle, Colo., April 30, 1905. President Theodore Roosevelt, who was on a hunting expedition in the area, addressed 200–300 people at a church service. (Rev. Horace Mann, Rifle Creek Museum)

Christmas, Easter and eighth-grade graduation in early June. Spring and fall programs usually included a basket social. The Young Citizens League, a youth group, also held programs twice a year in many schools. National holidays frequently were occasions for programs and community get-togethers. Small schools were the center of rural social life, so teachers would organize special programs for Valentine's Day, Washington and Lincoln's birthdays, Arbor Day, Memorial Day, Parent's Day and May Day, with its maypole dance and recessional.

A typical program featured community singing, two or three readings of humorous or inspirational pieces and then musical solos on accordions, violins, pianos or whatever instruments were handy. Programs concluded with an address by a local resident that included community news. A teacher who did not have a successful program might not be rehired for the coming term. Teachers' contracts often stipulated that they present at least two programs a year.

Schoolchildren performed in buildings so crowded that some spectators had to stand along the edges of the schoolroom, in the entryway or even at open windows outside the building. In *Fairview: True Tales of a Country Schoolhouse* (1981), Lettie B. Zion describes the enthusiasm of an eastern Colorado audience for such events:

> A flurry of excitement filled the place on these occasions, and the children usually found places to sit—but couldn't sit still—they twisted, turned, wiggled and squirmed, or had to get up and go outdoors often before it was time for the program to begin. Many people had to stand up as there often was not enough seats—even with wagon seats and planks laid across nail kegs.

At a program at Clark School, District No. 14, in Douglas County, S.D., in the 1930s, the crowd was so large that gas lamps on the school walls would not burn because there was not enough oxygen left in the room.

Of all the special events held at the schoolhouse, none had more importance than the Christmas program, the gala occasion of the year. Some teachers began to prepare for the program as early as October, although most began rehearsing plays, poems and recitations immediately after Thanksgiving. Not a single child was ever left out; frequently, lessons stopped two weeks in advance so that the entire school could make final preparations. Gifts and candies were ordered by mail, and parents packaged nuts and fruits. At noon on the day of the program, the teacher dismissed school. Parents returned in the afternoon to help decorate the tree so it would be a delightful surprise for their children. Toddlers who came to watch their brothers and sisters perform began to look forward to school. Many children saw their first Christmas tree at the school Christmas program. In the days when trees were lighted by candles, men were posted on either side of the tree as firewatchers. One innovative farmer in South Dakota in the 1930s lighted the school tree with electric lights powered by a radio battery.

At a 1914 Christmas program near Towner, N.D., every person in the community crowded into the school despite temperatures outside of 40 degrees below zero. Occasionally, blizzards on the evening of the program forced everyone to stay at school overnight. At one North Dakota school where this occurred, the children performed the program

Consolidated rural school, Sonora, Calif., c. 1918. An elaborate May Day celebration, complete with a decorated Maypole, brought together parents and students. (California Historical Society Library)

School, Hughes County, S.D., 1925. Diplomas in hand, proud graduates and their parents posed at an eighth-grade graduation ceremony. (South Dakota State Historical Society)

twice to help pass the time. Afterwards, they wrapped themselves in coats and went to sleep on the floor, while the adults conversed and played cards through the night.

In the mining communities and company towns of southern Colorado, coal companies provided a bag of Christmas goodies for each schoolchild, delivered by a person dressed as Santa. After the bloody coal miners' strike in Ludlow, Colo., in 1914, the unions grew stronger and supplied the Christmas bags themselves.

Because of crowded conditions in her one-room school at Soldier's Summit, Utah, in the 1930s, Roberta Ogden, the teacher, decided to hold the Christmas program in the local bar one year. She remembers:

> We all got prepared for Christmas Eve—we even brought the piano down from the schoolhouse. We had all the gifts and costumes and treats laid out, but for some reason the barkeep decided to go to the next town that day, where he got drunk, and he didn't come back. When we went to have our program, we couldn't get in—he had locked the place up. A couple of men decided to break the lock on the door, and we went in and had a great time. The next day the barkeep came home and said he had hidden $65 in the coal hod under the coal and that we had burned it up when we started a fire in there. Well, the party cost us $65, but in spite of that everything went pretty well.

The only event that generated as much excitement as the Christmas program was the end-of-school picnic in early June, which was often coupled with the graduation for eighth-grade students. Sack races, horse races, baseball games and horseshoe contests followed a picnic in a shady grove near school. This celebration was held to honor even a single graduate, as was often the case. John H. Wood, Honey Creek School District correspondent to the Eureka, Kans., *Messenger*, described the last-day-of-school dinner held in 1896 at the Honey Creek School in Greenwood County, Kans.:

> We spread out the school boards on each side of the room and thereon spread tablecloths—white as the snow. . . . within were seventeen different kinds of cake, pickled pigs' feet and hot coffee, jam, jelly, pies and other things too numerous to mention. . . . one of the most social times we ever had on dear old Honey Creek.

## Social Gatherings

In country schools, music served as the great socializer, bringing together diverse members of the community, including non-English-speaking immigrants. The German-Russians, Swedes, Norwegians and Italians may not have spoken English well, but for their children's programs they learned to sing patriotic songs in English. At singing sessions, known as singing schools, students learned hymns such as "Rock of Ages" and "Bringing in the Sheaves." Many of the young people who attended these singing schools probably were as interested in meeting members of the opposite sex as in learning new songs.

A musical concert with fiddles, guitars, zithers and accordions was often the highlight of a winter evening. As the community's economic status improved, the school board bought an organ or piano. Teachers who could play the piano were hired, so prospective teachers often listed their musical skills along with their academic background in letters to school board members.

At the Liberty Eagle School near Hamilton, Mo., in the 1930s, the teacher, Walter Ashworth, recognizing musical talent in his students, organized the Shoal Creek Band, which included such simple instruments as harmonicas, jew's-harps, paper and combs, tambourines, snare drums and a guitar. In this band, most of the students had their first experience in playing or singing before the public. The band became so popular that it was invited to other rural schools, to a nearby district high school and to local churches. The students worked hard to learn their solo and instrumental numbers, and Ashworth had to squeeze in music lessons along with the 45 other daily lesson preparations.

Although concerts were held in country schools and an occasional soloist would perform as part of a winter revival meeting, the music that was appreciated most was that played at community dances, which were always well attended. Older people came to share their knowledge of dances from the old country and younger people to try out the new round dances. Young parents brought their children and bedded them down on the benches. Lillian Grace Chadwick Warburton of Grouse Creek, Utah, remembers a dance held in Etna, Box Elder County, when she was teaching there in 1918:

> They decided they would have a real dance, so we pushed back all the desks and benches against the wall to make as many seats as we could for anybody who came. We erased anything we had on the board such as phonics and wrote, "Come one, come all, come short, come tall, come jump the tracks in Etna Hall." They got an accordion player, and he played the polka and the Virginia reels and all the square dances you could think of. Those boards just hopped along with the rest of us. It was really lively. There wasn't room for everybody to get on the floor at once. We had a really good time.

On the night of the country school dance, everyone rushed to get their farm and household chores done ahead of time so they could clean up, put on fresh clothes and head for the schoolhouse. The first people to arrive at the schoolhouse had to stoke up the fire, set the desks around the perimeter of the room and sprinkle a little cornmeal on the hardwood floor to protect it from the dancers' shoes. The musicians arrived to tune up their instruments—a few guitars, maybe a piano, always a violin. Families arrived in wagons that they pulled up into the schoolyard. When enough people had arrived, the fiddler standing on the teacher's platform would stamp his foot and call for friends and neighbors to "gather around, grab a partner and find the turkey in the straw." The children danced too and played around the wood stove and out in the stable. Toddlers slept on the desk tops, and even the older children took naps despite the din. Several men would appropriate the front steps as their spot for drinking, so no respectable woman ever went to the privy by herself. Half a dozen times the dancing would stop and groups of women would go together to the outhouse. Around midnight the musicians had to rest. Out came enormous quantities of food and strong black coffee. Then the fiddler would warm up again, and the piano player would call for the supper waltz, during which everyone was supposed to dance with his or her beloved. If two cowboys were courting the same girl, she had to be diplomatic, or someone might get hurt.

Rural school, Muskogee County, Okla., 1940. A boy stoked the fire for the evening's pie supper. (Russell Lee, FSA)

Rural school, Muskogee County, Okla., 1940. Homemade pies were the highlight of a February evening pie supper or box social. (Russell Lee, FSA)

Enthusiasm for dances often resulted in damage to the building. Pete King, a student at the Evergreen School, Hot Springs County, Wyo., remembers gasoline lanterns going out during a school dance because the dust raised by the dancers clogged the air vents in the lanterns. Schoolhouse dances were often an occasion for fighting, for if two people had a grudge to settle, the schoolyard seemed as good a place as any. At the Upper Cattle Creek School near Glenwood Springs in the Colorado Rockies in 1950, a fight broke out at a schoolhouse between two cowboys, one of whom had lost his wife to the other. The dance floor cleared as the two men went down wrestling. The outraged husband got in a few licks, but his adversary drew a pistol and began to shoot. John McNulty, a former student present that night, recalls:

> They all tried to get the gun. As near as I can figure it, five shots were fired. The bad part of it was that the school desks were pushed up against the walls, with little children asleep on them. One bullet went right through the top of a hardwood desk and buried itself in the wood. A baby sleeping on the desk was unhurt. Another bullet went through a bookcase.

After the man had emptied the gun, local ranchers and farmers dragged him out of the schoolhouse and severely beat him. He was lucky. At a country school dance near Meeteetse, Wyo., in the 1920s, a troublemaker was beaten to death.

Usually, when the dance ended, people went home. Tired cowboys swung into the saddle, and married couples bundled up their babies in the buckboard and put hot rocks or sadirons in buffalo robes at their feet. Sometimes, however, after putting the desks back and setting the building in order, the families would stay a while longer in the school. Occasionally, one of the men would pick up a Bible, read a few verses, preach a short sermon and lead the group in prayer.

Box socials held at the schoolhouse generated almost as much excitement as dances. To finance improvements in country schools, conservative farmers preferred a one-time donation at a play or box social to an increase in taxes or a mill levy that would stay on the books forever. For that reason, every kind of fund-raising activity imaginable took place in country schools. Schools sponsored box socials, pie socials and ice cream socials; in lean years, they even had cornmeal mush socials. In this way, country schools made enough money to pay for playground equipment, water containers, clocks or anything else that might be needed  A single box social could raise enough money to buy an encyclopedia, new textbooks, a pendulum clock, a globe or extra desks for the school.

The typical pie supper, or box social, began with the auctioning off of dozens of well-wrapped boxes, usually shoe boxes, stuffed with homemade pies, breads, jellies, sweet potatoes, baked potatoes and huge chunks of beef or pork sandwiched between rolls spread thickly with butter. Most boxes were sold for less than a dollar or, at the most, for a few dollars, although occasionally a man particularly determined to impress a woman might bid as much as $30 or a month's wages. A few suitors bid more money than they had in their wallets and had to sell some of their possessions to settle their debt. Bidding on the schoolteacher's box was an eagerly anticipated event because the successful bidder got to eat with the schoolteacher. One man might bid on his neighbor's wife's box and get a perfectly good chicken dinner for 90 cents, while a cowboy fresh in from line camp might spend half a month's salary just to sit with the schoolteacher and eat her biscuits, which might be as hard as rocks.

## Literaries and Debates

Literary societies evolved from lyceums, organizations sponsoring lectures, concerts and the like, which sprang up in the eastern United States in the mid-19th century. In many cities, the winter lecture series of lyceums had become a fixed institution as early as 1858. The most popular of the summer lyceums was the Chautauqua Assembly, an annual summer educational and recreational assembly begun in 1874 and held in Chautauqua, N.Y.

Isolated homesteaders were often starved for poetry and music. Many settlers were literate people who had abandoned their books when they moved west but had not lost their love of knowledge or eagerness for a good debate. In the early 1900s Ford County, Kans., had 50 active literary societies that met in the country schools. At the Yarnold School in Douglas County, Kans., adults voted to form a debating society in 1902 "for our mutual improvement, for the entertainment of our friends and for the cultivation of the amenities of social life" (quoted by Goldie Piper Daniels in *Rural Schools and Schoolhouses of Douglas County, Kansas*, 1978). Men over 15 years of age were charged a fee of 10 cents.

Audiences in the East sought speakers of eloquence, presence and reputation, but on the frontier, people would flock to hear almost any speaker, no matter what his or her credentials. Wandering minstrels and traveling photographers, for example, found eager audiences in country schools. On the frontier, literary meetings, or literaries, were a practical form of entertainment because they required no stage and no special arrangement of school desks. The literary would usually begin with recitations, dialogues (usually from Shakespeare) and readings (primarily from the McGuffey readers). In her novel *Lantern in Her Hand* (1928), Bess Streeter Aldrich describes the Stove Creek Precinct Literary Reading Circle, which met at the Woodpecker School in eastern Nebraska. During the winter of 1876, "the schooner Hesperus was wrecked, little Paul Dombey died, Hamlet met his father's ghost and the Raven quothed more times than there were meetings. . . . "

After the recitations would come a short recess, followed by the highlight of the evening—the debate. One frivolous debate topic, a favorite in Kansas and Nebraska, was, "Which is the most useful, the dishrag or the broom?" Other issues debated were whether a boy born on a farm should stay on the farm, whether a soldier serves his country more than a farmer (usually decided in the negative) and whether a farm woman works harder and has less recreation than a farm man. Serious topics—the value of the Taylor Grazing Act, which restricted access to open range in the West, women's suffrage and the question of entry into World War I—could lead to serious debates. One debate topic of the 1920s raised the question of whether a tractor or horses were more profitable to the farmer; on one occasion, a person in the audience laughed and replied that he needed his horses to go into town to get tractor parts. Debates in the Black Hills of South Dakota covered such topics as whether a person is morally bound to obey a law that he or she believes to be wrong and whether humankind would benefit if charging and collecting interest were made illegal. In the latter debate, the affirmative won handily. At literaries, men and women who would later launch political campaigns, enter the professions or become involved in land and cattle empires got their first introduction to Robert's Rules of Order. Some debates did, however, degenerate into fistfights.

In addition to singing, recitations and debates, another favorite lyceum activity was dramatic performances. The repertoire might include *Aaron Slick from Punkin' Crick, The Irish Detective, Robin Hood and His Merry Men, Let Toby Do It* and other melodramas and spoofs. In the early 1900s, one production earned enough money for a rural school district in Spirit Lake Township, Kingsbury County, S.D., to pay for a new floor.

### Political Events

Politics, too, brought community members to country schools. Issues such as the populist movement, the Farmers Alliance, the temperance movement and women's suffrage stirred heated discussion. Schools served as polling places for county, state and national elections and as

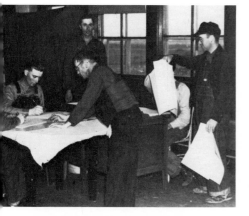

Beaver Creek School, McIntosh County, N.D., 1940. An election committee met to verify the number of registered voters. (John Vachon, FSA)

meeting places for water boards, the Rural Electric Association and the Farmers Union. In Iowa the Grange held open meetings and occasional oyster suppers in schools. The Nonpartisan League, a progressive farm-oriented political movement that flourished from 1916 to 1924, met in rural schools in North and South Dakota and in Kansas. Later the Farm Bureau met in the same buildings to discuss graveling county roads and improving rural mail service. In the West the vicious range wars between cattle and sheep ranchers were mediated in one-room schools.

The schoolhouse was the logical place for politicians to address a community. On April 30, 1905, President Theodore Roosevelt took time out from a hunting expedition to speak at a church service at Blue School, south of Rifle, Colo. In *Outdoor Pastimes of an American Hunter* (1905), Roosevelt recalled the occasion:

> One Sunday we rode down some six miles from camp to a little blue school-house and attended service. The preacher was in the habit of riding over every alternate Sunday from Rifle, a little town twenty or twenty-five miles away; and the ranchmen with their wives and children, some on horseback, some in wagons, had gathered from thirty miles round to attend the service. The crowd was so large that the exercises had to take place in the open air, and it was pleasant to look at the strong frames and rugged, weather-beaten faces of the men; while as for the women, one respected them even more than the men.

Country schools still serve as polling centers and township halls throughout the United States, just as their urban counterparts do.

## Church Services

Rural churches grew out of congregations that originally met in country schools. All groups used the school as a pulpit—Presbyterians, Baptists, Lutherans, Methodists, Adventists and Catholics. Church elders would meet once a month at the school to make plans for their congregations.

Board-and-batten and clapboard school, Oklahoma, c. 1910. Indians and whites attended Sunday School and church services in this one-room school. (National Archives)

Circuit-riding ministers, in addition to conducting services, would hold baptisms, confirmations, weddings and even funerals at the school. In *Our Yesterdays* (1970), Verda Arnold describes the Sunday interdenominational services at the Lame Johnny School in western South Dakota:

> Sunday gathered together Roman Catholics, Episcopalians, Christian Scientists, Methodists, Baptists and folks of any denomination who happened to be among us. We sang hymns. Hazel Howe played the organ, and we had classes learning Bible verses and Bible stories and we got our lessons from them.

Congregations met sometimes for decades in schoolhouses. The Dakota Congregational Church in southern Kingsbury County, S.D., met for 20 years in the Brown School. The Bethel Mennonite Church of rural Marion, S.D., met in the West Vermillion School, District No. 17, from its construction in 1883 until a church building was erected in 1892. Congregations that met in schoolhouses in coal-mining communities expected the schoolteacher to teach Sunday school three Sundays a month. Neglecting this obligation could cost the teacher his or her job.

Winter evenings were a favorite time for revival meetings. In *A Son of the Middle Border* (1917), Hamlin Garland describes revival meetings held in a one-room schoolhouse near Burr Oak, Iowa:

> As I peer back into that crowded little schoolroom, smothering hot and reeking with lamp smoke, and recall the half-lit familiar faces of the congregation, it all has the quality of a vision, something experienced in another world. The preacher, leaping, sweating, roaring till the windows rattle, the mothers with sleeping babes in their arms, the sweet, strained faces of the girls, the immobile wondering men, are spectral shadows, figures encountered in the phantasmagoria of disordered sleep.

Traveling preachers conducted funeral services in country schools, and the students would "mingle with the burying"—i.e., pay their respects to the deceased. In some instances, a cemetery would be next to the schoolhouse. Both the Moore Hill School in Crook County, Wyo., and the Little Greenbrier School and Church in Elkmont, Tenn., for example, had adjacent cemeteries.

## Community Service

On the frontier, schoolhouses served as forts and shelters from Indian attack. During the summer of 1880, settlers from Mancos, Colo., fled to a one-room school and stockade that had been built for protection from the Ute Indians. A sod schoolhouse near the western South Dakota border was boarded up at the time of the Wounded Knee Indian massacre, and local settlers stayed inside the 24-inch-thick walls. In neither instance did Indians attack, and after a few days the settlers rather sheepishly went home.

Country schools also saw use as hospitals. In 1917 the tiny community of Tructon, Colo., on the high plains east of Colorado Springs, built a new two-room school. The school board officers had installed a hardwood floor, woodwork stained mahogany and two Waterbury stoves, but before the building was completed it was used as a temporary hospital for victims of the Spanish flu.

During the devastating drought and crop failure in Kansas and Nebraska in the mid-1890s, relief committees worked out of schoolhouses. During the 1913–14 coal strike, a southern Colorado community prepared breakfast at the school for schoolchildren. During the Great Depression, children who had nothing except boiled onions for breakfast could look forward to a decent lunch of stew donated by people in the community and of milk provided by a school board member's cow.

Teachers dipped into their own pocketbooks to buy mementos for the class and to help clothe students whose pants were threadbare and whose shirts were in tatters. Country school teachers also organized their pupils to help neighbors in need. In the 1930s a farmer living near Carbondale, Colo., was dying of cancer and so could not handle his potato crop, which needed to be dug, bagged and stored in the cellar to be safe from the coming winter. In his condition, he could not get his crop in and make the money necessary for his family to survive a few more months. When he finally went out to try his hand in the fields, he found there many neighbors who had come to help—the teacher had dismissed school for the day so the youngsters could lend a hand. Later she commented that the farmer needed their assistance and that the children learned more in the potato field that day than they would have in school.

Rural school, Wyoming, c. 1905. Community members supervised voter registration on election day. (American Heritage Center, University of Wyoming)

### Moonlight Schools

The light-hearted social atmosphere in country schools during the evenings gave way to serious study in the 1920s, when country schools were used at night for adult education, hence their name "moonlight schools." The idea originated with Cora Wilson Stewart, an enterprising county superintendent of schools in Rowan County, Ky. Dismayed by the number of adults in her county who could neither read nor write, Stewart pledged the full support of her office to enlist country school teachers in a campaign to educate adults. She describes the phenomenal success of her project in her book *Moonlight Schools for the Emancipation of Adult Illiterates* (1922).

The schools taught adults between the ages of 18 and 86 how to read their Bibles, write letters to their children and sign their names with more than just their mark. As night schools burgeoned in the cities, moonlight schools began to reach people in the country who had never had a basic education. Teachers visited the homes of illiterate people and encouraged them to come to the moonlight schools to learn to read and write.

School trustees often joined adults who attended moonlight schools, many of whom had been too busy working or too ashamed to attend local schools during the day and sit with little children. When the program was initiated in 1911, Rowan County, Ky., school board members estimated that three students would attend each school, for a total of 150 students in the county; instead, 1,200 persons attended the first session and 1,600 the second session.

Children encouraged their parents and grandparents to come, and they did. In her book, Stewart wrote:

I stood in the door of New Hope school-house one evening and watched the throng come trooping through the moonlight to school. There were farmers and farmers' wives, and their grown sons and daughters; there were former school teachers who had seized this opportunity to break up the stagnation which had overtaken them; there was the community carpenter, the district blacksmith, the postmaster and his wife, the country doctor, the cross-roads merchant, the mill-owner with his crew of illiterate men, all coming joyously, hopefully, in quest of knowledge. It was "new hope" indeed to them. Some came to learn, some to teach, but all learned, for those who taught developed amazingly.

Within three years, the movement had spread to Alabama, Minnesota, Oklahoma, North Carolina and Tennessee and helped reduce substantially adult illiteracy in the rural areas of these states.

The country school served utilitarian purposes unique to any building of its size in rural areas of the United States. Many people grew up with the schoolhouse as the center of their lives. Everything important took place there. They attended school there as children, it was the focus for social events, it was the place for cultural activities, including church and Sunday school, and it offered the best education they could afford for their own children. The more isolated the community, the more significant the schoolhouse was.

Rock School (1867), Fillmore, Utah, 1930s, with furnishings arranged for lectures and a variety of community activities. (HABS)

# Country Schools and the Assimilation Process

During the 19th and early 20th centuries, immigrants thronged to America in search of freedom and opportunity. This country offered people the opportunity to make their own way—in mountain mining camps or on homesteads on the Great Plains. Naturally, the large numbers of foreign-born residents had a profound effect on local education.

After the Civil War, immigrants from northern and southern Europe, Russia, Canada and Mexico came in waves across the Dakotas, in lines of wagon trains across the prairie and by train to the end of the railhead. Men worked as section hands for the railroad and as miners in coal, gold and silver mines; others farmed. In the mountains and plains states, for example, between 1870 and 1890, 58 new counties in Kansas were settled with recent arrivals from eastern states and foreign shores. In Nebraska, Irish immigrants settled in Holt County in 1874 and Greeley County in 1877; Germans settled in Madison, Stanton and Thayer counties between 1867 and 1870; Swedes moved into Polk, Saunders, Phelps and Burt counties; and Bohemians began colonies in Knox, Colfax, Saunders and Saline counties. In the 1870s Germans from Russia as well as Danes, Poles and French immigrated to Nebraska. In 1890, one year after North Dakota achieved statehood, 43 percent of the state's 191,000 people were foreign-born. In the same year, one person out of seven of the population of Wyoming came from abroad. In 1900 immigrants made up 47.6 percent of the population of the 11 western states. In Utah, Montana, California and Nevada, they were in the majority. Immigrants composed 77.5 percent of the population in North Dakota, 74.9 percent in Minnesota and 61.1 percent in South Dakota. Most of the current population in the West and Midwest is descended from these pioneers.

Assimilation proved difficult for those who spoke a different language, ate strange food, wore unusual clothing and did not understand the American legal or monetary system. Many groups stayed in close-knit colonies, to provide support for each other and maintain their traditions. Individual families that lived apart from other immigrants became Americanized much sooner than their peers, but every family experienced great difficulties. In "German Immigrants and Parochial Schools" in *Issues in Christian Education* (1967), Frederick C. Luebke writes:

> When the typical non-English speaking immigrant arrived in America, he knew that he would have problems of adjustment to life in a new land. He expected language difficulties, climatic differences, unfamiliar units of measurement or of money, or strange political practices. Rational men could foresee these. But there was nothing in the typical immigrant's experience that could prepare him for the myriad frustrations, disillusionments and negative encounters with American people and American customs, the sum total of which we today call cultural shock.
>
> To his dismay and confusion, the immigrant found that the marks of his self-respect in Europe, the signs which granted him status in his old-world community, were of no account in America.

*opposite*
Ojo Sorco School (c. 1900), Ojo Sorco, N.M., 1943. This one-room school in a mountainous, isolated Spanish-American community had two teachers who taught in Spanish, the children's first language. (John Collier, OWI)

Of the 17 million people who passed through Ellis Island, many initially went no further than the tenements of New York City; others migrated to Cleveland or Chicago, Boston or Pittsburgh. But some dreamed of unplowed soil and of acquiring estates far larger than they could hope to own in the old country. Some could read and write their own language, but most could not. Some groups spurned education while others embraced it. But for all immigrants who lived in rural areas, the country school played a major role in their assimilation into American culture.

## Immigrants' Views on Education

One group that typified many immigrants' attitudes toward education was the Germans from Russia. For 200 years, Germans had lived in Russia as a little island of Germanic culture. There they farmed successfully and developed a turkey-red wheat, which, when transplanted to the Great Plains of the United States, made the region the breadbasket of the world. To keep their children from becoming assimilated into Russian culture, the German-Russians kept strict prohibitions concerning marriage, education and the church. As economic, political and religious conditions in the Ukraine and along the Black Sea worsened, they emigrated. From the 1870s until World War I, German-Russians streamed into the United States and Canada, settling on land that earlier immigrants thought unfit for farming. Many came to work in the sugar beet fields. By 1920 nearly 200,000 German-Russians had settled in Kansas, Colorado, Nebraska and the Dakotas. As immigrants to the United States, the German-Russians found conditions similar to those their ancestors had experienced on the Russian steppes. Again, prairie stretched as far as the eye could see; again, they had to toil hard to survive.

The German-Russians valued land more than education for their sons and daughters. In the village schools in Russia, they had learned little. Illiteracy was the rule, not the exception. "What would I need an education for, except to preach or teach?" asked Reuben Goertz, of Freeman, S.D., a son of a German-Russian immigrants. "Those were the only acceptable alternatives to staying home to farm. Otherwise, education introduced you to worldly things which would lure you away not only from the community but from the church and the old traditions." One American school practice that many Germans were suspicious of was the hiring of women schoolteachers, for in Russia women were not allowed to teach. The German-Russians were accustomed to the rough voice and firm hand of the "Schulmeister." Because of these attitudes, many of the children of the German-Russian immigrants attended school only sporadically.

In the United States, however, the German-Russians could own land for the first time, and they were protected by constitutional religious freedoms. Within a generation, the cultural bonds that had held them together through droughts and depressions in Russia began to loosen. In country schools in Colorado, Wyoming, Kansas, Nebraska and the Dakotas, German-Russians began to adopt a new culture and change the long pattern of isolation they had maintained in Russia.

Italian-Swiss Colony School (c. 1900), Asti, Calif. The parents of these students were brought to this community to help start the California wine-making industry. (California Historical Society Library)

## From Parochial Schools to Public Schools

St. Joseph's School, Hays, Kans., 1884. Students and teachers at this Catholic school posed in front of their frame schoolhouse. Many parochial schools were similar architecturally to public schools. (CSL)

Many immigrant groups—including the German Mennonites, Italian Catholics, Swedish Protestants and Latter-day Saints, or Mormons—established in their communities parochial schools, intended to provide religious and language instruction for their children. In many communities these parochial schools were the only schools. Within a generation, however, these communities had to accept secular education. The younger generation did not feel it necessary to speak only German or Swedish or Norwegian, and the parochial schools declined. Moreover, states passed laws requiring longer attendance at public schools. Beginning in 1915, Kansas required that all students in the German parochial schools attend public school for three months; the state then increased compulsory attendance to five months, seven months and, by 1930, nine months. Other states followed suit. In "A Recipe for Nationality Stew" in *Dakota Panorama* (1973), Douglas Chittick writes, "Before and sometimes after the compulsory school attendance law was passed in South Dakota in 1915, a person of immigrant stock could be born, reared, married, could farm and be buried without knowing much if any English." Because the immigrant communities could not afford to finance both parochial schools and public schools, such laws gradually eliminated parochial schools and forced immigrant children into the mainstream.

The German Mennonites followed the pattern typical of immigrant groups that established parochial schools. Between 1873 and 1884, approximately 18,000 Mennonites settled in the Midwest. Devout in their religious beliefs, church elders organized parochial schools to teach the German language and the Bible. Writing, arithmetic and other elementary subjects were included. At the 1877 Western District Conference, the 70 Kansas Mennonite ministers and teachers recommended that Mennonites try to dominate local schools whenever possible; if it was not feasible to do this, then the conference recommended that they establish church schools. The conference also recommended the learning of English as well as German to facilitate communication with neighbors and to help extend the Kingdom of God among the English-speaking people. This theme is repeated throughout the history of midwestern country schools; tightly and well-organized communities dominated the local school boards and controlled public instruction.

Mennonite education entered a second phase when public schools were organized in local counties by state laws. Unwilling to give up German and religion as subjects of instruction, Mennonite congregations tried to support both their own and the public school systems. When the territory was first settled, it was easy to do this, because school terms rarely exceeded three or four months, and the laws governing the curriculum were liberal. Local districts could do as they pleased by stretching the statutes, permitting German to be taught regularly in some public schools and allowing an hour to be set aside each day before and after the official school hours for further instruction in religion, hymn singing and German culture.

## *The Public School Experience*

The public school was the institution that played the major role, directly or indirectly, in acculturating immigrants. In the company of friends and neighbors, immigrants could cling to their native customs, but the states required their children to attend public school, and there all instruction was in English. As the children adopted American mannerisms, their parents gradually abandoned their native customs. Where the child went, the adult followed. Immigrant children taught the English they learned in school to their brothers and sisters, and the children in turn taught their parents. Children became the bridge for their parents to cross into this confusing new culture.

Of all the difficulties that immigrant children experienced in their first years in country schools, the most trying was their inability to speak the English language. At home, they, their parents and grandparents spoke the language of the homeland. Nora Mohberg, in *A Home for Agate* (1966), describes the difficulties her Norwegian grandparents encountered in their one-room school:

> [S]chool to the Flatabos was as painful as pulling teeth. It was not that they objected to learning. To the contrary, their storytelling father had instilled in them a sincere love of learning. But the first school days for each one were a humiliating and painful warfare of tongues.
>
> The Norwegian language was still spoken at home. The children were all taught to read and write in the mother tongue at the same time that they were supposed to learn English. Even the smaller ones early learned the Norse alphabet, numerals, and nursery rhymes. But they learned no English until they started to school. And when they finally did learn to speak it, it was shed like a cast-off garment as soon as school was dismissed. The older children had learned to speak English fluently, but since they never used it at home, the twins knew only a very few words. They were in utter terror of both the new teacher and the new language. . . . "You see," Amelia said much later, "we couldn't understand what the teacher said most of the time. And we were too scared to answer her even when we did understand."

Children learned English because they had to and because they wanted to—they wanted to be able to communicate with their peers. Gladys Webster, who taught children of 12 nationalities at a one-room school in Dunn County, N.D., in the early 1920s, believes that the children were motivated to learn English so that they could talk to one another on the playground.

Reuben Goertz, who attended South Dakota schools as a child, remembers the discrimination he encountered in school because of his thick Russian accent:

> They were calling us Rooshians, damned Rooshians and Rooshian peanuts because of the sunflower seeds we all ate. We were made to feel, on our home turf, that we were out of the mainstream of the American lifestyle. . . . I really had no social intercourse with other kids. I had two lives, a school life and one at home.

Schoolchildren thought it was funny when an immigrant child would inadvertently twist the language, and they delighted in playing pranks. In his book *In Reminiscence* (1963), Harry Mollhagen recalls one such prank:

> Since my folks always talked German to us youngsters, I knew very little English when I started to school. I was a bashful kid so the folks thought best not to send me to school until I was seven years old. . . . On one occasion the report was circulated that the county school superintendent was to visit the school that morning.

The older boys told me that the superintendent was coming out to give us all a working over or "licken." I believed them and slipped away from school and spent the morning in the neighbor's cornfield! I did not show up until the horse and buggy had left the school grounds. Fortunately, the boys did not tell what had happened to me. I did get a lot of kidding from those whom I had believed.

In Utah mining camps, the situation was different. Valentine Vouk, a Slovene-Austrian, describes his experiences in 1910, when he was 14 years old:

> I mean to tell you we had a rough time. We had to fight our way to school, and we had to fight our way back . . . till they learned to leave us alone. . . . We were the only [Slovene-Austrian] family here, and boy, everybody was on us. The Frenchmen were on us, and we had to whip them. The Italians were on us, and we had to whip them. The Mormons were on us, and we had to whip them, too. Finally, we got so we got along together.

Because children of immigrant families were needed to work on the family farm, as were many rural children, they often missed school. Carl Peterson, a Swedish boy who attended a country school near Colon, Neb., in the 1890s recalled:

> Father used to come to school quite often and tell me to go and get the cattle off the neighbors' land. Sometimes Father would come at 11 a.m., and by the time I would get the cows home it would be noon. He would say, "Well, it's dinner time now, so you might as well herd the cows this afternoon." So it went. School was a side issue, it seemed. In all, I went to school three winters and finished the third grade.

If in the 1890s boys and girls on the Great Plains were kept home from school to help with chores, as late as 1920 immigrant families in the remote mountain areas of Colorado persisted in keeping their children out of school. In a letter dated February 1, 1921, and written to the superintendent of schools for Gunnison County, Colo., George Streber, who ranched near Somerset, Colo., complained about poor attendance at the Muddy Creek School, which he had helped organize:

> In regard to som of the children here some of the kids told me to Hell with the School. and we have 10 children so far. and going to have 3 more in a short time. but theyre are three Families below here in 3 miles and the wont send the kids. the told me to Hell with it.
>   So I think it be up to the Board of the District to make am go. to my believ the dont want the kids to go to school they want am to work at home.
>   So—kindly advise me what to do. Theyre is George Volk. He wont send his need am at home to feet Stock. and Voolojich his kids told me go to Hell with the School. and Mr. Voolopich said He wont send am

Often, in large farm families, the oldest girl was expected to stay home on washday to help with the laundry and care for the smaller children. In many instances, the oldest girl did not attend school at all. Bertha Boyum, 12 years old, who lived near Milnor, N.D., had been overjoyed with the prospect of attending school in the fall of 1894. Her mother, however, insisted she stay home to help. Bertha was heartbroken but knew better than to contest her mother's wishes. That first morning, Bertha watched with tears in her eyes while the others left for school. Aware of her disappointment, her father hired, by the end of the day, a servant girl so that Bertha could attend school. Most immigrants, however, could not afford to hire household help.

Wyatt School, Weld County, Colo., 1934. Students at this school reflected a wide range of ethnic backgrounds. (Greeley, Colo., Municipal Museums)

The situation could be difficult for both immigrant children and teachers who did not speak their language but still tried to communicate. Paul Swaniga attended a country school near Calhan, Colo., in the early 1930s and spoke only the Slovenian of his parents. That first week, the teacher asked him to come to her desk and, not understanding English, Paul did not comply with her request. Irritated, she told Paul to go home. He knew what a terrible beating he would receive for being sent home, so he hid in the haystack. When his brothers and sisters returned from school, his father learned what had happened. In a rage, he tore off his belt and started after his son, who tried to escape by running out of the haystack and back to school. The boy barely reached the classroom before his father was on him, cursing and flailing the heavy leather belt. The terrified teacher explained that Paul had committed only a minor infraction. The father, who spoke broken English, understood. Never again did the teacher send anyone home early from school.

Anna Brown Pummer, who attended a one-room school in the early 1900s in Rawlins County, Kans., recalls that the first year she went to school she could not speak English and the teacher knew no Bohemian. About all Anna learned that year was how to crochet. One North Dakota teacher had 13 French-speaking pupils, who spoke French to one another at school. Their comprehension of English was very poor, and school was difficult for pupils and teacher.

Difficulties in school extended beyond the classroom. Occasionally, because of ethnic sensitivity, teachers often could not find suitable places to live in the community where they were to teach. As late as 1910, permits had to be issued to untrained local people to teach in schools in eight communities in North Dakota where the majority of students were German-Russians; parents refused to accommodate teachers who were not of German origin.

The reception that a teacher received varied from place to place. Mattie M. Martin found teaching Polish and Italian pupils in the Gordson one-room school near Bryan, Tex., an interesting experience. Before 1922 only one family that was not Polish and Italian lived in this community. Most of the older parents had come from Poland or Italy as young people, and many of them spoke poor English or none. The children in the first and second grades had some difficulty in learning because of poor English. The parents often visited her school for special programs and holiday fun. They always praised her work and encouraged her to use strict discipline in correcting their children; they seemed to look up to her, although she was only 18 years old.

Acculturation worked both ways; teachers learned ethnic traditions from the children they taught. Laina Laitala Tilley explains how teachers in Finnish communities in Minnesota took on Finnish nicknames, whether they themselves were Finnish or not. Tilley describes how teachers were invited into Finnish homes for "sauna nights" and to enjoy ethnic foods and holidays. Unfortunately, teachers did not always understand the customs of the immigrant children they taught. Icelandic women retained their original family name after marriage, a practice some Americans thought shocking. The Icelanders' sons carried their father's surname and daughters their mother's surname, so a brother and sister had different surnames; this practice confused and annoyed some teachers. Another Icelandic tradition that was often misunderstood was the Ash Wednesday practice of pinning a bag of ashes onto the teacher's clothes. American teachers would sometimes severely punish pupils for this prank, which was acceptable humor in the children's culture.

At a country school near Hatton, N.D., Guri Sand had to restrain the teacher from whipping her sister, who, like most Norwegians, could not correctly pronounce her *js* and *ys*. A Colorado student, a German-Russian named Mary Lind, remembers a teacher who hit her brother on the head with a ruler because he would not answer questions and speak up. He would not answer the question because he did not know English, and the teacher made no attempt to teach him.

In the Dutch community east of Castlewood, S.D., the teacher would show students pictures of familiar objects and then teach them the English word for the objects. In this way, students were encouraged to learn and use English. Clarine Boyken recalls teachers of one-room rural schools who taught English to immigrant children by using a Sears, Roebuck catalog as a reference book.

Dedicated teachers became role models, examples of success in this new and complicated society. Solomon Schneider, a German-Russian who attended a country school in Colorado in the 1930s, relates how important it was for the teacher to come to dinner at his house once or twice a year. She always stayed in the guest bedroom, and his mother fixed an elaborate evening meal as well as a lunch for her the next day. Solomon deeply respected his teachers, and he taught in a country school for a few years.

Insensitive teachers only exacerbated the problems of shy immigrant children fumbling to speak and read a language they had never heard, but some teachers tried to help. A few attempts were made to incorporate immigrant values and traditions into country school classrooms. In *Helpful Hints for the Rural Teacher* (1924), Laura Bassett and Alice Smith advised:

> If your district is a foreign one, be sure to have one of your very earliest programs, "A Program of All Nations." Encourage the children to have parents bring pieces of all kinds of their native handwork, lovely Hardanger embroidery, Russian needlework, Italian hand carving. Put on folk dances in costume, encourage old folks to put on costumes, sing songs, play instruments. Let this night belong to the foreign patrons. Show your appreciation of their efforts and your admiration of their ability. Be sincere in this. The Old World has much to give us that is really worth while and infinitely better than much of the tawdry jazz and bunkum we accept from each other these days.

If in 1924 some teachers were being encouraged to recognize value in the cultures of their immigrant students, for the most part such contributions were completely ignored. The children of immigrants and Native Americans came to believe that their language and traditions had no meaning or substance. Teachers made few attempts to educate their pupils within the context of the culture in which they had been raised. The attitudes of the time made cultural pluralism impossible.

In "German Immigrants and Parochial Schools," Frederick C. Luebke accurately states, "As a rule American public schools took no account of the cultural background of the children. Their special needs and capacities were ordinarily ignored. Old World customs, dances, music and folklore were denigrated, often unwittingly, by teachers who were anxious to instill a love of America in their charges."

Slowly, cautiously, the children of each group began to find their way into the mainstream of American culture. Clara Ehrlich, a German-Russian who received her schooling on the prairies in Colorado, wrote nostalgically in "My Prairie Childhood" (1962):

> We little ones were often very tired toward the end of the session—then one put one's head on one's arms folded over one's desk and dreamily studied the light coming in the large windows, three on either side of the room, one wondered about the authors whose pictures adorned the walls, one grew very familiar with the faces of Lincoln and Washington who were hung in a place of honor over the long blackboard which covered the whole north wall of the room. . . . The simple room designed for the teaching of the three R's in a rigid and formal way, became a part of one's very tissue—a room to love and remember.

The portraits of Lincoln and Washington defined patriotism for thousands of immigrants who came to the United States: Washington was the father of the country, while Lincoln symbolized the rise of the common people. Slowly, the children of immigrants became Americans, as Alfred C. Nielsen describes in this insightful passage from *Life in an American Denmark* (1962):

> For a thousand years my people had lived among the lakes and hills of Jutland, Denmark. Some of the well-meaning, if misguided, teachers of the vacation school had told us that we owed our first allegiance to Denmark. We did not argue with them . . . but when we children played war on the playgrounds we were not divided between Danes and German. . . . No! We fought the battles of Lexington, Bunker Hill, Gettysburg and San Juan Hill all over again.

## Native Americans

World War I intensified discrimination against Germans, but such prejudice had long been experienced by Native Americans who had struggled to maintain their culture against forcible suppression by the U.S. government. At the end of the 19th century and the beginning of the 20th century, young Native Americans attended boarding schools to be educated. In these large, multiroomed schools they were forced to discard their native dress, speech and customs. The traditional long hair of the boys was cropped close, and Indian girls accustomed to loose-fitting blouses and skirts were required to wear tightly buttoned dresses that covered them from their ankles to their necks. Hundreds of Native Americans were forced to attend boarding schools, although many longed to be home and closer to their families.

South Dakota State Superintendent Charles H. Lugg, in his biennial report for 1916, stated, "While our schools are not yet what we wish them to be, we may congratulate ourselves on the fact that illiteracy among the whites is but seventy two hundredths of one percent. The non-white population of the state is almost wholly Indian, and the illiterates among the Indians are still wards of the federal government for whom our schools are not responsible." For years, the federal government too had ignored its full responsibility to Native Americans,

Log school, Fort Yates, N.D., 1875. Indian girls at this school wore their hair in traditional long braids and wrapped trade blankets around their shoulders. (State Historical Society of North Dakota)

who remained even more culturally isolated than the immigrants who were homesteading their tribal lands.

Boarding schools for Native Americans failed to achieve their education objectives because their graduates could not easily be assimilated into mainstream American culture. Yet, with the skills and training they had received at school, they were also uncomfortable on the reservations, to which 95 percent of them returned.

Other Native Americans attended isolated one-room schools established by missionaries on the reservations. Gradually these few missionary schools gave way to public district schools, known as day schools, supervised by state school superintendents, many of whom were uninterested in Native American education. The federal government discontinued financial support to day schools in 1900, but local county governments would not accept Native American children into their schools. The segregation that plagued black country schools for almost a century also inhibited Native American education. Local schools were controlled by the Bureau of Indian Affairs, not the Native Americans themselves. The first serious attempts to educate Native American children in their own communities did not occur until the 1930s.

Each day school consisted of a schoolhouse in a small, loosely knit community of houses usually built of logs, up to one-fourth to one-half mile from each other. Besides the school there was a house for the teacher and his or her family, a building that served as kitchen, dining room and washroom, and sometimes a shop for the boys to work in. There was usually a garden somewhere in the vicinity, usually in a valley or good garden spot. The teacher worked all year round with a short vacation sometime during the summer. A man teacher served as teacher, janitor, carpenter, projects leader, gardener. His wife was cook, teacher and canner of all harvested produce for use during the winter, as well as mother and wife.

The day schools were officially designated by number, but like other one-room schools across the country, local residents gave the schools local names. Schools in the Pine Ridge reservation in South Dakota included Red Shirt Table School, Wakpamini School, Wounded Knee School, Lone Man School and Porcupine School. On the Cheyenne River reservation, day schools had names such as Red Scaffold, Bridger, Iron Lightning, Thunder Butte, Four Bear, Green Brass, Bear Creek, Moreau River and White Horse.

During the depression, teachers came from throughout the United States to take jobs on the reservations. Most of the children attending school in South Dakota spoke only Lakota, the language of the Dakota people. If cultural differences created difficulties when rural school teachers were teaching immigrants, the difficulties were even more acute when they were teaching Native Americans.

Attendance varied considerably; children came when they felt like it. Often, families would visit relatives on other parts of the reservation and not return for months. Harold Shunk began teaching at Cherry Creek Day School on the Cheyenne River reservation in 1936. Only two of the 40 or 50 children in the community came to school speaking English. Those children were part white, and they lived away from the community before moving back. Shunk began by using pictures of objects the children knew—pictures of deer, chipmunks, skunks, crows and trees—and printing the English word under the picture.

The children learned well. However, all the textbooks described scenes and situations utterly foreign to their culture. Shunk began with 21 pupils, and soon he had 52 children to teach in his one-room school. Lakota values are different from those of white society, and the children could not understand the reason for competition in the classroom. And if a child experienced difficulties, as most of them did, Native American parents felt no obligation to keep him or her in school. Poor roads, impassable in winter because of drifting snow and deeply rutted with mud in spring, did not help the attendance.

Schools taught and administered by whites did not reflect Native American beliefs, so discipline faltered. Confusion reigned. Shunk's supervisor told him to make the children "dance Indian" at school, hoping that they would then maintain regular attendance. Often children came to school late, or not at all, because they had been attending ceremonial dances. Part Native American himself, Shunk did not like the idea of requiring the children to do traditional dances in school, but the issue had been forced and his job was in jeopardy. One morning he pushed the desks back and told the children to do their dances. The next day, three irate Native American mothers arrived; he explained what his instructions had been. One parent demanded to see the supervisor, who, on her next trip to the schoolhouse, was told in no uncertain terms that Native American children were to go to school to learn from books. Dancing was to be the sole responsibility of the parents.

Parents who had been exposed to a formal education sought the same training for their children. Mildred Watson taught in the Wolf Mountains of Montana, where winter temperatures often dipped to 30 degrees below zero. She remembers that, despite the snowdrifts, "Several Indians rode horseback to school six or seven miles when they felt like it. But a Cheyenne Indian family wanted their children to go to the white school so badly that they parked their wagon and set up their tepee close to the schoolhouse. Mike, Claude and Mamie Little Wolf never missed a day of school."

Veronica O'Dea homesteaded with her family in western South Dakota near the Pine Ridge reservation in 1907. Her sister taught a country school on the reservation for six years; the school served six Native American families. The men had gone to the Haskell Institute, a well-known boarding school in Lawrence, Kans., and two of the mothers were registered nurses. The children were bright and attended regularly, and there were no discipline problems. The Christmas programs were successful joint efforts between the white and Native American children, a rare occurence because of persistent school segregation. Where schools were integrated, children learned well together, as in the one-room Bugtussle School (1909) near McAlester, Okla., which had an enrollment of between 50 and 60 students, including Irish, Italians and Choctaws.

Because schools in southern Utah refused to admit Native Americans, the Episcopal Church established St. Christopher's Mission in Bluff,

Utah, to help the Navajo. The mission set up a small country school and tried to maintain two teachers because the pupils ranged in age from one to 85. Helen Sturgis, the principal of the school, said that although the Navajo learned slowly, they loved having the opportunity to learn: "They were very eager for school. One little sheepherder would come down at night. He would take the sheep down to the water and look around to see if the parents were looking and then run into the school, grab his pencil, and work feverishly for a few minutes. Usually the parents came after him."

Few Native Americans, however, succeeded in receiving a good education on the reservation, and many who did try to make their way in the "outside" world soon returned to their own land and traditions. Not until World War II did Native Americans begin to enter the cultural mainstream.

### Black Americans

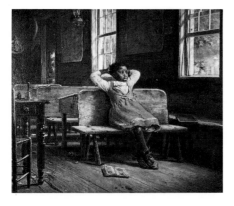

*Kept In* (1888), by Edward Lamson Henry. This student, who is being disciplined, has not been allowed out at recess. (New York State Historical Association, Cooperstown)

Black school (c. 1910), Marcella Plantation, Mileston, Miss., 1939. (Marion Post Wolcott, FSA)

Black schools in rural areas of the South had none of the meager educational benefits that Native Americans enjoyed. Native American education was clearly a responsibility of the federal government, which hired competent, although sometimes culturally indifferent, schoolteachers. No black public schools existed in the antebellum South.

Before the Civil War, in many southern states it had been against the law to teach blacks to read and write. Slaves who had been freed, called freedmen, attended freedmen's schools, but when the war broke out most of those schools closed. When Edward Stanley became governor of North Carolina in 1862, his first official act was to close the freedmen's schools. After the war many whites who employed black servants would not allow them to work if they attended school. Northern teachers who had come south to educate blacks were denied room and board; their school buildings were burned, stoned and shot at. Henry Allen Bullock wrote in *A History of Negro Education in the South* (1967):

> The education movement was not imposed upon Negroes by overzealous Northerners. It seems that wherever teachers carried their seeds of knowledge, they always found some fertile soil in which to plant them. They found in their Negro charges not only a desire for literacy but also a willingness to endure the hardships necessary to attain it.

For some blacks, those hardships included migration from the South to the western frontier in pursuit of the same education and economic freedoms sought by immigrants. Blacks from Kentucky, Missouri and Tennessee settled on the western prairies of Kansas and started major black settlements in Hodgemen, Barton, Rice, Marion, Logan and Graham counties. The most famous settlement, before the well-publicized black exodus from the South in 1879, was Nicodemus, on the Solomon River in Graham County, Kans. By 1880, 700 black homesteaders had taken up land near Nicodemus, and many managed to hold onto their farms despite droughts, political strife and crop damage done by marauding cattle herds. Residents of Nicodemus built a one-room school, staffed it with a black teacher and encouraged their children to acquire the education they themselves had been denied.

Black school (1917), District No. 1, Nicodemus, Kans. Built in the black "Exoduster" town of Nicodemus, this frame school was in use until 1955. (Clay Fraser, HABS)

Nicodemus flourished in the 1880s, and, although the railroad did not come through as expected, population grew steadily until 1910. The Nicodemus community represented a black migration from rural areas in the southern and border states to rural farming areas in Kansas, much like the European peasants who also migrated to the plains. Many blacks were unable to read and write but were adamant in their desire to educate their children. One black man vowed: "I am going to school my children if I have to eat bread and water" (quoted in *Exodusters: Black Migration to Kansas After Reconstruction*, 1977, by Nell Irvin Painter).

An eloquent statement by one black, also quoted in *Exodusters*, could apply equally well to what immigrants experienced:

I wants my children to be educated then I can believe that they tells me. If I go to another person with a letter in my hand, and he reads it, he can tell me what he pleases in that letter, and I don't know any better. I must take it all for granted; but if I have got children who read and write, I will hand them the letter, and they will tell me the contents of that letter, and I will know it's all right, as he says it.

Rural immigrants had difficulties with the English language, but at least they had schools to attend. Southerners bitterly resented the intrusion of teachers from the North, who had often been invited by Union generals, yet most southern whites remained unwilling to take even the smallest steps toward establishing rural schools for blacks.

After the Civil War, on the southern coastal islands, white Christian missionary women began black schools. Charlotte Forten, as a black agent of the Freedmen's Aid Society, had taught her own school on St. Helena Island during the war. She wrote in her essay "Life on the Sea Islands," published in the *Atlantic Monthly* in 1864:

> But after some days of positive, though no severe treatment, order was brought out of chaos, and I found but little difficulty in managing and quieting the tiniest and most restless spirits. I never before saw children so eager to learn. . . . Coming to school is a constant delight and recreation to them. They come here as other children go to play.

Blacks' enthusiasm for education after the end of the war is also echoed in Booker T. Washington's autobiography, *Up from Slavery* (1901). He wrote:

> Few people who were not right in the midst of the scenes can form any exact idea of the intense desire which the people of my race showed for an education. As I have stated, it was a whole race trying to go to school. Few were too young, and none too old, to make the attempt to learn.

The Freedmen's Bureau, an agency set up during Reconstruction, established 4,239 schools, many of them rural, but the bureau was in operation only for five years before it was dismantled for political reasons in 1875. Blacks were forced to form schools wherever they could and to make use of a wide variety of buildings.

When black rural schools finally were established, they were crude, vernacular and often abandoned structures that had frequently seen other uses as houses or shelters for livestock. Blacks often adapted the structures themselves and hired their own teachers by paying a subscription fee, a technique for financing education that dates from the colonial period. Teacher qualifications posed a serious problem. Immigrant teachers rapidly became assimilated and prospered within their local communities, but educated black teachers usually left their rural areas as quickly as possible to find better opportunities in northern cities. An outstanding example is the young Fisk University student W. E. B. DuBois, who taught a black rural school in Tennessee in 1886. DuBois wrote in *The Souls of Black Folk* (1903):

> The schoolhouse was a log hut, where Colonel Wheeler used to shelter his corn. It sat in a lot behind a rail fence and thorn bushes, near the sweetest of springs. There was an entrance where a door once was, and within, a massive rickety fireplace; great chinks between the logs served as windows. Furniture was scarce. A pale blackboard crouched in the corner. My desk was made of three boards, reinforced at critical points, and my chair, borrowed from the landlady, had to be returned every night. Seats for the children—these puzzled me much. I was haunted by a New England vision of neat little desks and chairs, but, alas! the reality was rough plank benches without backs, and at times without legs. They had the one virtue of making naps dangerous—possibly fatal, for the floor was not to be trusted.

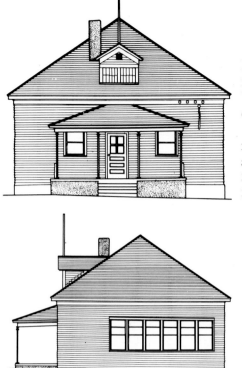

Black school (1917), District No. 1, Nicodemus, Kans. (Everett L. Fly, HABS)

The myth of the little red schoolhouse and egalitarian education proved totally false for rural blacks, who were often lucky to have any schools in session at all. D. E. Williams, who served as state agent for Negro education in Florida from 1927 to 1962, is quoted in *The Education of Black People in Florida* (1974):

> The most tangible and visually impressive need observed in my first visits was the need for schoolhouses. Most of the 866 Negro schools in operation in Florida during the early years of my employment were conducted as one-teacher and two-teacher schools in churches, lodge halls, [and] turpentine or sawmill camp residences. There were a few county-owned schoolhouses. . . . Often trees and bushes served for toilets, and surface privies, when provided, were usually so filthy that children preferred to use the bushes.

Because of inadequate funding for construction of suitable school buildings, black educators turned to northern philanthropists to help finance school construction. Laurence J. Jones founded the Piney Woods School in Piney Woods, Miss., in 1910 in an abandoned slave cabin. Like many other prominent black schools in the South, the Piney Woods School grew larger because of contributions and donations from northern philanthropists. At the suggestion of Booker T. Washington, in 1914 Julius Rosenwald announced that he would provide money for the construction of black rural school buildings. In 1917 the money became available to southern communities willing to build schools according to plans approved by Rosenwald Fund directors. Blacks could receive $300 toward schoolhouse construction provided they raised an equal amount from public funds or their own resources. In Florida alone, 128 Rosenwald schools were constructed. The Rosenwald Fund also offered library books to rural schools at two-thirds of the cost.

Black school, Destrehan, La., 1938. Although the building was plain, it received a dignified bell tower. (Russell Lee, FSA)

An equally serious problem was the critical shortage of rural black teachers. To address this need, the Anna T. Jeanes Fund was established in 1907 with the intention of training rural schoolteachers and assisting in the establishment of better rural schools for blacks. Private funds were necessary because public school financing simply did not exist for rural black schools. The Slater Fund had been established in 1897 for the purpose of providing high school opportunities for southern blacks, but those funds were also used for building county training schools such as the Tangipahoa Parish School (1911) at Kentwood, La. Today, only the Old Dormitory remains, a simple pine structure sheathed in clapboard. The building lacks embellishments or ornamentation of any kind and is thus representative of the humble beginnings of the county training schools designed to prepare blacks to teach.

Tin-roofed frame school for blacks, Daufuskie Island, S.C. (Daufuskie Island Historic District)

Unlike rural immigrants who controlled their local schools, southern blacks could not participate in school board elections because of voting restrictions. After the Civil War blacks eagerly sought an education, but because they could not vote they had no voice in the administration of local schools, set up for them for the first time. The county superintendent's position remained a plum of political patronage. Superintendents frequently squandered fiscal assets or diverted funds from black schools and applied them to white schools, which enjoyed better-qualified teachers and longer school terms.

In his oral autobiography, *All God's Dangers* (Theodore Rosengarten, 1974), Nate Shaw describes his schooling—what there was of it—at the turn of the century in Alabama. Shaw relates:

> The white schools would all be floatin along, runnin on schedule; colored schools doing nothin, standin waitin for a chance to open. When the colored did start to school, we had to supplement the money the state give us with our own money. . . . down through the years when my children was goin, they'd send out word from Beaufort, "Close the schools down. Money's out, money's out." Sometimes school wouldn't run over a month and a half or two months and they'd send out word from Beaufort, "Close the schools down, close the schools down. Money's out." Colored had to close their schools down, white folks' schools was runnin right on till May.

The pitiful state of rural black education before World War II is best illustrated by statistics. In 1930, when the average national expenditure per pupil was $99, for blacks it was $12.44, with two southern states spending only $6.50 per student per year—black or white. In rural counties expenditures for black education were roughly one-third less. Horace Mann Bond states in "A Negro Looks at His South" in *Harper's Magazine* (1933), "In the county where these lines are written, the county receives from State funds $7.88 for every child, black as well as white. Of this amount, a little more than two dollars is spent on Negro children, per capita, while all the balance goes to the white schools, together with all of the local county and district taxes for school purposes."

Unlike one-room schools in the Midwest or West, black one-room schools did not hasten assimilation. Instead, they provided only a minimal education and contributed to cultural isolation—already a serious problem because of enforced segregation. In 1932, 74 percent of black school-age children in the South attended 17,087 one-teacher schools and 4,252 two-teacher schools in 17 southern and border states. Class terms shorter than white school terms by one and a half to two months were not unusual. L. N. Taylor in his article "Our Colored Schools" in *Kentucky Progress Magazine* (1932) wrote:

> One-twelfth of the school children of Kentucky belong in our colored schools. It is the policy of our people to provide an efficient system of schools throughout the state, without discrimination as to rich or poor, white or colored, rural or urban. We provide separate schools for the colored. Our policy is segregation without discrimination.

Taylor went on to note that the rural black population was moving away from farm tenancy toward industrial life, but he added, "School authorities generally undertake to carry on their colored schools with the same integrity with which they carry on their white schools," except in the case of school districts in small towns, "which devote their entire revenue to their white schools," leaving it up to county boards of education to fund rural black schools.

When journalist James Agee visited Alabama in 1936, he did not see rural black schools in quite the same light as L. N. Taylor. Agee wrote in *Let Us Now Praise Famous Men* (1941):

> The school population of this county is five black to one white, and . . . not a cent of the money has gone into negro schools. . . . The negro children, meanwhile, continue to sardine themselves, a hundred and a hundred and twenty strong, into

stove-heated one-room pine shacks which might accommodate a fifth of their number if the walls, roof and windows were tight.

Yet, despite their inexcusable buildings, blacks worked to get an education in their one-room schools. They saw education as their only weapon against ignorance and a requisite step toward greater freedom and opportunity. Country schools for blacks, like country schools for immigrants, provided a sense of community and social cohesion. W. E. B. DuBois looked back on his one-room school students and wrote that "their weak wings beat against their barriers—barriers of caste, of youth, of life." He understood their poor attendance and the excuses given him by parents who wanted their sons home to work the fields and their daughters home to mind the babies. He wrote in *The Souls of Black Folk*:

> I have called my tiny community a world, and so its isolation made it; and yet there was among us but a half-awakened common consciousness, sprung from common joy and grief, at burial, birth or wedding; from a common hardship in poverty, poor land and low wages.

The legacy of the one-room school for southern blacks was not the well-furnished, white-clapboard structures of New England, but the sense of community, of belonging to a family of children and their larger families, was the same for country school students and teachers of any race, in any state. The poor condition of southern black schools was inexcusable, but a building, after all, is only four walls and a roof. Illiterate blacks, like illiterate immigrants, gained an education because they wanted one. The deplorable state of segregated rural schools in the South could not stop blacks who were truly committed to learning.

## Hispanic Americans

Like the children of other immigrants, Spanish-speaking students had difficulties with the language when they entered school. But unlike immigrant children, Hispanic Americans were often in the minority in one-room schools. Black children attending country schools had a sense of community with their classmates, but the children of migrant workers never stayed in one place long enough to make fast friends and to get to know their teachers. Anglo teachers generally made little effort to asist their Hispanic students and gave them low grades as punishment for their poor language skills. Quiet Hispanic students, confused by instructions and books in English, seemed timid and uninterested in learning when in fact they were just trying to comprehend the classroom.

Their parents spoke little or no English and justifiably saw education as a threat to their culture and their parental roles—as did German, Norwegian and Swedish parents. The migrant workers, however, had no ties to the community, no stake in ownership of the land. As late as 1952 an estimated 40,000 to 50,000 children moved with their parents to supply the harvest labor in the Sacramento, San Joaquin and Imperial valleys of California. These Hispanic children may have attended rural schools only one or two months a year and brought to class as first graders an English vocabulary of two words—"shut up!"

For them one-room schools were an exercise in futility because they simply could not adjust in a short period of time to all of the English rules, requirements and restrictions. It is to their credit that they learned as much as they did, but for Spanish-speaking students whose parents were farmers, ranchers or miners, the story is different.

In parts of Arizona, Colorado, New Mexico and Texas, where people have lived and spoken Spanish for more then two centuries, problems with assimilation and unsympathetic Anglo teachers have occurred, but there were also Spanish-speaking teachers who knew what difficulties their students faced and willingly helped with the adjustment.

Escolasticia Salazaar Martinez attended all eight grades in the 1920s in the Malachite one-room school in Huerfano County near Gardner, Colo. At home her mother taught her to read and write in Spanish although she herself had received only a second-grade education in a one-room school in Chama, Colo. The mother learned under a Spanish-speaking teacher, but the daughter was not as fortunate. Her teacher did not know Spanish, and Martinez spoke only her name the first day of school and nothing else. She says:

> A lot of things I missed, I guess, because I didn't understand my teacher. It was rough. I memorized everything so my grades weren't too bad. I could memorize the stories in reading but they didn't have much meaning. They thought because you didn't know the English you were slow in learning.

To complicate matters, as she walked home from school a boy student threw stones at her because she was Hispanic. Because of his antagonism, she did not go out for recess for two years. Gradually, however, she became friends with his sister and his hostility dissipated.

A problem for Hispanic students from large families was the need to purchase all textbooks and paper for school. The expenses drained limited budgets. Another problem was school lunches and the harassment children received for eating Mexican food. Martinez said, "I didn't like to bring the tortillas so I usually took biscuits or light bread and sandwiches." In the assimilation process, even traditional foods had to be sacrificed.

But Martinez worked to finish the eighth grade, and at the age of 18 she began teaching in her own one-room school, the Pass Creek School in Huerfano County, where she had as many as 60 pupils. She taught there for seven years. Her students were all Hispanic, so classwork progressed slowly because she had two languages to teach. In an interview she recalled: "I started with them by translating words. I would not have gotten the school unless I promised a Christmas program. I figured that I would have some Spanish plays, too. That's what they liked the most. And the children learned Spanish very fast." Martinez taught both Spanish and English for 20 years in one-room schools. She remembers that fellow teachers from New Mexico taught even more Spanish than she did. In Colorado's San Luis Valley some schools used textbooks in both Spanish and English. These one-room school teachers in the Southwest taught bilingual education long before it became mandated by law. They knew the discomforts they had experienced and they wanted to help other children forced to straddle two cultures.

Eulalia Bourne taught 23 children in the 1930s at Baboquivari School in southern Arizona, close to the Mexican border. In her book *Nine Months Is a Year* (1968), she writes about using Spanish in a school program at the Pozo Nuevo Ranch:

> Had there been a chauvinistic critic present I might have been "defrocked," as the law insisted that all Arizona schools be taught in the English language. This wasn't exactly school and yet in a way it was. We had composed this play and studied the parts and rehearsed it during school sessions. Yet I felt that honoring their language would help parents to be more interested in their community school and cause them to cooperate in its aims and programs.

## The Americanization Movement

At the turn of the 20th century, faced with a wave of new immigrants from southern and eastern Europe, educators feared that the new groups would not be quickly assimilated. The nativism of the 1830s and the Know-Nothing attitude of the 1850s had become xenophobia by the 1890s. Traditionally conservative Protestant church and business club organizations throughout the United States believed that the republic would be threatened unless the immigrants adopted American culture, mores and values. Teachers felt obligated to Americanize their students to protect the country.

On July 10, 1915, Supreme Court Justice Louis Brandeis gave his famous speech on "true Americanism" (quoted in Philip Davis's *Immigration and Americanization*, 1920):

> What is Americanization? It manifests itself, in a superficial way, when the immigrant adopts the clothes, the manners and the customs generally prevailing here. Far more important is the manifestation presented when he substitutes for his mother tongue the English language as the common medium of speech. But the adoption of our language, manners and customs is only a small part of the process. To become Americanized the change wrought must be fundamental. However great his outward conformity, the immigrant is not Americanized unless his interests and affections have become deeply rooted here. And we properly demand of the immigrant even more than this. He must be brought into complete harmony with our ideals and aspirations and cooperate with us for their attainment. Only when this has been done will he possess the national consciousness of an American.

In a speech delivered in New York at Carnegie Hall three months later, Theodore Roosevelt stated (quoted in *Immigration and Americanization*):

> There is no room in this country for hyphenated Americanism. When I refer to hyphenated Americans, I do not refer to naturalized Americans . . . a hyphenated American is not an American at all. This is just as true of the man who puts "native" before the hyphen as of the man who puts German or Irish or English or French before the hyphen. Americanism is a matter of spirit and of the soul. Our allegiance must be purely to the United States. We must unsparingly condemn any man who holds any other allegiance. . . . The one absolutely certain way of bringing this nation to ruin, of preventing all possibility of its continuing to be a nation at all, would be to permit it to become a tangle of squabbling nationalities. . . .

Carnegie Hall may be a long way from the Dakota plains or the mining camps of the Rockies, but such speeches increased the pressure on local school districts to deal more thoroughly with the "foreign element" in their schools. Pressure could be applied more easily in cities than in rural areas where large enclaves of immigrants had settled

Rural school, Fowler, Colo., c. 1918, with students participating in a patriotic program. (Pueblo Library District)

entire counties. The outward allegiance was evident—immigrant children celebrated all of the conventional American holidays, including the presidents' birthdays, Columbus Day and the Fourth of July. The only holidays they retained from their own cultures usually centered around religious themes.

As the storm clouds of World War I swept over the nation, to speak German in public implied sympathy with the Kaiser. In 1919 Kansas passed legislation providing that all public, private and parochial schools use English as the only language of instruction. Mennonite parochial schools that had been operating since the 1880s closed their doors. According to the historian Richard Sallett in *Russian-German Settlements in the United States* (1974), "one out of every ten bills introduced into the Nebraska Legislature during January of 1919 reflected the German language question." South Dakota followed suit. School law was amended in 1889 to read "in the English language only" before the list of subjects to be taught. A second act extended this prohibition to private elementary schools and made it a misdemeanor for teachers and school officers to violate it.

In 1919 South Dakota legislators passed the Americanization Act, which required youths between the ages of 16 and 21 who could not speak, read or write the English language on the fifth-grade level to attend night or day school classes. The state paid one-half of the cost of instruction; the local school district, perhaps in retribution for its previous failure, was to foot the rest of the bill. Because of this law, Hutterites committed to their religious beliefs and to Germanic culture disposed of their lands in South Dakota and moved all but one of their colonies to Canada. It would be 20 years before they returned.

Most of the groups affected, in order to eradicate the stigma of foreignness, complied with these laws. Moreover, at this point many immigrants and first-generation Americans took steps to become naturalized American citizens. Country schools began programs to introduce these groups to American history, American civics and the English language. As late as 1928 in Albany County, Wyo., Alberta Seaman, a rural school teacher, helped prepare immigrants for American citizenship. She remembers, "I also had night school at the camp for six men who were learning to read and write English so they could take their tests for naturalization in Laramie in the spring." A few accommodating teachers held special evening sessions for adults who wished to learn to speak and read English. In North Dakota in the 1920s, Delrey Webster instructed a 40-year-old Swede in English during recess and often held spelling bees in the evening for adults who wished to sharpen their language skills.

The Young Citizens League was an exercise in cultural assimilation aimed directly at the children and grandchildren of immigrants; unlike other clubs springing up in the United States, it had its roots in one-room schools. Michael M. Guhin started YCLs in 1912 in Brown County, S.D., while serving as county superintendent of schools. He claimed to have borrowed the idea from a Minnesota Department of Public Instruction bulletin entitled "The Little Citizens League," prepared by Anna Stelland Williams. By July 1919 Guhin had been appointed state director of Americanization, under the supervision of the South Dakota superintendent of public instruction.

The goal of the Young Citizens League was to promote patriotism, citizenship and character-building in country schools. Although YCLs spilled over into Colorado, Montana and Wyoming, they remained most popular in North and South Dakota—states with heavy concentrations of immigrant children in the public schools. As with other groups that originated during the Progressive Era—such as the Boy Scouts, Girl Scouts and Boys' Clubs—the Young Citizens League sought to create morally upright, socially conscious, healthy patriotic citizens experienced in participatory democracy.

Forty chapters of the Young Citizens League had been started in Brown County, S.D., by 1915. At its height in 1927, the YCL could boast 3,415 chartered chapters and 60,092 members. Prospective members had to receive a majority vote of current members and to memorize the motto "Help Uncle Sam, one another, our school and our community." Committee work formed the basis of the YCL, and its four standing committees included the committee on information and programs, the committee on health and sanitation, the committee on physical training and the committee on patriotic aid. A "Manual

Victor School, Weld County, Colo., 1918. To show support for the allied cause, these schoolchildren displayed the American flag and President Wilson's portrait. Many children of German-Russian immigrants attended this school. (CSL)

The American flag symbolized for children in isolated, one-room schools the larger whole to which they belonged. (Andrew Gulliford)

for League Officers" gave instruction for conducting formal business meetings.

Through shrewd manuevering on the state level, South Dakota county superintendents voted in 1925 to make it mandatory for public schools to sponsor YCL chapters before they could be eligible for state aid. Each year, the YCL sponsored major projects in rural schools, such as recataloging, reconditioning and building up school libraries; music appreciation and the purchase of musical instruments; and art appreciation and the addition of art works to school classrooms. In 1926 alone, the South Dakota clubs raised a phenomenal $83,408.

For 40 years, the Young Citizens League march song was part of the heritage of rural school pupils in the states of North and South Dakota, Colorado, Wyoming and Montana. The chorus ended with these words:

> In all the winds of heaven
> There breathes a patriot's creed . . .
> Clean hearts and minds and bodies
> Serve best our country's need . . .
> That creed we hold, America,
> Enshrined in heart and soul;
> A deeper sense of duty
> And better lives our goal.

As rural schools closed because of school consolidations after World War II, the Young Citizens League also declined. Never an organization that focused on town schools, the YCL slowly faded away. The role it played in Americanizing rural schoolchildren cannot be overestimated.

Describing his native North Dakota, archivist and historian Daniel Rylance sums up the Americanization of immigrants in one-room schools:

> Country schools were an important institution in the growth and development of North Dakota. From the earliest days of settlement, the small white frame schoolhouse stood as a lonely ship on a sea of prairie grass. The country school symbolized both continuity and change for all engaged in the process of settlement. For the seasoned older American, used to moving further West every few years, the school stood for continuity. It symbolized the continual reestablishment of a basic pattern of American civilization from the East Coast through the old Northwest and now onto the Great Plains. For the newly arrived Norwegian or German-Russian, the school stood for change. It also epitomized, however, a new civilization and the inevitable process of Americanization.

Thousands of immigrant and minority children attended rural one-room schools. Whether their parents were black or Hispanic, northern European or southern European, native-born or foreign-born, the children received their basic education in country schools—both from books and from interaction with their teachers and peers in the classroom and on the playground. The role of rural schools in the assimilation and Americanization process was significant, however physically remote and culturally isolated the schools may have been. Some immigrant and minority groups supported country schools far more than others, but for most of these children the rural one-room school played a critical role in expanding their horizons while providing a firm and secure sense of continuity and community.

# Country Schools Today

Country schools, which were the norm throughout the United States until World War II, are the exception today. Of the approximately 835 one-teacher schools still in use in 1984, Nebraska has 360 and Montana and South Dakota each have approximately 100. Twenty-one states no longer have one-room schools in operation. The last one-room school in Louisiana closed in 1980; the final bell sounded for Rhode Island's only operating one-room schoolhouse in 1982. The last one-room school in Iowa, the Fairview School at Kalona, closed in May 1984 after a 4-3 vote by school board members.

Throughout this country, there always will be families who choose to live in remote areas and for whom the one-room school is a vital part of their children's education as well as their community life. Most remaining one-room schools stay open because they serve communities so isolated that no other public education options exist. In the South, the East and the Midwest, where it is easy to transport children to consolidated schools, few one-room schools remain in use. Where the terrain is rugged—in the mountainous western states, in the narrow valleys of northern New England, on islands off the coast of Maine and Washington and in Alaskan villages—country schools still operate. In some areas of the northern Great Plains, distance prohibits consolidated schools. In Montana, for example, large cattle ranches and wheat farms represent huge financial investments, and farm families willingly support one-room schools to keep their children close to home.

Nebraska has more one-room schools than any other state today. One-room schools continue because of lower taxes and long-standing traditions. In the fall of 1983, Al Hodge attended the same one-room school in Brown County that his mother and his grandfather had attended; his teacher, Lucky Pike, of Ainsworth, had taught in one-room schools for more than 30 years. Saunders County, which borders the urban areas of the eastern part of the state, has 16 one-room schools, some less then five miles apart. Sioux County, in the Sand Hills, has fewer than one person per square mile, but parents are unwilling to give up their Class I district schools (which provide instruction through the sixth grade). They believe that they will lose some basic education values, and they know that their property taxes will increase.

School financing is a touchy issue in Nebraska. In 1980 Gerald Koch, chairman of the education committee of the Nebraska legislature, proposed to cut the number of school districts in half by 1985. Koch initially had sought to abolish all one-room schools in favor of districts with kindergarten through 12th grade. Koch stated in the *Denver Post*, "Most Class I districts are tax shelters and the reason for their existence has absolutely nothing to do with education—taxes, yes, education, no." He continued, "Many people know we should reorganize, but politically it's a dangerous position." Koch's bill never made it out of committee, and his constituents voted him out of office in 1982. He had touched a sensitive nerve.

*opposite*
Duett School (c. 1915), Bowling Green, Fla., 1983. Students sit on the steps of Florida's last one-teacher school.
(© 1983 Barbara Hansen)

113

Class VI district schools (high schools) often charge high tuition fees for students coming from the Class I schools, thus forcing them to consolidate and expand their tax base. In 1980 one-room school districts in Douglas County, Neb., paid $4,800 each to send their children to high school. Lancaster County charged $5,000 each, and Dodge County charged $7,000 each. So far the consolidation attempt has not succeeded, although some wealthy Class I districts are also a part of a Class VI district such as in Adams County, which surrounds Hastings, Neb. Housing subdivisions that encroach on Class I districts' taxable lands may contribute $500 per house to district revenues but may also contribute additional children whose per-student expense may be $1,500 each. In those cases, the one-room school districts have increased their revenues although they suffer a net financial loss.

No small common school districts are left in western South Dakota since reorganization took place in the 1960s. Every one-room school is part of a larger school district that often covers hundreds of square miles. But these schools carry on much as they did when they served smaller areas.

The Albany County, Wyo., school district covers 4,374 square miles and is one of the largest school districts in the continental United States. The district recognizes its obligation to serve all the children living there, even if some of them live 90 miles from Laramie, the county seat. In 1981 the district operated four schools with only one pupil each: Cozy Hollow, River Bridge, Palmer Canyon and Indian Guide. Eight distant rural schools are in the north end of the county, and five are closer to Laramie. The distant schools are 50 to 125 miles from Laramie; five do not have telephones. In one case, the one-room schoolhouse has given way to a modern trailer where the teacher lives in one end and teaches in the other half.

In this county, parents who live in remote areas are asked to deliver their children to the nearest school so that the school district is not obligated to provide a school bus. Under a statute reviewed regularly by the state legislature, parents receive isolation payments to help defer expenses incurred in transporting their children to school. In 1983 one family drove 60 miles daily to take their children to school; the parents were reimbursed $18.60 a day, a rate of 31 cents per mile. A second type of isolation payment is for families who live on ranches and must board their high school children in town. Families are reimbursed $100 or more per month to pay for room and board depending on the number of children attending school. The third type of subvention, known as a family move, is given families when a parent, usually the mother, boards in town with the children. The allocation for a family move is a maximum of $200 per month. Like all other types of isolation payment, funding comes from state property taxes and is reimbursed to the school district, which then reimburses ranch families. For seven years, Shirley Lilley would leave her home, 20 miles west of Laramie, Wyo., to stay with her children during the week as they attended school. She says, "I didn't like being away from home each week of the school year. . . . I'd get home Friday evening and have to start baking and cooking for the next week ahead. You live out of a box—one box for the ranch and one box for the trailer in town."

### Teachers' Lives Today

Montero School (1918), Leonard Creek Ranch, Paradise Valley, Nev., 1980. Teacher Sandy Kearns gives individualized instruction to one of her four students. (Andrew Gulliford)

Today, as in the past, a variety of natural hazards plagues country school students and teachers. In Albany County, Wyo., snowstorms can come up at a moment's notice, and teachers and ranchers alike must be prepared to buck eight-foot-high drifts that close roads and isolate schools. Some of the schools do not have telephones, but all have citizens band radios and extra supplies of food and water. Teachers are required to take survival courses before assuming their duties. Concerned parents do not want to worry about their children being stranded in a school.

Isolated from friends and family members, teachers new to rural communities often feel alienated. In Montana, one-room school teachers on their first rural assignment have been known to run up hundreds of dollars worth of long-distance telephone bills. Coping with inadequate social opportunities can be a serious problem. Alan Zelter, dean of education and director of the Rural Education Center at Western Montana College, wrote in the *National Rural Project Newsletter* (1980): "The largest problem confronting new rural teachers in the plains and mountains of the northern Rocky Mountains region is the reality of rural living." Zelter notes that the problems of loneliness and cultural deficiency are compounded when "access to supermarket shopping, medical services and commercial entertainment represents a drive of many miles that may not be possible during the winter months."

"North county" teachers in Albany County, Wyo., try to get together once a week to share food and fellowship, and as long as the roads are clear they may drive 90 miles one way for dinner. Such meals are important occasions in which to discuss classroom activities and to plan class parties. Typically, they plan joint celebrations for Halloween, Thanksgiving, Christmas, Valentine's Day, St. Patrick's Day and the end-of-the-year picnic, and each group party is a major event for both teachers and students.

In northern Nevada, the Leonard Creek Ranch one-room school is still in operation and had four students in 1981. The school is located 90 miles north of Winnemucca and has served children of the Montero family since 1918. In 1981 the teacher, Sandy Kearns, received a salary of $9,800, a free trailer, free meals and even free gasoline for her pickup. After two years of teaching at Leonard Creek Ranch, however, Kearns wanted to give up her position for one in town because "the 90 miles out here is pretty hard. . . . I was scared coming out here, but I gave my word and couldn't go back on it. To go to a party, it's 40 miles to the nearest neighbors. After school you go out and saddle up your horse and separate cattle until dark. Then you come back for supper."

Kearns had under her tutelage two children of Frenchy Montero, who has become a close friend. "I was lonely coming out here, but they accepted me as one of the family. We went to a wedding recently, and Frenchy introduced me as his daughter. Frenchy works hard to find single cowboys in the area that I might like, but the last time he tried it, the scheme backfired. The one I liked moved to California. . . ." She also noted, "If you got yourself on the wrong side of a parent out here, you'd be in real trouble."

Dan Vogeler, who taught from 1979 to 1982 at the one-room Brown's Park School in northwest Colorado, had an hour's drive for groceries and a two-hour drive to pick up extra school desks in Craig, Colo. As Vogeler found out, in a rural school there is an implied obligation to conform to community values, but there are also opportunities for independence and innovation. In 1981 Vogeler had seven pupils in six grades and at least 50 chickens, ducks and turkeys in a pen near the one-room school. "The school board didn't mind," Vogeler says about his small flock, "and roosters help keep the kids awake!" Although some teachers remain outsiders in close-knit rural communities, Vogeler got along fine with local families. However, he notes, "Someone who didn't like to hunt and fish would be at a loss."

Brown's Park School (c. 1910), Moffat County, Colo., 1981. After lunch, teacher Dan Vogeler reads to his students in their one-room school, made of two small buildings placed end to end with the end walls removed. (Andrew Gulliford)

Housing for rural school teachers always has been a critical problem. Most country school teachers must live adjacent to the schoolhouse. Paul Adams, who taught in a small consolidated school in Montello, Nev., in 1981, said of his housing, "This trailer is a palace compared to some I've seen. When I went for an interview at a one-room school near here, the trailer was unfit for human habitation, but I didn't know that at the time. They had conveniently lost the keys so I couldn't see inside."

Because teachers live so close to the school, they have little privacy from their students. Vogeler, who lived with his family in a trailer a dozen yards from the schoolhouse, remembers, "Everyone came over to the trailer for coffee in the morning after they dropped off their kids, and my wife would still have neighbors there at noon. I never got away from the kids. Our friends had children in school, and then after school was out, you'd see the same people and the same kids, over and over again." Vogeler now teaches in a small consolidated school in Iowa where his children can get an education from someone other than himself. "One of the hardest things," he says of his one-room school teaching career, "was trying to keep a parent-teacher relationship separate from the good friendships that we formed."

"Low pay and teacher isolation are perennial rural school problems," says Eugene J. Campbell, Colorado Department of Education certification consultant. Although pay scales have risen in recent years, rural teacher housing shortages have been common for half a century. There is also sex-role stereotyping. A young, single, woman school teacher in Nevada states that her rural school superintendent had told her, "You are hired unless I can find a man." He believed that in a conservative community a man was better suited to teach and assist the older boys.

To keep down costs, teachers at one-room schools today, as in the past, often are responsible for their own building maintenance. Donna M. Chrouser, who teaches with her husband at the Rock School near Rio Blanco, Colo., wrote in *The Small School Forum* (1980), "The furnaces must be checked at every cold snap as the pilot lights may go out. . . . One must not travel during winter vacations or on weekends unless he seeks out a responsible rancher to check the buildings [school and teacherage] to prevent freezing up."

Such problems continue to plague remote one-room schools, where even dedicated teachers find it difficult consistently to generate enthusiasm for their job. No colleagues are available for advice or for grading papers or standing in when they are ill. The entire responsibility for educating the children of tiny rural communities rests on the teachers' shoulders.

Audrey Allmon has taught for 25 years at the Battle Rock School in McElmo Canyon near Cortez, Colo. To help teach responsibility, she engages the students in a range of projects, including a school garden. The students plant, tend, harvest and sell produce, thus learning about business, mathematics, botany and how to earn money. They stage traveling talent shows, study nearby Indian ruins and teach each other everything from cake decorating to how to build a Navajo hogan. Allmon, the 1973 Colorado teacher of the year, says that her first goal is to see that each child has a positive self-image: "If you have that, you can adapt to anything," she said in the *Rocky Mountain News.* "When you've got a child from kindergarten through sixth grade, you can't blame a student's poor performance on the teacher behind you. You've got to tune into each child's educational needs and interests. There is a great deal of responsibility."

Springhill School (1889), District No. 20, Gallatin County, Mont., 1983. Today, as in the past, music is an important part of the curriculum, and many one-room schools have a piano. (© Cliff Willis)

## Criticisms of Country Schools

Historian and writer Dorothy Weyer Creigh wrote in 1980, "There are unfortunately a number, an appalling number, of one-room country schools *still* in existence in Nebraska, with outdoor privies, incredibly slipshod teaching, with a criminal lack of books and other teaching tools. As a member of the Nebraska State Board of Education, I know the present-day one-room country schools for the anachronisms they are, and am eager to dispel the myth of the rural schools now as the be-all and end-all of educational excellence. For their time they served a purpose. Their time is long past."

Criticisms of rural schools have focused on inadequate preparation of teachers, poor design and maintenance of the school building and insufficient curriculums. Graduates and school board members alike agree that if the teacher is incompetent, a school year in a country school can be a total loss. Many rural schools still have trouble attracting well-qualified teachers. A teacher at a three-room school in northern Nevada said of the older teacher who had taught 20 years in the same school, "She wouldn't flunk a kid if her life depended on it. She doesn't make them mind and be quiet. They scream and holler and carry on. She can get away with it in a rural school." Men teachers are harder to keep in rural areas, and the ones that a community would like to keep frequently move on. A parent in northern Nevada complained, "Then there are poor teachers, and it's almost impossible to get them fired. It takes an act of God." Because communities are small, no one wants trouble with their neighbors, and if one of the neighbors is a weak teacher, parents sometimes believe that they have little recourse except to keep their child out of school or move to another school district.

The condition of the school building also is often an object of criticism. Maintaining one-room schools at a level commensurate with state building codes proves exceedingly difficult because most of them were built more than 60 years ago. Most are poorly insulated and far from energy efficient; many need new roofs, new wiring and new plumbing. Renovating these buildings to meet modern health and safety regulations is sometimes difficult and expensive.

An academic disadvantage of country schools is that competition is limited. With only a handful of students in a classroom and sometimes only a single student in a grade, the competitive spirit wanes. Students will not necessarily challenge themselves, and young, inexperienced teachers may not know how to motivate their pupils. Consolidated schools can offer elementary school students a far richer curriculum with a wide range of options. Some critics of rural schools argue that the broader education base in consolidated schools allows rural students to perform more efficiently on a variety of standardized tests. In comparison with all American children, rural children pass through school more slowly, score lower on standardized tests, are more likely to drop out of school before graduating and are less likely to continue with formal education after graduation. However, standardized tests often have an urban perspective. Rural children have never been evaluated by tests that take into account the particular strengths and

Decatur School (c. 1950), Decatur Island, Wash. A second-grader works at his own pace on an art project in this frame school, which has a small, primarily symbolic cupola atop the gabled entrance. (Brent Olsen, Superintendent of Public Instruction)

weaknesses of a rural education.

Social isolation can seriously impair students in their adjustment to the wider world. At consolidated rural and urban schools, students can mingle with classmates of their own age, but students at one-room schools have limited opportunities to form peer relationships. Many do not have the opportunity to learn and play with students their own age of both sexes. Brown's Park School, located in the far northwest corner of Colorado, is so remote that students attend from the neighboring states of Wyoming and Utah, which are only a few miles away. Neilene Foulks, who was graduated from the eighth grade in 1983, was the only girl in the school for eight years. Other girls attended periodically when their parents worked at a nearby mine, but none for any longer than a few months at a time. Foulks had no choice but to become accustomed to being the only girl in the school. Some students do not adjust as easily, and this social isolation can breed timidity.

At one-room schools in the West, the student population is frequently made up of children whose parents own ranches and children whose parents work on ranches or for federal agencies such as the Bureau of Land Management, the National Park Service or the Forest Service. If parents argue about state and federal bureaucracies and increased fees for mining or grazing permits, the same arguments also take place in the schoolyard. Also, distinctions among the students are sometimes made on the basis of economic status, racial characteristics or whether or not the child's family owns land in the school district. Cliques form, and it can be difficult for children to feel wanted or accepted if they are newcomers.

Because of the isolation, lack of equipment and lack of participants, rural students have little opportunity to participate in organized sports. In some schools, the only organized activity is aerobics.

Moreover, leaving the familylike atmosphere of a one-room school to enter a larger school can be devastating. Graduates of rural schools who enjoyed special privileges with their teacher and the respect of younger students find it acutely uncomfortable to be just another face in a large junior high; their sense of self-worth is threatened.

In "Consolidating Rural Schools—Is Bigger Better?" in *Country Journal* (1980), Tom Gjelten addresses the problem of the broader social world to which rural school children are introduced when they move to town schools. Country schools have been thought to encourage isolationism, but Gjelten does not agree. He believes that the students can and should be exposed to thoughts and ideas beyond those of the immediate community.

## Closing Country Schools

Country schools can be legitimately criticized on major academic, economic and social issues. Proponents of consolidated schools agree that consolidated schools, because of their wider tax base, can provide better services and a better quality of education—better-paid and better-trained teachers, extracurricular options and hot lunch programs, as well as some health care.

The education provided by large consolidated schools, however, has begun to draw extensive criticism. J. Myron Atkin, dean of Stanford University's School of Education, believes that "for the first time, it is conceivable to envision the dismantling of universal, public, compulsory education as it has been pioneered in America." Complaints today against public education center around the poor teaching and lack of discipline found in many schools, particularly urban schools. More than one-third of high school seniors must take remedial courses if they are to graduate. A 1979 federal study found that 13 percent of high school seniors were functionally illiterate, as was 20 percent of the adult population. Parents are angry at overgrown education systems that do not teach students to write a complete sentence.

Bruno Bettelheim, head of the University of Chicago's School for Disturbed Children and professor emeritus of the University of Chicago, stated in 1981 in *Psychology Today* that public schools treat children "like idiots." Said Bettelheim, "If I were a first grader in one of the suburban schools, I would conclude that schools are geared toward two important things: lining up for lunch and putting the chairs on the desks at the end of the day. Everything else in the classroom is more or less laissez-faire. All sorts of distractions are allowed." He sees little hope for most public schools today, contrasting them with one-room schools:

> Children in the one-room school had a common background; they would normally have played together, too. So, without any effort, the teacher could understand what life was like in their families. In addition, a one-room school can't function unless the older children help teach the younger ones. Now, having worked with highly disturbed children and academic failures, I've found that having some children help teach is the best way for all children to learn. The older child learns material that can be mastered only by rote much better by teaching it to a younger child. The one-room school was the best school we ever had.

The one-room school concept appeals to parents who are dissatisfied with contemporary education. Consequently, one-room schools may be making a comeback, not in rural areas but in urban ones. Mario Fantini, dean of the University of Massachusetts School of Education and a supporter of one-room schools, believes that their numbers may increase because they provide an alternative to the "bigness and bureaucracy" found in most contemporary schools. In an interview in 1984, Fantini said, "The trend in education today is toward smaller, more community based, more intergenerational settings." He believes that in many schools "students have lost their sense of identity" and that because "we've separated young people from adults," we have "weakened the very fabric of the educational process."

Unless urban and consolidated rural schools change significantly, suggested Fantini, "there may be a continued exodus" toward other types of nonpublic education that take on "the characteristics of the one-room schoolhouse." Many of these new schools are private or parochial schools with ties to the home schooling and community schooling movement of the 1960s and 1970s. Other such schools represent not liberal but conservative thinking.

The Wisconsin Evangelical Lutheran Synod Board for Parish Education lists 36 affiliated one-room schools for 1983–84, down only

Amish school, Lancaster County, Pa. This one-room school is part of the Amish parochial system, which provides education through the eighth grade. (Pennsylvania Dutch Visitors Bureau)

three from the school year 1977–78. According to executive secretary Donald Zimmerman, "Most of the schools which our congregations open begin as one-room schools." He explains, "They usually add other rooms within a year or two. However, some of the schools retain their one-room character for more then several years."

In Pennsylvania, 100 Amish one-room schools enroll 3,000 students each year. The Amish seek to insulate their children from external influences, but as late as the 1950s the Amish attended the existing one-room public schools in their districts. When Pennsylvania forced consolidation of one-room schools, the Amish lost their voice on local school boards. They became concerned about the secular nature of education and resented compulsory attendance in physical education classes. In his book *Amish Society* (1980), John A. Hostetler writes, "In the one-room country schools, children were taught largely by oral means and by example; discipline and basic skills were stressed. Those aspects of schooling that were not considered relevant were tolerated." Hostetler continues, "With consolidation all this changed. The Amish have struggled to retain a human rather than organizational scale in their schools to make them complementary with their way of life." As the one-room public schools came up for auction, the Amish bought the buildings and now use them for private schools. By utilizing these schools for their original purpose, the Amish are following the best precepts of historic preservation.

Another religious group with deep convictions about schooling are the communal Hutterites, who are successful farmers in 30 colonies throughout eastern South Dakota. Hutterite children come to school speaking German, the native tongue of their ancestors who arrived in

America more than a century ago. The children follow strict rules; the girls wear dresses and bonnets, and the boys wear pants with suspenders instead of belts. Like the Amish children, Hutterite children attend school only until they are 15, and then they assume adult roles within the commune. At the Gracevale Colony near Winfred, S.D., Barbara Hyink had 23 students in grades K-8 for the school year 1983–84. Throughout the winter months German school is held in the one-room school building a half hour each morning before regular class begins. As with other teachers in Hutterite colonies, Hyink is a non-Hutterite who lives outside the commune and whose salary is paid by the local school district. Although the one-room school at the Gracevale Colony operates as a private, parochial school, it is really a free, public school, but the only students who attend are Hutterites.

## *Measuring Up to an Ideal*

In spite of the hardships and disadvantages of country schools, the rewards for students and teachers can be enormous. Bill Martin, who taught in the Cozy Hollow School in Albany County, Wyo., comments, "These kids are blessed with remoteness. There aren't many others around for them to copy or try to impress. They have to draw upon themselves. They have time to think, to use their own imaginations." Former students of Edith Clymer at the Valley View School in Albany County remember the enriched education she provided. She taught the students not only the standard subjects but also, during the lunch hour, how to fish and cook the fish for lunch, how to start fires on the ice, how to skate, how to play the piano and even how to do ballet steps. Today, as in the past, rural teachers must have an extraordinary repertoire of skills and strengths to do their job well. In an interview with Brent W. Olsen in *Your Public Schools* (1983), Rebecca Corey, the teacher at Winton Elementary, a one-room school built in 1915 east of Seattle, said, "I have the same children each year. Here, if there's a problem, I can stop it before it gets to be very bad. I'm not starting from scratch each year."

Cheryl Carstensen, the teacher at the one-room Alfalfa Valley School, S.D., says, "I feel that younger and older students learn from each other, not only subject matter but how to give and take. They learn how to work with and cooperate with others, despite vast differences."

Ranch families live and work together, and few of the fathers go off to a daily job in which their family has no part. The ranch *is* the family job, not just the father's responsibility, and that makes for close family ties and more personal contact between teachers and parents. As Carstensen said, "There is closer contact with *both* the parents of students in a rural school."

Country schools offer unusual opportunities for studying science. The Ocracoke School in Ocracoke, N.C., has been involved in an environmental science project in which students examine food chains in the inlet's marsh areas, measure erosion and determine the extent of pollution in the tiny bay around which the village lies. The project encourages students to think about their future on the inlet and how best to use the land and water in the Ocracoke area. The Rock School,

Rio Blanco, Colo., is in the middle of a valley with one of the largest deer herd migrations in the United States. As a recess activity, students tan and prepare deer and elk hides that hunters leave at the school, and they make a sizable amount of money. The proceeds are used to finance field trips.

Country schools have been criticized for producing graduates who lag behind their peers in urban schools. Yet, some former country school teachers insist that their students score higher on achievement tests and in district competitions than pupils of a similar age in town schools. In Montana, students do score successfully on standardized tests; the state ranks fourth in the nation in scoring on the College Board exams. Three of the last four Montana spelling champions came from Rock Springs School, a one-room school with a student body of three to five pupils.

Country school students develop independence, resourcefulness and a sense of who they are as individuals and as members of the school community. Ivan Muse, professor of education and director of a rural education teacher-training program at Brigham Young University, says, "Rural school graduates are highly self-confident. They may receive poorer grades, but once they begin college they are easily motivated and usually succeed. They quickly compensate for any curriculum deficiencies."

As for basic skills, country schools never stopped teaching them. Terms such as "open concept classroom," "peer teaching" and "individual learning centers" all refer to techniques that have been used for years in one-room rural schools. The one-room school is open in that students in different grades and with different backgrounds all work together. Peer teaching is practiced effectively, as older students help younger ones, thereby reinforcing learning. As for individual learning centers, for decades teachers in country schools have helped students on a one-to-one basis. Moreover, "mainstreaming," putting learning disabled or educationally handicapped children back into the classroom, is not applicable to country schools, for these children were never excluded. In *No Easy Answers: The Learning Disabled Child* (1981), Sally L. Smith writes:

> The learning disabled child needs more time to grow, more time to do his work, more time to learn. He must work hard. His parents and teachers must work hard with him and provide him with the support he needs in order to learn properly and to behave appropriately. Those are the only reliable cures at this point. . . . The one-room schoolhouse of yesteryear allowed for slow maturing. The heterogeneous groupings allowed a child to proceed at his own pace.

In *Where the Rainbows Wait* (1978), Trent Jones describes his work in the one-room schoolhouse in Terlingua, Tex., near Big Bend National Park and the Mexican border. Nominated as the nation's outstanding elementary school teacher, Jones left a secure job to take this position near the Chisos Mountains at half his former pay. Jones believes that "one of the teacher's most important jobs is to create an atmosphere in which children want to learn. If a student sincerely wants to learn, to pursue his natural curiosity, then half the teacher's battle is won." One of Jones's most rewarding experiences was with a slightly retarded boy who had been in a special school in El Paso

Franklin School (c. 1920), Hodabird, S.D., 1983. Teacher Kay Meyers helps one of her students with a reading lesson at this one-room school, which has students from first through eighth grades. (Jeff Almen)

and whose mother was unsure whether he could succeed in a normal classroom. In the one-room school environment, he gradually began talking and identifying objects and eventually learned to count to 200 and even to read.

## *Community Support*

Parents help out not only in the classroom but also in other ways. In Squabble Hollow, Vt., parents help maintain the schoolhouse, built in 1881, and last summer repainted the entire building. Similarly, the 100 full-time residents of Shaw Island, Wash., maintain their school building, which has been in continuous operation since it was built in 1890. Listed in the National Register of Historic Places, the one-room school frequently serves as a community center. The children of the island, many of whose parents and grandparents attended the school, have a strong sense of continuity. They are proud of their school, and vandalism is rarely a problem.

Near Davis, Calif., the Fairfield one-room school has been reborn on a two-acre site five miles west of town. The red cinder-block building, built in 1969, was closed for two years because of budget cuts. Parents reopened the building in 1981 by promising the board of education that they could operate it for $30,000 less than the estimated cost. Parents have been performing daily and weekend chores ever since. During the week, they volunteer as aides, crossing guards and playground supervisors. They also serve hot lunches transported from another elementary school. The result is community-centered education supported by community-minded parents.

The same demographic twists that caused rural schools to close because of declining enrollment are now taking another turn. In the 1970s, for the first time in 160 years, population growth in the United States was higher in rural and small-town communities than in metropolitan areas, a reversal of a movement toward urban areas that began before the Civil War. People are leaving the cities and seeking different values for themselves and their children. The number of small farms in New England is increasing. More than half the population in the western United States today was born elsewhere.

Across the nation, parents and teachers have banded together to support rural schools. Universities are finally taking a serious look at how they train rural teachers and are developing programs to help prospective student teachers interested in careers in rural education. Because a "small" school is generally defined as having fewer than 150 students, these groups and programs do not specifically apply to one-room schools, but they have a profound effect not only on efforts to halt consolidation but also on such vital areas as teacher preparation and adjustment to rural life.

Of the nearly 17,000 public school districts in the United States, more than 13,000 are rural, and 32 percent of these rural districts have student enrollments of fewer than 300. Yet, according to James D. Jess, an Iowa school superintendent, in 1977 only six of 2,000 teacher training institutions in colleges and universities had rural teacher education programs. Western Washington University, Bellingham,

Shaw Island Elementary School (1897), Shaw Island, Wash., 1981. In continuous use for almost a century, this one-room school is the pride of the community, which maintains it. (Brent Olsen, Superintendent of Public Instruction)

Wash., is home of the National Rural Development Institute, which regularly publishes a newsletter that lists rural school positions in special education. Colorado State University has a Rural Education Association and publishes *The Rural Educator*. Special summer workshops on rural education are held at Western State College in Gunnison, Colo., and at Western Montana College in Dillon, Mont. Research, both on microfilm and in reprints, is available through ERIC/CRESS, a computer clearinghouse on rural education at New Mexico State University, Las Cruces, N.M.

The largest rural parent-teacher support group is the Iowa-based People United for Rural Education (PURE), which was formed in 1977 and now has 3,300 members, among them parents who believe that they have the right as well as the responsibility to educate their own children in their own communities. Winner of the National Volunteer Activist Award in 1977, PURE promotes high-quality rural education by working closely with parents, teachers, state agencies and public officials. Other states, such as Kansas and Utah, have similar groups, as does Texas.

One-room schools are also being analyzed objectively. Bruce Barker of Texas Tech University and Ivan Muse and Ralph Smith of Brigham Young University are preparing a descriptive study of the one-teacher schools in the United States still in operation. The survey focuses on the teachers, students, school programs and community. Direct contact with the various state offices of education confirmed a total of 837 such schools for the academic year 1983–84; the list of one-teacher schools that appears on page 276 is derived from this study.

Demographics point to growth in rural populations, but one-room schools may not survive long enough to profit from rural resettlement. At the 12th Annual Dakota History Conference in 1980, Marian Cramer, in a paper on country schools in South Dakota, said, "The rural one-room school is dying. . . . If we examine what was good, what was useful in the one-room school and translate this to our modern educational system, we shall have achieved a great deal."

New information technologies can be used to compensate for the smallness and isolation of country schools. Through the use of computers, students can get technical training close to home, however remote their school. According to Quality Education Data, 78 percent of single-building rural schools have microcomputers. Efficient use of a computer in a one-room school should increase the competitive edge of these students.

With the successful use of educational television, minicomputers, videotape machines, calculators and tape recorders, country schools show that they can adapt to 20th-century demands. Although isolated geographically, they represent the synthesis of education ideals: small class size, individual instruction, students helping students, and the involvement of committed parents and community members. Quite possibly the future of successful education in this country depends on a return not only to the basics that were consistently taught in country schools, but also to the community values that country schools represent.

The schoolhouse stood in a rather lonely but pleasant situation, just at the foot of a woody hill, with a brook running close by, and a formidable birch-tree growing at one end of it. From hence the low murmur of his pupils' voices, droning over their lessons, might be heard in a drowsy summer's day, like the hum of a bee-hive; interrupted now and then by the authoritative voice of the master, in the tone of menace or command; or, peradventure, by the appalling sound of the birch, as he urged some tardy loiterer along the flowery path of knowledge. Truth to say, he was a conscientious man, and ever bore in mind the golden maxim, "Spare the rod and spoil the child."—Ichabod Crane's scholars certainly were not spoiled.

Washington Irving, "The Legend of Sleepy Hollow," 1819–20

In the country the repository of art and science was the school, and the schoolteacher shielded and carried the torch of learning and of beauty. The schoolhouse was the meeting place for music, for debate. The polls were set in the schoolhouse for elections. Social life, whether it was the crowning of a May queen, the eulogy to a dead president, or an all-night dance, could be held nowhere else.

John Steinbeck, *East of Eden*, 1952

*opposite*
Lafayette School, near Groton, N.Y., 1907. A barefoot boy, standing by the teacher's desk, reads his lesson. (Verne Morton, permission of Verne Morton Collection, DeWitt Historical Society)

*left*
*Country School* (1890), by E. L. Henry. This painting shows a schoolhouse interior around 1870, when more women were becoming teachers. (Mable Brady Garvan Collection, Yale University Art Gallery)

*below*
Engraving of Ichabod Crane's classroom, by Darley ("The Legend of Sleepy Hollow," 1919–20). The schoolmaster has a rod on his lap for disciplining students and even larger cudgels under his desk. (Library of Congress)

*above*
Painting (1876) by an unknown artist. Colonial schools earned the nickname "blab" schools because of the noise and confusion that accompanied the recitation of lessons. (Library of Congress)

*right*
One-room school, mountain region, Utah. The schoolmaster stood in the middle of the row of students in front of the school, which was probably made of log and then covered with rough-cut clapboards. (Utah State Historical Society)

*I will read and study to prepare myself,*
*for some day my chance will come.*

Abraham Lincoln

*left*
Clapboard school (c. 1890), Seneca, Neb. This two-room school was created by adding onto a one-room structure without changing the basic design. (Nebraska State Historical Society)

*below*
First Mahoning School (1890s), Minnesota, 1900. The bell had yet to be raised in this recently built one-room school, where the girls all played London Bridge. (Edith L. Beardsley, Minnesota Historical Society)

*right*
School interior, Fort Lupton, Colo., c. 1890. This well-furnished one-room school boasted wallpaper, wainscoting and a gas lamp. (Hazel E. Johnson Collection, Greeley, Colo.)

*below*
Douglas Flat School (c. 1870), Calaveras County, Calif., 1947. The square, enclosed bell tower is a type built generally before 1880; later bell towers had open sides. (Challis Gore, California Historical Society Library)

When I was three years old, Pa carried me three miles to show me a schoolhouse. . . .

The building was painted white. Pa lifted me from his back to the ground—the first schoolground that I ever put my feet on. Pa pulled a bandanna from his overalls pocket and wiped the sweat from his face and neck.

"I got this house for you, son," he said. "Since I didn't get any education, I don't want my youngins to grow up in this world without it. They'll never know what they're missin' until they don't have it. If I could only read and write!"

Though Pa couldn't read and write, he served for twenty years as school trustee for the Plum Grove district. I don't believe that a man with a good education could have done better. Pa left his corn in the weeds to go over the district getting the people to petition for the new schoolhouse. He cleared off the schoolhouse and built the toilets. He built a cistern. There wasn't anything within his power that he wouldn't do for the Plum Grove school.

Jesse Stuart, *To Teach, To Love,* 1970

*right*
Canadian School (1885), later called Cowdry School, North Park, Colo. Students and teacher posed with the horses they rode to school. A horseshoe was nailed above the doorway for good luck. (Colorado Historical Society)

*above*
A school class embarking on an outing in the 1890s. The U.S. Bureau of Education stated that "the best wagons are built so that drivers sit inside with the children." (Frances Benjamin Johnston, Library of Congress)

*right*
Slate Creek School, Summit County, Colo., 1894. Teacher Pearl Harper and a student posed with their bicycles. (Denver Public Library, Western History Department)

*left*
School (c. 1920), Morton County, N.D., 1942. Sleds proved useful for recess fun. (John Vachon, FSA)

*below*
Breathitt County, Ky., 1940. Students often walked home from school, which in this county usually began in July and ended in January because most of the children had insufficient winter clothing to travel the long distance. (Marion Post Wolcott, FSA)

*above*
A "standard" school wagon, manufactured to transport students to consolidated schools. (Wayne Company)

*above*
Lancaster County, Pa. Roller skates shortened the trip to this Amish boy's parochial school. (Pennsylvania Dutch Visitors Bureau)

*above, left*
Montero School (1918), Leonard Creek Ranch, Paradise Valley, Nev. All-terrain vehicles have replaced horses for some rural school students. (Andrew Gulliford)

*left*
Lancaster County, Pa. Amish students are pulled home on sleds by genuine mule power. (Pennsylvania Dutch Visitors Bureau)

*The boy with his sister behind him rode bareback on the little Indian pony. Flossie trotted along slowly, knowing well where she was headed. The log schoolhouse was four miles away, down a mountainside, across the creek, and back up the other side of the canyon.*

*"Listen now," the boy said. "See if I can say it all the way through without forgetting." And he began to recite "Horatio at the Bridge" . . . "With weeping and with laughter still is the story told, how well Horatio kept the bridge in the brave days of old."*

*It was Friday, the day everyone spoke a piece.*

Clark C. and Margaret Ewing, *Early McCoy,* 1976

*right*
Morton School, District No. 4, near Groton, N.Y., 1907. Students work on individual assignments. (Verne Morton, permission of Verne Morton Collection, Dewitt Historical Society)

*below*
School, Barnes County, N.D., c. 1910. Globes and dictionaries such as the ones here were frequently purchased with money earned at pie suppers and box socials. (State Historical Society of North Dakota)

*above*
Metzgar District, N.Y., school, 1901. A young girl recites for the class. (Verne Morton, permission of Verne Morton Collection, DeWitt Historical Society)

*left*
Lafayette School, near Groton, N.Y., 1907. The teacher calls the roll before work begins. (Verne Morton, permission of Verne Morton Collection, DeWitt Historical Society)

*above*
Page from a book used in southern Colorado rural schools. The curriculum of country schools had little consistency; in some cases, students used a different series of texts each year they were in school. (CSL)

*left, top*
Spencerian charts of writing (1874). Spencerian handwriting technique required both correct placement of the pen on the paper and specific body positions. This boy is demonstrating the right-side position, favored for the greatest uniformity of letters. (Library of Congress)

*left, bottom*
Little Red Schoolhouse, Crossville, Tenn., 1930s. Second- and third-grade students read their lessons to the teacher. The benches were not adjustable and were uncomfortable for short students, who often sat on a book. (FSA)

*left, top*
Pages from *McGuffey's Eclectic Primer,* which were among the first that a 19th-century child would read in school. The readers, written by William Holmes McGuffey, were termed "eclectic" because they incorporated the work of many authors.

*left, bottom*
Brookside School, Aberdeen, S.D., 1949. Attentive second-graders practice their vowel sounds for the teacher. (National Archives)

*below*
Title page of *The Illustrated Primer* (c. 1870), published by George F. Cooledge and Brother, N.Y. (Library of Congress)

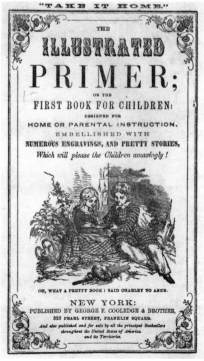

137

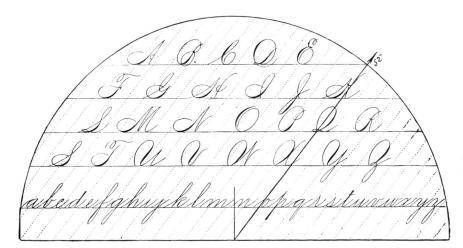

The class work is showing more and more those who are earnest about their education, those who have a determined purpose to get all there is to be gotten out of a year's school work, and those who are careless seemingly, or do not desire to benefit themselves with these opportunities so freely offered.

These nice spring days require an effort for boys to tear themselves away from their tops and horse shoes and come to school. Yet he who does so conquers in manhood, and yes in womanhood, too, for in the intellectual realm man has found his peer in woman.

*Rifle Reveille,* Rifle, Colo., 1896

*above*
Centennial library paste, which came in quarts, pints and tubes and was "guaranteed to give satisfaction." (Centennial School Supply Company, Denver)

*left, top*
Scale showing desired angle for slanting letters. From "Real Pen Work, Self-Instructor in Penmanship." (Lone Star School, Centennial Village, Greeley, Colo.)

*left, middle*
A coal bucket and scuttle, a chart of the alphabet and punctuation marks and a paddle for administering discipline—essential elements of a country school education. (Andrew Gulliford)

*left*
Award for perfect attendance received by Lydia Harms, District No. 2, Richardson County, Neb., 1933. Despite ill health, bad weather and poor roads, many country school students attended class every day to earn such coveted awards. (CSL)

*left*
*The Country School,* by A. Kollner. In this stylized depiction, the country school resembles a summer cottage, and the students playing tag in the fenced schoolyard are well dressed.

*below*
Stereograph (1899), by Strohmeyer and Weyman. The students' positions and playground activity were carefully staged by the photographer in front of a schoolhouse. (Library of Congress)

*right, top*
Stereograph (1923), by Underwood and Underwood. Each person is posed, from the teacher gazing out the window to the younger boys standing quietly in line for their turn at bat. (Library of Congress)

*right, bottom*
Jones School, near Groton, N.Y., 1907. Students prepare a portion of the school-yard for a garden. (Verne Morton, permission of Verne Morton Collection, DeWitt Historical Society)

*below*
Hampton School (c. 1890), Breathitt County, Ky., 1940. The crowded play-ground shows the conditions that helped speed school consolidation in Appala-chia. (Marion Post Wolcott, FSA)

*left, top*
Roller School (c. 1920), near Ardmore, S.D. Only a giant stride swing remains at this abandoned school. (Andrew Gulliford)

*left, bottom*
Rural school, Morton County, N.D., 1942. "Fox and geese" or "cut the pie" was played during recess. (John Vachon, FSA)

*below*
Consolidated two-room school, Sparta, Tex. Boys play softball, while the girls and teachers watch. (National Archives)

*The day at school goes as rapidly as it used to when I was the sponge instead of the ladle. I feel considerable pride in being able to say this, for the first day was a whole month long, and the decrease in length has been regular and gradual, very gradual. Then, when four o'clock comes, I have a romping game of tag with the children (which always makes me wonder at myself); split my kindling (and occasionally my thumb); sweep my dusty little room; close the shutters, lock the door, shoulder my dinner pail, and swing out. . . . When I reach home, I scrub for an hour in a room 8 degrees below zero, with hard, limey water. By this time, it is nearly supper time. After this meal, where I eat enough for a man, there is only an hour or an hour and a half until bedtime (8:30).*

Letter from Mabel Townsley to Helen Myers, February 17, 1900

*above*
Mabel Townsley, who taught in a rural school near Hartford, S.D., 1899–1900. (Lawton, CSL)

*above*
Esma Lewis, who moved from Dongola, Ill., to Silt, Colo., in 1909 and taught for 60 years in country schools in Garfield County, Colo. (CSL)

*right*
*The District School Teacher* (1867), by A. R. Ward. In the mid-19th century, women were urged to become teachers to fulfill their duty by educating and elevating humanity. (*Harper's*, Library of Congress)

*Her name was invariably Grace, Charity, or Prudence; and if names had been always a descriptive of the personal qualities of those who bore them, she would have been entitled to all three. . . . She was somewhat angular and rather bony. Her eyes were usually blue, and, to speak with accuracy, a little cold and grayish, in their expression—like the sky on a bleak morning in Autumn. . . . In manners and bearing, she was brisk, prim, and sometimes a little "fidgety," as if she was conscious of sitting on a dusty chair. . . . She was careful of three things—her clothes, her money, and her reputation. . . . The man who courted her must do so in the most sober, staid, and regulated spirit.*

J. L. McConnel, *Western Characters,* 1853

*left*
The *Schoolmistress* (1853), by Darley. One stereotype of the schoolteacher was the aging, embittered spinster. (John L. McConnel, *Western Characters,* Library of Congress)

*below*
Leadville, Colo., schoolteachers in a formal portrait, 1901. Teachers meetings provided the only opportunity for rural teachers to exchange ideas and socialize with their peers. (Colorado Historical Society)

*right*
Second-grade certificate to teach in Dawson County, Neb., awarded to Mattie J. Billingsley, 1886. She was the 43rd teacher to be assigned to a school in Dawson County that year. (CSL)

*below*
Watson Ranch School (c. 1900), Nebraska, 1904. A man schoolteacher stood with his students in front of their schoolhouse, while parents waited on the porch. (Solomon D. Butcher Collection, Nebraska State Historical Society)

*"One o' my girls had her heart set on bein' a school teacher, but I talked her out of it. Teachin' school is too much like bein' a preacher's wife. It's a high callin', but people expect you to give mor'n they pay for."*

Aunt Hettie, in *Heritage of Our Schools, the Pride of Kansas*, 1934

*"It is quite possible that it was never intended by the good Lord that I should be a schoolteacher. At least not so soon after the turn of the Twentieth Century, when they were definitely a distinct species. . . . Early in the 1900's, women teachers suffered most of the restrictions of nuns, with none of the advantages they enjoyed. . . . Nobody defined exactly what a teacher's place was, but everyone knew she should keep it."*

Maude Frazier, in *Maude Frazier: Nevadan*

*above*
Myrtle Cottier, of Golden, Colo., 1899, one of many women schoolteachers on the frontier who were married after teaching for only a short time. (CSL)

*above*
Six-month contract with Ethel Sherar to teach in Carbon County, Wyo., for $70 a month, 1911. She was also responsible for the janitorial work and could be dismissed at the whim of the school board.

*top*
Mason Valley School, Lyon County, Nev., 1889. The teacher, at right, is distinguishable from the students by the large book and the identification on her apron. (Nevada Historical Society)

145

*A fellow came riding into Cut Bank, Montana, one day and stopped at the livery stable to rest his horse. He asked the blacksmith if he knew where any of the Kipp family members lived in the area. The Kipp family was one of the first white settlers in the area and there were lots of them. "Well, you know it's too bad about them Kipps," the blacksmith said. "Oh, what happened?" "Well, they had a big family reunion at the Old Star School. It was the only building big enough to hold 'em all. Well, they got to dancin', drinkin', and cavortin' around so much, that someone hit the stove and the stove pipe fell down on 'em all and killed all but a hundred of 'em."*

Western lore

*left*
Glendale School, Washoe County, Nev., c. 1940. Nevada pioneers gathered to celebrate a half century in Nevada. (Nevada Historical Society)

*above*
Scenic School, District No. 26, North Dakota, 1943. Students wore handmade masks for a class party. (CSL)

*left*
Lakeland School (c. 1870), Minnesota, 1895. Parents as well as students posed for school photographs. (Minnesota Historical Society)

*above*
School near Groton, N.Y., 1912. Students and teacher celebrated Arbor Day with a picnic. (Verne Morton, permission of Verne Morton Collection, DeWitt Historical Society)

*right*
Waterford School (1882), Waterford, Minn. Students and visitors created a photographic still life during a picnic. (Minnesota Historical Society)

*Prairie View was the official name, so far as it had any, of a country school district in southeastern Kansas. Its capital was a small white-painted building which was not only the schoolhouse, but the center—educational, social, dramatic, political, and religious—of a pioneer community of the prairie region of the West.*

Marshall A. Barber, *The Schoolhouse at Prairie View*, 1953

*above*
School, Woodland Park, Colo. The double entrances and the lack of a steeple suggest that this is a one-room school, here being used for a funeral service. The six pallbearers are women. (Colorado Historical Society)

*left*
Fairfield School, District No. 11 (c. 1910), Fairfield, Iowa, 1951. Community members turned out to give this four-room school a fresh coat of paint. (National Archives)

*left*
Rural school, Gee's Bend, Ala., 1939.
Juanita Coleman, teacher and National
Youth Administration leader, listens to
an 82-year-old student, who had just
learned to read and was the best in the
class. (FSA)

*below*
Rural school, Coffee County, Ala.,
1939. Men and women, holding their
children, attended an adult literacy class
conducted by vocational teachers.
(Marion Post Wolcott, FSA)

*right*
German-Russian immigrants at the Bismarck, N.D., train station after their arrival from the Ukraine, 1900. (Hiram H. Wilcox, Haynes Foundation Collection, Montana Historical Society)

*below*
Eight- and 10-year-old immigrant children on a farm near Sterling, Colo., 1915. They worked in the beet fields from 5:00 a.m. to 7:00 p.m. (Lewis W. Hine, Library of Congress)

*Depressed and heart-sore Peder had dropped into the seat. He felt utterly sick and weary of everything. All the eyes back of him pricked his neck like pins. Directly in front of him hung the blackboard; at the top of it was written in a beautiful hand, "This is an American school; in work and play alike we speak English only!" He read the commandment twice; a feeling of shame came over him and he slunk even lower in his seat.*

O. E. Rolvaag, *Peder Victorious*, 1929

*The Bohemian and Scandinavian girls could not get positions as teachers because they had no opportunity to learn the language. Determined to help in the struggle to clear the homestead from debt, they had no alternative but to go into service. . . .*

*If I told my schoolmates that Lena Lingard's grandfather was a clergyman, and much respected in Norway, they looked at me blankly. What did it matter? All foreigners were ignorant people who couldn't speak English.*

Willa Cather, *My Antonia*, 1918

*left*
Black children, West Memphis, Ark., 1949. Four grades of students were jammed into the pews of a Baptist church, their only classroom, which had no plumbing or heating. (Ed Clark, Life Magazine, © 1949 Time Inc.)

*below*
Black mother in Transylvania, La., in 1939 taught her children numbers and the alphabet in her sharecropper home. (Russell Lee, FSA)

*right*
Atlanta School, Atlanta, Idaho, 1983. A young student gets a few words from teacher Jody Clay during recess. (© John Blackmer)

*below*
Atlanta School, Atlanta, Idaho, 1983. Standing by a wood-burning stove for warmth, teacher and students from three to 13 say the Pledge of Allegiance at the start of the school day. (© John Blackmer)

The school greets me like a series
of sentence fragments sent out to recess.
Before I hit the front door
I'm into a game of baseball soccer.
My first kick's a foul; my second sails
over the heads of the outfielders;
rounding third base, I suck in my
    stomach
and dodge the throw of a small blue-
    eyed boy.
I enter the school, sucking apples of
    wind.
In the fifth-grade section of the room
I stand in the center of an old rug and
    ask,
Where would you go where no one
    could find you,
a secret place where you'd be invisible
to everyone except yourselves;
what would you do there: what would
    you say?
I ask them to imagine they're there,
and writing a poem. As I walk around
    the room,
I look at the wrists of the kids,
green and alive, careful with silence.
They are writing themselves into fallen
    elms,
corners of barns, washouts, and alkali
    flats.
I watch until a tiny boy approaches,
who says he can't think of a place,
who wonders today, at least, if
he just couldn't sit on my lap.
Tomorrow, he says, he'll write.
And so the two of us sit under a clock,
beside a gaudy picture of a butterfly,
and a sweet poem of Christina Rosetti's.
And in all that silence, neither of us
can imagine where he'd rather be.

Donovan Welch, "Poet in Residence at a
Country School," 1980

*right*
Atlanta School, Atlanta, Idaho, 1983.
Because the rope to the school's bell was
broken, a student had to climb the 10-
foot tower to ring the bell at the end of
the day. (© John Blackmer)

## Country Schools Today

*There are not many haunted one-room schoolhouses left now, I suppose; some are rotting on back country roads and a very few have been preserved as quaint antiquities. But rather than battlefields or museums for the student of Americana, if he could visit those ancient schools, he might better feel the presence of our history.*

Eric Sloane, *The Little Red Schoolhouse,* 1972

*above*
Brown's Park School (c. 1910), Moffat County, Colo., 1981. Teacher Dan Vogeler and a young student review arithmetic exercises. (Andrew Gulliford)

*right, top*
Springhill School (1889), District No. 20, Gallatin County, Mont., 1983. A young student reaches into his desk for materials. (© Cliff Willis)

*right, bottom*
Three-Way School, Erath County, Tex., 1982. Teacher Lillie Gibson gives her younger students a test during their English lesson. (David Kent)

*far left*
Van, driven by a parent, that transports students to the Rock School (1897), Rio Blanco, Colo. (Andrew Gulliford)

*left*
Log school, Bondurant, Wyo. Teacher Barbara Slager stands on the front steps outside this remote school. (Andrew Gulliford)

*below*
Franklin School (c. 1920), Hodabird, S.D., 1983. Country schools today have playgrounds and swingsets, but most do not have enough children for a real game of softball, football or soccer. (Jeff Almen)

# COUNTRY SCHOOL ARCHITECTURE

# Little Red Schoolhouses—and Others

Few images in American mythology are as revered as that of the little red schoolhouse. Yet, most of America's country schools were not red. They were indeed little, generally rectangular or square, one room and one story. But if a color is to be used to describe country schools, it would be white—with touches of green, red, blue or brown in the trim. "There *were* red schoolhouses," observes Fred E. H. Schroeder in "The Little Red Schoolhouse" (*Icons of America*, 1978). "But the color probably became fixed in the popular mind in poets' and artists' renderings." Poems, paintings, songs and memories softened by time all have helped build a popular image of the small rural school that differs somewhat from the architectural truth.

In paintings such as Winslow Homer's *Snap the Whip* (1871) and *New England Country School* (1872), an atmosphere is portrayed that Schroeder calls "clear, sunny and warm; the children playing snap the whip at recess are thoroughly happy in their play, while the children inside the schoolroom are fully attentive to their studies ("The Little Red Schoolhouse"). The reality is that many country schools were crowded, dark and cold, and the interior arrangements and equipment did not lead particularly to attentiveness or order in the classroom. James Johonnot, author of an 1859 architectural plan book for schools, noted that rural schoolhouses were outside the mainstream of progressive advances in American architecture:

> They are the most unsightly buildings in the district . . . exposed to the depradations of stray cattle and unruly boys. Its style is nondescript, being too small for a barn; too deficient in the elements of just proportion for a dwelling, too lonely and too much neglected for the outbuilding of a farm, and in short, too repulsive in all respects, and exhibiting too many marks of the most parsiminous [sic] economy to be anything but a schoolhouse.

Johonnot's despair echoed that of many school administrators such as Samuel Young, who complained to the New York State legislature in 1844, "No subject connected with the interests of elementary instruction affords a source of such mortifying and humiliating reflections as that of the condition of a large portion of the school-houses." In a survey he reported, "one-third only were found in good repair; another third . . . barely sufficient for the convenience and accommodation of the teachers and pupils; while the remainder, consisting of 3,319, were to all intents and purposes unfit for the reception of man or beast."

In their size, scale, materials and construction methods, country schools often resembled houses, especially on the frontier. The teacher and his or her charges were like a big family, further increasing the association of schools with houses. In many instances, school architecture reflected the design of churches; such schools had separate entrances for girls and boys, a square or round bell tower and a gabled vestibule and were painted white. In regions of the country just being settled, where the resources were especially scarce, country schools tended to resemble crude farm buildings built from whatever materials were

*opposite*
*Snap the Whip* (1873), by Winslow Homer. In this lithograph based on his painting, the artist helped enshrine the little red schoolhouse as a national icon. This vernacular frame school has, typically, only one shutter for each window. (*Harper's Weekly,* Library of Congress)

available. This type in particular was seldom meant to be more than a temporary solution; such structures have been demolished, weathered by the elements and replaced by more substantial schoolhouses.

The design of country schools has been, above all, an architecture based on limitations. Early builders were limited by materials on hand; they used rough logs in all frontier areas, sod on the prairie, adobe in the West and even dugouts cut into the land. The construction ability of settlers also was limited, and professional architectural assistance was almost nonexistent in most rural areas; school builders used whatever construction techniques they knew. Communities have been limited in the amount of money that could be devoted to schools, producing structures that had only the most functional value; style was an extra that was seldom affordable. The first schoolhouse in a community also was only a temporary construction, to be replaced when the community's resources and population were not so spare. Schools, like churches, were built in a hurry in many places, intended to be erected quickly to help mark a civilized settlement. The size of country schools also was limited by an often overlooked factor: the range of the human voice. The classroom had to be small enough to give the lone teacher control over a disparate group of pupils and allow him or her to hear their recitations. The interior arrangement had to provide for accommodation of students of different ages, for circulation and for a prominent focal point for the teacher. Schools were sited wherever land was available, within equal walking or riding distance of their students.

Yet, no single building type in American architecture more vividly represents the communal efforts of the settlers, who donated time, labor and materials to provide places of learning for their children. In the East, the first structures raised by settlers were churches, but in the West, where ethnic backgrounds and religious beliefs were more varied, schools took priority. A community with a school was a community with a future. German immigrants built schools in Douglas County, Kans., without even bothering to register the deeds. The schools took priority; the paperwork could come later. The same was true on the northern plains, where Norwegian immigrants highly valued free education. In Nebraska, schools were built at the rate of approximately one each day between 1870 and 1875; for the next quarter century, the pace slowed to one every two days.

The best workmen in the community were drawn to the construction of a new school even more than to a barn raising or cabin framing. The erection of a schoolhouse wholly by donated labor was of such importance that family and social events were calculated from the date of construction of the schoolhouse. If farm work was slow, the volunteers would take off a few days to build the new schoolhouse, the time depending on the size of the building and the number of families with school-age children. Laying up the sod blocks, adobe brick or heavy logs would be left to the most experienced builders in the community. Women helped by serving meals and gallons of hot coffee they had prepared at home and warmed up at the school site. Country schools were community schools, and everyone took pride in what they had accomplished—a few schools even were named Pride,

Nathan Hale School (c. 1720), East Haddam, Conn. In 1773–74, at age 18, Nathan Hale taught in this vernacular clapboard school with rare 12-over-12–light windows. (HABS)

Claim shack used as a school, south fork of Bad River, S. D., c. 1904. (South Dakota State Historical Society)

Pride School (1888), District No. 41, Ness County, Kans. Teacher and students posed in front of their new schoolhouse, which the community built for $600. (CSL)

such as Pride School (1888), District No. 41, Ness County, Kans.

Money, in addition to education, could be derived from the construction of a school, particularly a frame schoolhouse built with local labor and finished, bought lumber. Cash-poor homesteaders profited from each wagonload of materials they charged to haul to the construction site from a railhead 40 or 50 miles away. Merchants also profited from selling nails, shingles, doors, window sash and paint. After school districts had been established, some community members in the West in the 1880s even paid themselves for building one-room schools. By taking out school bonds over a 10-year period, certain families could profit from constructing the schoolhouse while all the families within the school district were obligated to pay off the indebtedness of the bond. In frontier communities, some families moved on simply to avoid these payments.

Colorado was one territory that took an innovative approach to financing school construction to reduce the tax burden on individual property owners. The second territorial legislature, when it convened in 1862, provided for the following supplement to school funds:

> That hereafter when any new mineral lode, of either gold bearing quartz, silver or other valuable metal, shall be discovered in this Territory, one claim of one hundred feet in length on such lode shall be set apart and held in perpetuity for the use and benefit of schools in this Territory.

W. J. Curtice, the first territorial superintendent of common schools, responded to his new position with this charge to the public to carry out the most important phase of the first school laws:

> It now remains for the people and their duly chosen school officers, to immitate [sic] the commendable zeal of the Legislative Assembly in behalf of education, by carrying into effect the school law and inaugurating a public school system in every county of the Territory. In discharging this duty, we shall not only remove a great barrier—want of schools—to the rapid settlement of the country, but will be developing an educational system among us, for the future, of greater value than the gold of our mountains, and a better safeguard to society than the effective franchise of standing armies.

## Schoolhouse Sites

For a new community ready to undertake the ambitious project of building a school, an early consideration was the site. A school "should overlook a delightful country, present a choice of sunshine and shade, or trees and flowers, and be sheltered from the prevailing winds of winter by a hill-top," advised Henry Barnard in his plan book, *School Architecture: Or, Contributions to the Improvement of School-Houses in the United States* (1838). Rolling meadows and wildflowers, however, were not the typical view from most rural schoolrooms.

Choosing the location for a school often caused serious squabbles among rural neighbors, according to John R. Stilgoe in *Common Landscape of America, 1580–1845* (1982). An acre of land for a school would be deeded to the school district by a farmer or rancher who owned acreage close to families with children who would be attending the school. If the families moved, the schoolhouse could be moved closer to the remaining residents in the district, and the land reverted to the original donor. However, many farmers did not want the school near their land because the schoolchildren would trample the crops and their dogs would harass livestock while the children were in school. So farmers often put schools in swamps, mudholes, floodplains or even sites adjacent to pigsties. Any sliver of land unfit for agricultural use was likely to be chosen as the site of the district school.

A country school in Vermont, notes Fred Schroeder, "served as one wall to a putrid swine pen, where unwanted calves were thrown to be torn and devoured by the hogs; this gruesome spectacle all in full view of the schoolchildren" ("The Little Red Schoolhouse"). A person who attended a one-room school in Texas recalls that "the biggest problem in getting to school was having to cross 'hog-wallers.' They were literally ponds, 6 to 8 inches deep and 10 to 30 feet across, and they seemed to be impossible to get around and still be heading in the direction in which you started" (Texas Congress of Parents and Teachers, *Journey from Ignorant Ridge*, 1976).

Rural schools had to be located within walking distance or at least pony-riding distance of the homes of the pupils. In New England, schools tended to be placed at the geographic center of the district they served and, consequently, were often far from the road, in the middle of woodlots or in swamps. Such locations often failed because many of the children lived disproportionately far distances from this center. Each surveyed township had 36 sections, and the Land Ordinance of 1785 designated Section 16 as the school section, but it often proved too distant from the corners of the township for children to walk to school. On the plains, however, fierce and frequent blizzards made parents eager to have the school located near their homes. Homesteaders on the plains did not have title to their land until they had lived on it for five years and "proved it up." Consequently, property disputes over placement of the school were minimal. And farmers who donated land for the school increased their prestige in the community at little loss to themselves, as they each received a quarter section (160 acres) to plow, plant and harvest. On the flat and open prairies, the rectilinear lots and section roads that posed a problem in the South, western Pennsylvania and northern New England were hardly an issue; nevertheless, in choosing the site of a school, property lines had to be considered. In the territorial era, South Dakota tended to replicate the eastern dimensions of two by three miles for a school district. Brookings County, along the Minnesota border, developed an average of five schools per standard congressional township of 36 square miles. District sizes ranged from 4 square miles to 12 square miles. Further west in South Dakota, schools per township were fewer still, but this state of nearly 80,000 square miles developed 5,011 one-teacher rural schools by 1916, its peak.

Construction did not necessarily mark the end of the site-selection process. Everett Dick, in *The Sod-House Frontier 1854–1890* (1937), explains:

> Near Superior, Nebraska, five or six men worked one-half day on a dug-out when another citizen asked them to move it one-half mile farther west. They agreed to accommodate their neighbor and started working in the new location. Another neighbor then requested them to move it one-half mile farther west so it would be

One-room school, Ormsby County, Nev., 1940. Surrounded by mountains, this school had a prominent bell tower and even a front porch. (Arthur Rothstein, FSA)

close to his place. They moved to accommodate him. This process was continued until they had moved four times and were two miles away from the original location.

Brick and stone schools remained where they had been built regardless of changes in the demographics of the school district. But frame and log schools, constructed without foundations, plumbing or wiring, could be put on skids and freely moved about. In the western states, schools were regularly moved to adjacent communities to accommodate shifts in population. In Wyoming, one log school even had numbers on the outside of the logs so that it could be easily reassembled at a new site.

Such moves did not always have the consent of the entire community. Not long after the Kansas Territory opened in 1854, settlers on the east side of a school district near Lawrence built a log cabin school. A few years later the population shifted, so late one night a group of west-side residents hitched their teams to the school and dragged it on its built-in skids to their side of the district. Several nights later, the east-siders stole back the school. Such occurrences were not uncommon on the frontier. Some schoolchildren, at least once during their rural education, walked to school only to find that during the night their schoolhouse had been moved a mile or so away. Such moves were the delight of the children, who liked to think of their schoolhouses dashing back and forth across the prairies under cover of darkness.

Alice Marsh describes how attached the people of Currie, Nev., became to their schoolhouse. Apparently, the school was on the property of a widow who wanted it removed:

> While warring with the chairman of the school board, she declared she was going to make the schoolhouse into a washhouse. Since it was on her land, it belonged to her, she said. One day, she actually boarded the morning train for Elko, to bring back the sheriff on the afternoon train to put us off as trespassers. Now, we knew that had the schoolhouse been on a concrete foundation, it might be proved to be attached to the land. It was, however, on piles of rocks at the four corners and the middle of the long sides. There was no time to get a legal opinion. As soon as the train had vanished around the bend, several teams of draft horses appeared as if by magic. The schoolhouse, the pupils and the teacher all rolled off and down the road a quarter of a mile to a bit of railroad property. The fence around the old lot was replaced, and every trace of our occupancy was removed. When the sheriff stepped from the train that afternoon, the school was in session as usual, and he could find no sign of its ever having been on the lot in town. Strange, too, the sheriff couldn't find a single person who had seen the school on that spot.

Such antics were not likely to happen in New England, where a school would serve the members of a family for generations and where communities were settled and taxes were established.

Even though the schoolhouses themselves might be made of rough-cut logs and other vernacular materials, their settings sometimes were exhilarating examples of natural beauty that made up for the crude architecture. According to Mary A. Riley, who attended country schools in Crook County, Wyo., in the 1930s:

> The setting was very picturesque—a little valley with forested hills all around, Devils Tower to the west, rimrocks to the east and the irrigated pastures and hay fields of the Campstool Ranch to the north. Chokecherries, gooseberries, strawberries and wild roses grew along the banks of Lytle Creek. Our drinking water came from the clear, cool stream.

Rural school (c. 1850) near Rensselaerville, N.Y., 1936. Soon to be abandoned, this school had 9-over-6–light windows and cornice returns on the gable end. (Carter, FSA)

## *The Architecture of Country Schools*

The architecture of country schools can be divided into four general categories: the vernacular, which includes both folk vernacular and, more commonly, mass vernacular examples, and the architect-designed, which encompasses structures based on plan books and, rarely, those commissioned directly from architects. This categorization of country school architecture has been developed by Fred Schroeder, whose insights have significantly helped guide the study of country schools as a special building type. "The categories are not important in themselves," says Schroeder in "Schoolhouse Reading: What You Can Learn from Your Rural School" (*History News*, 1981), "and the specific features of a given building will overlap in a way that is certain to frustrate purists." Like much of American architecture, country schools evolved through a number of stages. They started generally as shelters using readily available local materials and showing strong regional or ethnic characteristics (folk vernacular), then were replaced with traditional designs using machine-made, commercially sold materials (mass vernacular) and, finally, were designed from standardized plans and built with stock materials. Few country schools bear the mark of a famous architect, although Frank Lloyd Wright's Wyoming Valley Schoolhouse (1957) in Wisconsin is an exception. Many of the rural schoolhouses that remain today can be viewed as eclectic—exhibiting their regional vernacular building traditions but often based on designs transmitted through architectural plan books or on a common cultural perception of what a country school should look like.

### *Vernacular Schoolhouses*

The history of one-room schoolhouse construction, in its initial phase, parallels the history of vernacular architecture in the United States. "Vernacular" means native, the panoply of traditional building materials and forms used in a given place, learned locally or imported with new settlers. Some architectural historians view vernacular architecture as "place-related inflection of culture" (Doug Swaim, *Carolina Dwelling*, 1978). John Brinckerhoff Jackson provides a good definition of the term in *Discovering the Vernacular Landscape* (1984):

> As generally used, the word suggests something countrified, homemade, traditional. As used in connection with architecture, it indicates the traditional rural or small-town dwelling, the dwelling of the farmer or craftsman or wage earner. Current definitions of the word usually suggest that the vernacular dwelling is designed by a craftsman, not an architect, that it is built with local techniques, local materials, and with the local environment in mind: its climate, traditions, its economy—predominantly agricultural. Such a dwelling does not pretend to stylistic sophistication. It is loyal to local forms and rarely accepts innovations from outside the region. It is not subject to fashion and is little influenced by history in its widest sense. That is why the word *timeless* is much used in descriptions of vernacular building.

In many cases, the form of vernacular buildings is shaped by local traditions, while details and decorative features may acknowledge current styles that filter in from other places. According to Schroeder in "Schoolhouse Reading":

> Folk vernacular is traditional and native down to the very materials used, such as sod, logs, hand-hewn planks, adobe, or fieldstone. Such buildings are rare survivors

because in most cases they were temporary pioneer buildings to be abandoned or recycled as soon as a more respectable schoolhouse could be built.

The design of a folk vernacular schoolhouse is more likely to resemble an agricultural outbuilding or primitive dwelling than a schoolhouse or other civic building. . . . Ornamental detailing rarely will be found because of the temporary nature of construction, but any that exists is likely to be unique folk carving or painting.

Mass vernacular is identifiable primarily by the use of commercial machine-made materials such as dimension lumber, standard-size bricks, concrete blocks, asphalt shingles, and commercial siding; prefabricated millwork such as barn sashes, standard doors, and casings; and manufactured hardware and fittings such as doorknobs, hinges, ventilating louvres, and bells. The design of mass-vernacular is likely to "look more like a schoolhouse" than a farm-building or home and to resemble other rural civic structures in the locale such as the town hall or church. It may have ornamental details or even fairly sophisticated architectural additions—a portico, a dormer, a bell tower—but these will tend to be provincialized.

Provincialization is discernible primarily in simplification of detail for reasons of economy or inadequate craftsmanship. For example, a vernacular school may have an overall classical design, but the columns will be square rather than round, they will not be fluted and may not even have a Doric capital; the pediment may be indicated by shallow overhangs and superficial moldings without dentils. A Gothic-style schoolhouse may be identifiable only by vertical board-and-batten siding and may lack entirely features such as gingerbread, window hoods, pointed windows, or even a high gable.

The mass-vernacular schoolhouse is as ubiquitous and undistinguished as Shep, the generalized mongrel dog.

Tarpaper schoolhouse, Wyoming frontier, c. 1890. (American Heritage Center, University of Wyoming)

Tent schoolhouse, Idaho frontier, c. 1900. This reinforced tent had a wooden foundation and even a wooden door. (Idaho Historical Society)

The important factor in these vernacular buildings, as Schroeder stresses, is that the "vernacularity is in the design, which is traditional: the builder (not an architect) builds not according to blueprints, but according to a cultural template in his mind of what a schoolhouse 'looks like' and what the current method of building construction happens to be. . ." ("Schoolhouse Reading"). Design elements in vernacular schoolhouses were transmitted westward by the process of cultural diffusion. The schools also reflected forms used in neighboring communities and other structures such as houses and agricultural and civic buildings.

Although published architectural plans for school buildings were available for schools as early as 1832, homesteaders throughout America struggled long after that to erect schools with the resources at hand; they had little inclination or ability to follow elaborate school designs. As the frontier moved westward and families sought to establish their roots in a strange wilderness, they used any building materials available, particularly any used for dwellings. When school officials could not purchase a door, they made one from log planks or a deer hide; if parents could not buy boards and shingles for a roof, they used poles, brush and soil. Often members of the school district were each required to bring a certain contribution of sod blocks, hewn logs or cut stone to the schoolhouse site.

Everett Dick notes in *The Sod-House Frontier 1854–1890* that the "first temple of learning in Alliance, Neb., was a tent." The first school in Blanding, Utah, also was a tent. Lucreti Lyman, a former student, recalled, "They used to board the sides of the tent with two rows of boards. They filled [the] walls with sawdust to insulate. A tent is quite warm, if you keep the fire going. The sawdust kept the wind out." The Blanding school grew quickly; several months later another tent had been erected, and the next year a frame schoolhouse was started.

Vernacular schoolhouse building was widely varied in place and time. In New England in the early 19th century, folk vernacular structures included schools of locally quarried stone. Using commercial machine-made materials, communities in Ohio, Indiana and Illinois were building brick schoolhouses with bell towers and separate entrances for girls and boys by the 1880s. At the same time, homesteaders on the plains sent their children to schools made of sod and adobe that were clearly in the less developed, folk vernacular tradition. And as late as 1900, tents were still being used as schoolhouses in frontier settlements in Nevada, Utah and Wyoming while ornate, two-story frame schools were built in North Dakota. Pioneers also used as schools whatever structures could be adapted, from abandoned farmhouses and log houses to chicken coops and, on the prairies, dugouts.

An important unifying element in the design and building of country schools was that they tended to follow a progression within each community of replacement by a sturdier and more pleasing specimen as resources would permit. It is unlikely, says Schroeder in "Educational Legacy: Rural One-Room Schoolhouses" (*Historic Preservation*, 1977), that "the oldest existing school building is the first one constructed in a district. These early folk-vernacular schools, in the forward-looking tradition of Americans, were never meant to be anything but temporary." Many areas, East and West, first built log structures, except for western territories where earthen materials such as sod and adobe and the ground itself were used (for dugouts or bermed shelters). By the 1870s small frame schoolhouses often replaced the simpler earlier structures. Late in the century designs reflecting plan-book and education reforms became more popular. While in the West in the last quarter of the 19th century parents were often building the first schools in a district, in New England during the same period old vernacular schools were being replaced by architect-designed buildings. And in the 20th century, particularly during the WPA projects of the 1930s, many schools were renovated or altered, some gaining electricity and even plumbing for the first time. As the old schools were replaced, their materials were often scavenged for new uses or the buildings left abandoned.

### Architect-Designed Schoolhouses

Many schoolhouses bear the imprint of an architect, even though in most cases it came via long distance, transmitted by an architectural handbook or plan book rather than obtained from a specially retained architect. Plan books played a significant role in shaping many American buildings, especially houses, during the 19th century. Through these books, architectural designs were made easily available for replication by carpenters and other builders anywhere in the country; they included sketches and elevation drawings as well as floor plans.

By the third generation of school building, school districts almost always followed architectural plan books. For those who chose to build such a "designed" school, the intention was to reform the places in which education was to take place or to adopt the style of the times,

Cold Creek School, White Pine County, Nev., c. 1905. The use of log ends extending beyond the wall plane is a centuries-old vernacular Scandinavian building tradition. (Northeastern Nevada Museum)

Board-and-batten school, Kentucky. This large school had the shape and proportions of a small, English three-bay barn common in the upland South. (Kentucky Department of Education)

or both. Popular American architectural styles were used or adapted for schoolhouses, reflecting the rise and fall of public tastes. Greek Revival, Gothic Revival, Queen Anne, Richardsonian Romanesque, classical revival, bungalow, Mission and the International Style all were used for country schools. But, observes Fred Schroeder in "The Little Red Schoolhouse":

> Despite these patterns, the architect-designed plans generally failed in rural schools. One way or another, the vernacular asserted itself. Exemplary schools might be built in the cities of New England, but invariably the scaling down of size along with the necessary paring down of appropriations simplified and obscured the mainstream styles, and, like irrepressible mongrels, the rural school houses continued to assert and reassert their homely design genesis as a house for holding school. The final product was a native American architectural style.

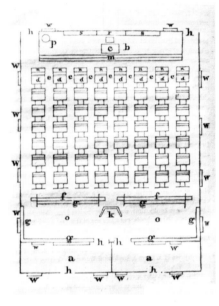

Floor plan showing suggested furniture arrangement, by William A. Alcott, 1832. (*Essay on the Construction of School-Houses*)

Yet, reformers, architects, some schoolteachers, government education departments and even product manufacturers first tried to create an appropriate country school architecture. By the third decade of the 19th century, sentiment had turned to ways of reforming school buildings to improve their performance and appearance. A key year in schoolhouse design was 1831. That year, William A. Alcott, a school-master, won a $20 prize from the American Institute of Instruction for his essay on the design of schoolhouses. Alcott's *Essay on the Construction of School-Houses*, published in 1832, reflected improvements made in Alcott's own school. Presented mainly through floor plans rather than elevation drawings, Alcott's suggested new designs included backs on the desks, which were to be arranged in rows to allow circulation room for the teacher and students; large windows for light and ventilation, arranged above eye level to avoid distractions; and space for storage and display of paintings, prints, engravings, maps, charts, a globe and other scientific equipment. He also suggested allowing space around the school for fresh air and recess play. Although his recommended Greek Revival style was not widely adopted for country schools, the new style of interior arrangement was.

Henry Barnard, another educator who also designed several schools and served in the Connecticut legislature, was responsible for *School Architecture,* first published in 1838. Barnard was state superintendent of education in Rhode Island and Connecticut and became U.S. Commissioner of Education when Congress created the office in 1867; he also was editor of the *American Journal of Education,* an influential journal. His classic handbook, issued in a revised edition in 1848 and in several other versions, presented plans in the latest architectural styles, addressing exteriors, interiors, yards, mechanical equipment and furniture. Barnard credits some of his ideas to Alonzo Potter and George B. Emerson's *The School and the Schoolmaster* (1842), 14,500 copies of which were distributed in New York State and Massachusetts in 1842–43.

Barnard believed that a well-built, impressive school building would inspire pupils in their learning. Consequently, two of his designs were Greek Revival schoolhouses because he was convinced that "every schoolhouse should be a temple, consecrated in prayer to the physical, intellectual and moral culture of every child in the community." Most school districts, however, were willing to settle for a simpler building that would not leave them in debt forever.

Several school designs adaptable to rural areas were published in Barnard's book, including a Gothic Revival board-and-batten primary school in Westerly, R.I., complete with a spire on the roof gable and decorative gingerbread trim under the front eaves. Barnard also provided designs for Greek Revival schoolhouses. One design, reflected in a school in District No. 6 in Windsor, Conn., had no windows flanking the massive door; the school looks like a mausoleum. Another Greek Revival design, used for a primary school in New Haven, Conn., has a dome in the middle of the roof, three windows on each side with louvered shutters and Doric columns on either side of the school entrance. Barnard's requirements included a separate entry or lobby for girls and boys.

Barnard sought to improve schools not only by giving them a standard external appearance but also by paying attention to the interior space, the placement of windows, ventilation, desk size and sanitary facilities. Barnard advocated at least 150 cubic feet of air for each occupant, requiring high ceilings that made the buildings extremely difficult to heat. He required enough room for each pupil to sit comfortably and to have freedom of movement. Architect-designed schools had more physical space than vernacular schools because they usually had the "one or more rooms for recitation, apparatus, library and other purposes" suggested by Barnard.

Lighting was a perpetual problem in rural schools. Direct north light meant undue exposure to the elements; Barnard thought that it also imparted "less of cheerfulness and warmth than [light] from other directions." Warning against the presumably worse dangers of cross-light glare and reflection, he recommended that windows be placed on only two sides of the room at least 3½ or 4 feet above the floor and that they not be directly behind the teacher. He suggested that every window be furnished with blinds and curtains. Barnard also attempted to alleviate lighting problems through use of skylights and included in his book a design by Ithiel Town and Alexander Jackson Davis for an octagonal schoolhouse with an eight-sided skylight (reprinted from Potter and Emerson's book).

Barnard's crusade for better school buildings did not initially alter the design of most country schools; the exigencies of time, money and construction sophistication prevailed, so the vernacular continued to shape the majority of schoolhouses. He nonetheless became a champion of education reform and the first of many plan-book writers who sought to improve learning by improving the school building. Barnard's *School Architecture* was reprinted as recently as 1970, indicating its value as an important research and historical document in the history of American education.

The next architect of note to produce a handbook of school design was Charles P. Dwyer of Buffalo, who in 1856 published *The Economy of Church, Parsonage and School Architecture Adapted to Small Societies and Rural Districts*. Dwyer's designs were imbued with the Gothic mania of the period, although he suggested that local materials might be used so that a design "could, in a thickly timbered locality, be constructed of hewn logs, and yet, with very little extra cost, be made

Elevation drawing for a primary school, Westerly, R.I., in the Gothic Revival style, by Henry Barnard, 1848. (*School Architecture*)

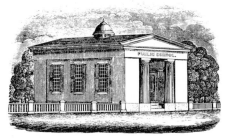

Drawing of a Greek Revival primary school, New Haven, Conn., by Henry Barnard, 1848. (*School Architecture*)

Architect's drawing for a country school resembling a church, 1873. No bell towers of these proportions were ever built for one-room schools. (*American Journal of Education*)

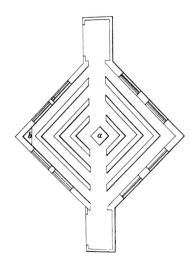

Plan for a diamond-shaped schoolhouse, by Charles P. Dwyer, 1856. (*The Economy of Church, Parsonage and School Architecture*)

Perspective of a schoolhouse, outbuildings and grounds, by Alonzo Potter and George B. Emerson, 1842. (*The School and the Schoolmaster*)

to look well." One of Dwyer's designs was a diamond-shaped school. Unlike Barnard, Dwyer paid little attention to interior plans and had students sitting on seats arranged in close rows, like pews. Two of his designs were for two-story schools in which the teachers would live above the classroom.

Other architects also drew schools based on their experience with churches. Rural schools of the second half of the 19th century, suggested Fletcher B. Dresslar in his *American Schoolhouses* (1910), derive from village churches of New England with their long, rectangular floor plans, windows on two sides and entrance at one end. In his 1873 annual report, Horace M. Hale, Colorado superintendent of public instruction, included as an illustration a woodcut, reproduced from the *American Journal of Education*, that shows obvious church influences. In the Kansas legislature's second biennial report for 1879 and 1880, Haskell and Wood Architects of Topeka, Kans., published details for a school recalling colonial churches except for a front facade with a double entrance and a Palladian window in the middle, with matching curved hood molds above the doors and double window. This school was built near Lawrence, Kans., in 1874, but ceased to be used as a school in 1955. Today, it is used as the Sunnyside School community center and the only voting place for Sarcoxie Township.

James Johonnot's *Country School-Houses* (1859) incorporated design elements from previous books, but he stressed that "the principles developed in city architecture are not applicable to the wants of the smaller district schools." The popular Greek and Gothic designs would

have to be scaled down considerably for the small schoolhouse, he said. Johonnot found Greek porticos and colonnades to be wasteful and more suitable to the gods than to children, asserting, "Their introduction into school-house architecture was unfortunate, and we trust the time is not far distant when they will fall into disuse. . . . A diminutive structure can never call up the emotion of the sublime; and . . . when the Greek forms are used . . . in small buildings, the old maxim is illustrated, that 'there is but a step from the sublime to the ridiculous.' " Johonnot was correct that most frugal farmers in rural areas had no money to spend on fluted pilasters. He also had disparaging words for the Gothic Revival style, because its ornateness seemed impractical for country schools and steep Gothic roofs might wear out sooner than lower-pitched roofs. Nonetheless, one of the designs in his book (many were executed by S. E. Hewes) has board-and-batten siding and decorative scrollwork reminiscent of basic Gothic motifs. Johonnot concluded:

> As society advances in intelligence, and education begins to receive that attention which its intrinsic merits demand, we feel confident that the subject 'Schoolhouse Architecture', will be more and more studied, until finally every new School-House erected will be a solid permanent structure, built with due regard to all the fundamental principles of architectural art.

By 1871, when a second volume of Johonnot's plans was published as *School-Houses*, a big market for schools and their furnishings had developed; this book was published by a furniture dealer, J. W. Schermerhorn. These designs showed greater window area, and one included a Renaissance Revival school.

Samuel F. Eveleth's *School-House Architecture* (1870) contained two designs suitable for rural schools. The first one included piazzas coupled with recessed windows that could open at both ends of the building to provide cross-ventilation. The second design presented another small school of the Gothic cottage type with a relatively large veranda intended as a "play room for rainy weather." These structures are really houses outfitted with double entrances for use as schools. The decorative work, cornices and balustrades were too ornamental for the serious wear and tear that country schools received.

The focus on styles raised questions for rural school builders. "How are we to achieve a one-room Romanesque, or a Florentine Palazzo in a cow-pasture, or a Palladian classic with school windows?" asks Schroeder in "The Little Red Schoolhouse." He suggests:

> The answer is that it can be done, and it has been done, but in all cases, the stylish motifs are reduced and simplified by the vernacular axioms. . . . Thus, "Queen Anne" in a one-room school is marked by the addition of one or more windowed dormers, these enclosing useless attic space, and by the characteristic Queen Anne use of small panes in the upper portion of a window with a single pane in the lower portion. With the possible addition of a bell-tower, we have one of the most common Midwest turn-of-the-century designs.

At the hands of a master architect, a country school could be made to fit function with innovative form. On land he donated, with plans made free of charge, Frank Lloyd Wright designed the Wyoming Valley Schoolhouse in Wisconsin in 1957. Robert C. Twombly, in *Frank Lloyd Wright: An Interpretive Biography* (1973), describes this two-

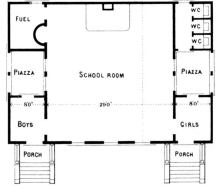

Elevation drawing and floor plan of a frame one-room school in the style of a Gothic cottage, by Samuel F. Eveleth, 1870. (*School-House Architecture*)

Wyoming Valley Schoolhouse (1957), Wyoming Valley, Wis., designed by Frank Lloyd Wright. (© 1958 The Frank Lloyd Wright Foundation)

Mosca School (c. 1930), Alamosa County, Colo. The strong vertical emphasis and ornamentation of this architect-designed, four-room school were key Art Deco motifs. (Edwin L. Dodds)

room school as consisting of "two classrooms separated from a gymnasium-cafeteria-assembly hall combination by a skylit central corridor under a forest of crossed beams. Its roof line almost exactly reproduced the contours of the hill behind it, and in its bucolic setting it was a quaint and simple expression of organic architecture." Supervised by Wright himself, the school was built of concrete block and redwood and a shingled roof. In defiance of the 80-year tradition of stoves and chimneys, plans called for a fireplace in each classroom. Observes Schroeder, "Frank Lloyd Wright's quixotic gesture appears to have rung down the curtain on the architectural history of rural district schools" ("The Little Red Schoolhouse").

Other architect-designed country schools built in the mid-1960s are less organic; many are scaled-down versions of their urban counterparts. The Cox Bar Elementary School, located in the Big Bar Forest Service Camp in Trinity County, Calif., and sited on a bluff above Trinity River, was designed by the California Bureau of School Planning, a division of the California State Department of Education. The plan of the interior resembles that of a model school built in Hays, Kans., in 1917. Not only is the cloakroom (now called the wardrobe) located in the same place, but the Cox Bar school also features a refrigerator and kitchen range where the Kansas model had a table for domestic science. After 120 years, the problem of glare has been solved with indirect fluorescent lighting and an extended overhanging roof that blocks the sun's direct rays. The Forks of Salmon Elementary School in Siskiyou County near Orleans, Calif., reflects International Style design. The roof, which incorporates a Native American motif, also extends out to block the sun's direct rays. Designed by Smart and Clabaugh, the flat-roofed school is in a dramatic setting of meadows and evergreens near the Salmon River. The Coffee Creek Elementary School is located near Trinity Lake, Calif., in a forest glade undisturbed except by a parking area and small playfield. Also designed by Smart and Clabaugh, the school has a single classroom of generous size with shelving and movable cabinets. Large glass windows offer a breathtaking view of the forest.

Vernacular one-room schoolhouses continue to be built. In 1981 a $40,000 modular schoolhouse was constructed on the Kendrick Ranch near Sheridan, Wyo. Named Hanging Woman School after the creek that crosses the ranch near the school, the building was paid for by the Kendrick family and will be used by the children of their ranch hands. The building is red with white trim, has a gabled room and in its simplicity is a legitimate descendent of the vernacular one-room schools of the 19th century.

## The Form of Schoolhouses

"Form ever follows function" suggested architect Louis H. Sullivan in 1896. Although this principle is not universally true of all building types—or all buildings—it rings true when the building type is country schools. While such schools may have been constructed of widely different materials, in widely varied terrains and climates, in a range of styles and colors, they nonetheless constitute a distinctive building

type. The form of country schools followed their function, relying on small utilitarian designs built with inexpensive, generally unprepossessing materials to shelter isolated, small groups of children brought together to get an education. A distinguishing mark of a building type is that its function has come to be readily recognizable by its form. Although a few country schools might be mistaken for rural churches or farm outbuildings, most can be quickly identified for what they are, or once were.

The vast majority of one-room country schools were rectangular, while some were square. The pivotal determinant of—and limitation on—the form of these schoolhouses was the carrying distance of the human voice: the teacher's to keep order, the students' to be heard by the teacher. Even before the plan-book architects and educators quantified the optimum size for country schools, vernacular builders intuitively were constructing schools to the maximum feasible size of no more than 30 by 40 feet. This is the limit recommended by William Alcott in his 1831 proposal, one echoed in later plan books. Classrooms of 25 by 32 feet were thought by Washington, D.C., architect Edward C. Earl in 1919 "to be about the practical limit of voice and vision for teacher and pupils." By the mid-19th century, other common sizes were 24 by 36 feet, 20 by 30 and 18 by 32. These sizes were ideal for the maximum of 30 to 40 students who attended most country schools. More students meant more teachers as well as more space.

Rectangular and square schoolhouses typically had three or four widely spaced, small-paned windows, generally 9-over-9 lights hung in double sash. Windows were placed on one or both of the long sides—the latter not favored by those who feared that light from two directions would harm students' eyes. The placement of windows on the north side, which produced even, year-round light, alleviated the problem but made the classroom even colder in winter.

Vernacular schoolhouses tended to have just one entrance door on the short side of the building, sometimes sheltered by a portico, porch or roof, but often opening out into the elements. Doors usually faced south or east. More like their residential namesakes, a few schoolhouses had an entrance door on the long side of the building, with the windows. Carrying through the form of the occasional religious prototypes, some schools were built with two doors, separating the girls and the boys. Many schoolhouses with double entrances—particularly west of the Mississippi—were built from an architect's plans; in some communities, the pragmatic people who constructed vernacular schoolhouses saw no reason to spend extra time or money on a double entrance. However, the double entrance appears in many vernacular structures such as schools and churches in other communities.

Roofs were usually simple gabled forms, with hipped roofs later recommended by the plan books. Almost all of the roofs were shingled, except for the early log and sod schools that had pole and brush roofs. Shake shingles were used in communities where timber of the correct dimensions could be obtained. By the late 19th century, clapboard schools made use of mass vernacular shingles, which were easy to acquire and inexpensive.

Stone School (c. 1850), near East Troy, Wis. This symmetrical stone school, constructed of native buff sandstone, had an almost archetypical schoolhouse form. (Herbert W. Bradley, HABS)

Marsh's Settlement School (1839), District No. 1, Lake County, Ill. The double entrances, gabled roof, rectangular form and clapboard siding were features shared by many country schools. (HABS)

Diamond Rock School (1818), Chester County, Pa. This octagonal school had a hipped roof and a central chimney. (HABS)

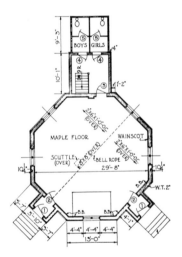

Octagonal school, District No. 17, Skaneateles, N.Y., first floor plan. (James M. Timmens, HABS)

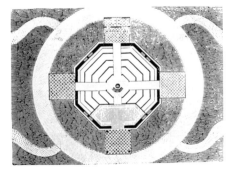

Plan for an octagonal school site, by Ithiel Town and Alexander Jackson Davis, 1842. (Potter and Emerson, *The School and the Schoolmaster*)

Unlike the rare dugouts, tents and other purely temporary schools—whose forms were unique unto themselves—octagon-shaped schoolhouses tended to conform to the typical characteristics of schools in most ways except for their shape. "Why continue to build in the same square form of all ages?" asked Orson Squire Fowler in his seminal book *A Home for All; or, the Gravel Wall, and Octagon Mode of Building* (1848). Even before this phrenologist and amateur architect popularized the octagon as an efficient form for houses and other buildings, eight-sided structures had been constructed throughout the United States. The Dutch colonies chose octagons for numerous buildings, including a trading post in Trenton, N.J., in 1630; Thomas Jefferson refined his use of octagonal shapes with Poplar Forest (1806–22) in Bedford County, Va. Between 1850 and 1860, the use of octagons for houses became almost a national fad, one to which schoolhouse builders were not immune. When plans for an octagonal school by Town and Davis were published in Henry Barnard's plan book, eight-sided buildings had already gained popularity.

One of the major attributes of octagonal schools was that they were compact and easy to maintain. With a wood stove in the center, these schools were economical to heat because less wall surface was exposed to the outside elements. The teacher's desk was usually situated in front of the door and faced the students or was on the opposite side of the room facing the entrance.

Octagon-shaped schools were built primarily in the mid-Atlantic states of Delaware, New Jersey, New York and southeastern Pennsylvania. In Bucks County, Pa., 10 octagon schools were constructed between 1775 and 1833. Only one remains—the Cedar Grove School (1802), also known as the Wrightstown Octagonal School House. The walls were built of uncoursed and roughly cut ashlar stone in several shades laid in a random pattern with rough quoins at the corners. A vernacular octagonal design also surfaced in Chester County, Pa., with the Diamond Rock School (1818), built by people of Welsh and German descent. Bills for the school's construction totaled $260.93 for materials; they were paid for by subscription from 49 patrons, who contributed $264.24. In use until 1864, it was restored in 1918 and has undergone no significant alterations. The school faced south and was built of stone, as was the Stone Jug octagonal school (c. 1830) in Wayne County, Pa. The Stone Jug School featured uncoursed rubblestone walls 18 inches thick with large stone quoins at the corners. Hand-hewn wooden plates 10 inches square were placed on top of the stone walls, and the rafters rose to a peaked center above them. The original windows were 9-over-6 with deep sills. Even the door was four inches thick.

Extensive documentation describes the Pleasant Hill Academy (1831) in Little Creek Hundred, Del., which was probably based on octagonal schools in nearby Pennsylvania. Although called an academy, the school served as a free school. The Act for the Establishment of Free Schools passed the Delaware general assembly in February 1829, and Pleasant Hill was started within two years. Construction continued through 1834, when School District No. 12 purchased 250 feet of white pine boards for $5. Interior furnishings came later and included soap, "1

wash Bason [sic], curtains, corn broom, two earthen vessels, watering pot, tin cups and one box Lucifers [matches] for twelve and a half cents." Octagonal schools waned in Pennsylvania with the publication of *Pennsylvania School Architecture* in 1855, edited by Thomas Henry Burrowes, which advocated "plain and neat" rectangular forms.

If any one color was used most frequently for painting country schools, it was white. According to Fred Schroeder, vernacular schools erected before 1870 were seldom painted because paint was expensive; the commercial production of linseed oil and manufactured pigments made cheap paint readily accessible after 1870, however. But the color typically used then was white, not red as myth would have it. For the Greek Revival buildings so popular with Americans during the 1830s and 1840s, as well as the other classical revival styles adopted into the 20th century, white was the color of choice (it was not known at the time that the ancient Greek models had been polychrome). In *The Rural School Plant for Rural Teachers and School Boards, Normal Schools, Teachers' Training Classes, Rural Extension Bureaus* (1917), S. A. Challman asserted that "pure ground white lead" should be used for proper schoolhouses. Country schools were seldom painted red, and when they were, it was an iron oxide red used for barns rather than the fire-engine reds available today. Gothic Revival and Queen Anne structures featured earth and forest tones, with some of the latter built of tan or yellow stucco.

By the 19th century, a belfry or bell tower, usually placed above the entrance to the schoolhouse, had become a status symbol for many school districts. Some schools had simple roofs over their bells; others had elaborate bell towers with ornate gingerbread woodwork and copper roofs with hand-hammered or etched designs. Schools built in the 1880s often had received a vestibule and bell tower by 1910. Some schools even flew flags from the top of the finials above the bell towers.

Early schools did not have such luxuries; teachers had to call students to class with hand bells. As a community thrived, a subscription was often taken up for a bell tower, which would serve both a decorative and a practical purpose. The tower itself would be ornamentation for the school, and the bell within it could be used to call children to school, to signal when someone was lost or hurt and to warn the community in case of danger, as when a prairie fire was coming perilously close. When the school bell pealed in the middle of the day in mining camps, the townspeople rushed to the mine, fearing for the safety of the miners. But the school bell also rang joyously at Christmas. In all communities the school bell was a source of community pride.

Later educators and school superintendents sought to eliminate bell towers on rural schools because they seemed to be a symbol of the past and did not represent 20th-century virtues of efficiency, economy and progress. S. A. Challman, commissioner of school buildings for Minnesota and author of the influential book *The Rural School Plant*, wrote:

> The belfry is a relic of the time when the school and the church were closely associated in men's minds. It served a useful purpose when reliable watches and clocks were uncommon, and telephones and gongs were unknown. . . . From an architectural point of view the belfry seldom adds anything to the attractiveness of

Harmony School (1894), Selden, Kans. This two-room school featured an impressive belvedere for its bell, as well as iron cresting atop the hipped roof. (Kansas State Historical Society)

a building, but more often becomes a grotesque excrescence on an otherwise pleasing exterior.

If superintendents saw bell towers as a problem, outhouses posed an even greater problem. "Usually one or two privies slouched in a corner of the schoolyard, but far too often to suit the educators there were none at all," notes Wayne E. Fuller in "Country Schoolteaching on the Sod-House Frontier" (*Arizona and the West*, 1975). For most country schools, one outhouse sufficed, but some rural schools had two, one for boys and one for girls. In one popular design, the outhouses were built as one structure, with a coal or wood shed in the middle, not only for convenience but also for added privacy. Most outhouses could accommodate only one user at a time, but two-seat privies and even three-seaters were not uncommon, with the teacher using a private outhouse a discreet distance away.

County and state superintendents minced no words in protesting the lack of proper sanitary facilities. A New York school superintendent said in the 1840s that "those miserable abodes of accumulated dirt and filth . . . debarred the possibility of yielding to the ordinary calls of nature without violent inroads upon modesty and shame." The Nebraska state school superintendent complained in 1872, "Too much cannot be said against the barbarous custom of providing no place of retirement whatever. One privy is scarcely better than none, and [in] some respects worse. How many ruined characters can trace their downfall to the scenes of their early school days, where, through force of circumstances, they lost that delicate sense of modesty, so essential to guard the virtue of the young." In 1894 Laura Eisenhuth, state superintendent of public instruction for North Dakota, called the poor condition of school outhouses in her state "the greatest moral question affecting schools." Too many, she noted, are "snowed full in the winter and too vile to enter in summer, leaving the pupils without the proper means to obey the call of nature the whole day. No wonder that their brains are inactive, their indigestion impaired and their circulation sluggish." She urged school boards to provide healthy outhouses and to "keep them free of all kinds of drawings and writings, immoral influences that burn and blacken the pure young souls of innocent children, and perpetuate and strengthen evil."

In the great push to improve rural schools in the early 1900s, county and state superintendents began circulating plans for "the sanitary privy" along with other architectural drawings. Soon rural school experts were addressing the problem with more specific information and suggestions. An entire chapter of *The Rural School Plant* was devoted to toilets, the author declaring:

> There should always be separate toilets for the sexes, and they should be far enough apart to avoid moral contagion. The main considerations are privacy and cleanliness. If these can be secured, all other matters are secondary. A latticed enclosure in front of the door of the toilet is always desirable.

Although school superintendents considered outhouses to be dens of iniquity, the children thought of them as safe bases for games of tag, convenient hideouts from other family members in school and fine places to conjure up plots.

Outhouses at a rural school, Denhigh, N.D., 1937. These outhouses were built to WPA specifications, which included brick foundations, double windows, double vents and railed staircases. (Russell Lee, FSA)

Outhouse design varied from ornate, pedimented Greek Revival outhouses with small, 2-over-2 windows on the sides to simple, unpainted vernacular structures with three walls, a door and flat roof. Virtually all of the outhouses were built of wood. Until the Works Progress Administration drew up plans for model outhouses in the 1930s, no thought was given to ventilation. The plans for better one-room schools disseminated by county school superintendents included plans for outhouses. The options included deep, underground vaults that had to be cleaned periodically, fly-proof pits that could be covered over and the outhouse moved, and buckets placed under the seats and filled one-third with disinfectant.

Another problem facing county school superintendents was teacher housing. Before 1900 teachers simply boarded with the families of their pupils. As rural schools became more modern and professional and as teachers sought decent wages, teachers also expected better housing. The idea of separate housing for teachers developed in Europe, particularly in the northern countries of Norway, Sweden, Denmark, Germany and France. In the United States, the first teacher's house adjacent to a school, or teacherage, was built in 1905 in Walla Walla County, Wash., under the supervision of the county superintendent of schools. Forty-three teacherages were in use in South Dakota in 1921, but few of the cottages remain. One of the few teacherages listed in the National Register of Historic Places is at the Markham School (1915), a red-brick, one-story building in the oil-boom ghost town of Markham, Okla. The teacherage, built in bungalow style at the same time as the school, has a hipped roof with clipped gables and two interior chimneys. The windows are all 1-over-1, single sash. The building is still in use as a residence.

The schoolyard was generally grass, usually not cut except along paths to the outhouses, and was well trodden in the areas where the children frequently played tag or ball. In North Dakota, some schoolyards had rows of trees or shelter belts planted along their perimeter, while in Ohio and Wisconsin fewer but larger trees marked the dimensions of the schoolyard. In the West, schoolyards were often fenced—not to keep children in, but to keep cattle out. An interesting variation on a common school feature is the wide variety of turnstiles used to enter the schoolyards. Turnstiles had to be simple enough for a first-grader to go through but sturdy enough to keep farm animals out. Most turnstiles were crude wooden devices that pivoted around a firmly set wooden fence post. The elaborate wrought-iron gate used at the one-room school (c.1900) in Jiggs, Nev., is an unusual turnstile. It is perfectly balanced and handsomely crafted and, as with true folk art, also serves a functional purpose. Today, the school is a post office and many of the adults it serves turned the gate years ago as children.

The form of country schools, in the end, was functional, "partly as a result of planning and design," observes Schroeder, "but mostly it proved to be functional because of the resiliency of the people within— the jack-of-all-trades teacher and the children, all gristle, not yet bone— who together managed to accommodate their processes and personalities to any schoolroom" ("The Little Red Schoolhouse").

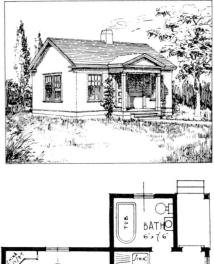

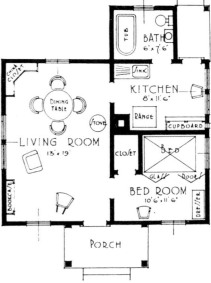

Elevation drawing and floor plan for a model teacher's cottage, Washington State, 1917. (S. A. Challman, *The Rural School Plant*)

Rural school (c. 1900), Jiggs, Nev. The metal turnstile to this schoolyard is a perfectly proportioned piece of folk art. (Andrew Gulliford)

## Materials and Techniques

Just about every type of building material was used for country schools, depending on the local availability or ease of ordering manufactured materials. Logs, frame with wood siding, stone, brick, adobe and sod all were used; dugouts partly tunneled into berms or sloping earth housed some students, while a few attended school in tents. Wood frame became one of the most prevalent building materials, representing an improvement over early log or earthen structures and one using a ·material commonly available throughout the country. North Dakota's stock of country schools is an example of the variety found in many states. In 1894, 273 schools were built in the state; of these, 263 were frame, five were stone, one was sod and four were log. By 1906 North Dakota had 3,700 schools; of the total, 3,554 were frame, 103 were stone or brick, nine were sod and 34 were log. By 1914–15, the last year in which such statistics were compiled, North Dakota had 5,150 frame, 252 stone and brick and 19 log and sod schools.

## Log Schoolhouses

In timbered regions, logs were the primary construction material for the first rural schools. Throughout the mountainous areas of the United States—in the Cumberlands, Appalachians, Rockies and Cascades, in the woodlands of northern Michigan and southern Missouri, in Maine, Minnesota, Wyoming and Wisconsin—early schools were made of logs. In the remote valleys and hollows of Kentucky, Georgia, Tennessee and the Carolinas, children walked to log schools that were braced on fieldstones; usually these schools did not have even a masonry foundation. In 1844 the superintendent of schools for New York listed 707 log schools in a statewide report. In 1890 a survey in Wyoming identified 141 schools built of log or sod.

Log schools were built by farmers and frontiersmen. The Swedes, Norwegians, Germans, Finns and forty-niners who built these schools with only a few tools exercised native craftsmanship and ingenuity. As with all vernacular structures, no two log schools were ever built alike, although their exteriors resembled each other more than their interiors. New York log schoolhouses averaged 18 or 20 feet by 26 or 30 feet (dimensions similar to those recommended by school reformers); walls were carried to a height of 10 feet with windows and doors sawed out. Logs were shaped, trimmed with an adz and then notched and joined with a V-notch, full dovetail or half-dovetail cornering technique. The schools were built with only a few window openings and perhaps a deerskin for a temporary door. Hair from the deerhide went into the lime and mud mortar used to daub the logs. The logs also were chinked with sticks split or hewn in the proper shape and held in place by wooden pins daubed with mud. In settlements where glass was not yet available, the school windows were covered with oiled paper or cheap factory cloth. The doors were made of thick boards or planks hung on wooden hinges and secured with wooden latchkey fasteners. Schoolhouses of green or unseasoned logs were often built in a day; teacher and students could delight in the branches that would sprout inside and out when spring came. Log schoolhouses

Ebenezer Academy (1823), Iredell County, N.C. The design of this school typified vernacular log schoolhouses. Teacher John Parris inscribed the interior with letters, maps and mottoes in the 1880s. (Gary Freeze, North Carolina Division of Archives and History; Iredell Historic Preservation Commission)

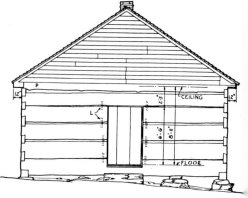

Little Greenbrier School and Church (1882), Elkmont, Tenn., 1936. This school reflected sophisticated building techniques for the time. (Charles S. Grossman, HABS)

were also covered with lime-based mortar (often removed by farm boys and used as ammunition on the playground or in school).

Schools built of hewn logs were fairly common in wooded frontier communities. Dressing the upper and lower surfaces of the walls made them fit better. Dressing the outer wall showed that the pioneers thought their school was important, and a hewn building was a sign of local pride. As finances permitted, clapboards could be added later to the hewn outer surfaces. Hewing the inner surfaces made the interior schoolroom walls safer for boisterous children and easier to clean.

Although most log schools were made of horizontal timbers, in Oklahoma, Colorado and Nevada another variety of school building was the stockade or picket type. It was made of smaller, shorter logs that were stood on end and toenailed to beams that made the sills of the school.

Log schools usually had planed pine boards on the floor. Often, the spaces between the boards were so wide that when the students swept the floor, they just pushed the dirt between the boards. Such floors had many splinters. In summer, children often attended school barefoot, and the teacher frequently had to interrupt a recitation to pick a splinter from one of her pupils who had come hopping to the front of the room for first aid. Log schools built in New York between 1820 and 1850 had large stone hearths and a chimney stack of earth, stones and sticks laid up in a wattle-and-daub style and covered with a thick plaster of mud. After the chimneys had seasoned, they would occasionally catch fire, or improperly selected stones might explode into the schoolroom, igniting the floor and gaining the attention of even the drowsiest student.

Log schools usually had pole roofs, which occasionally had tenants—such as the wood rat that frequented the Disappointment Creek Valley School in southwest Colorado in 1897. Nellie Carnahan Robinson, a teacher new to the area, was not impressed with her little log school, as she wrote in her diary (quoted in Michael L. Husband's "The Recollections of a Schoolteacher in Disappointment Creek Valley," *Colorado Magazine,* 1974):

> I am sure there was not another schoolhouse in the whole country as primitive as this one. There couldn't have been. It was made of logs and had been built in a day by the men in the settlement. The dimensions were about fourteen by sixteen feet. The logs were chinked and daubed with adobe mud. In many places the mud had fallen out. If a child wanted to look at anyone passing, he would peek between the logs.
>
> The roof was made by first placing a layer of poles across which was the ceiling. The poles were then covered with straw and over the straw was a thick coating of adobe mud. From the ridge pole on each side were unfinished boards. There was little slant to the roof, but it kept out the rain.
>
> On some days we had occasional showers of dirt when a wood rat would be prowling up there. The floor was of unfinished boards, and if a child dropped a pencil he learned to be quick to retrieve it or it rolled through the cracks under the floor. At times we would have a general upheaval at the noon hour when the boys would take up the floorboards and reclaim the erasers, pencils, chalk and various other articles the wood rat had hidden under there.

An outstanding example of a log school is the Little Greenbrier School and Church near Elkmont, Tenn., considered one of the finest log structures in the Great Smoky Mountains National Park. Construction began on this school on January 1, 1882, and only the best "corner men" in the community were selected to notch and fit the logs. Joining up logs at corners requires great skill, and each of the four men knew that it was a mark of distinction to be selected for this job of building the school, which would also serve as a church.

Huge poplar logs, so large that only one at a time could be hauled, were dragged to the site by oxen. Each log was split in two, the hewn half forming the inside of the wall. Ephraim Ogle, one of the corner men, helped "line" each log to see that it split straight. A string dipped in powdered charcoal and water was stretched from one end of the log to the other and snapped, leaving a black line on the log, which was then cracked along the line with a pole ax to start the split straight and to keep splinters from running off where the split had begun.

A man astride the split log first scored or trimmed it with a double-bitted ax; a broad ax was then used to dress the log halfway down its face. The log was then turned over and hewn on the other side to keep the thickness uniform and to prevent the hewer from "running under," causing one edge of the log to be thinner than the other. The big poplar logs were also edge-hewn to make their width uniform at all points. Billie Ogle bolted, or cut, the smaller logs to make shingles to cover the roof. He split the bolts with a maul and froe. The shingles were of 18-inch riven poplar, the gables sawn poplar weatherboarding and the door white pine dressed on both sides. The sills were locust, 10 by 10 inches. The floor joists were 7-inch-thick oak logs with the top hewn to a line. The original floor was made of wide pine boards, the ceiling of hand-dressed sawn chestnut boards. Ceiling joists were 8½-inch-thick pine logs pinned to the rafters with 1¼-inch square locust pins. Length of construction time is unknown, but the use of materials shows a good understanding of local woods.

For 50 years the Little Greenbrier School and Church served the people of the community with both teaching and preaching. School terms during the first years were seldom longer than two months because the teacher received a poll tax of only $1.25 per child. During the noon hour the preacher would frequently hold revival meetings in the school. The older people would gather inside while the children played outside. In the 1930s Elkmont and the surrounding area became part of the Great Smoky Mountains National Park. The school has been restored and is open to tourists.

Almost none of the original log country schools still exists, having been replaced by frame schools built of dimension lumber and smooth clapboard or shiplap. The log schools that remain are often in ruins, as is the Castle Park School at the bottom of Yampa River Canyon in Dinosaur National Monument, Colo. One log school that has been in continuous use since 1889 is the Cottonwood Community Center near Stillwater, Okla. This school, made of cottonwood logs, measures 20 by 43 feet, has a gabled roof and is still in excellent condition.

*Earthen Schoolhouses*

West of the 100th meridian and east of the Continental Divide lie the Great Plains, once called the Great American Desert because of the low annual precipitation and few trees. Permanent settlers came to the high plains after the Civil War. Without trees to fell for logs, stone to quarry or a readily available source of brick, homesteaders built schools with the only materials at hand—the earth and prairie sod. These were strictly folk vernacular schools, intended to be used only until the community could afford to replace them, usually with a frame school built of dimension lumber. Out of necessity, the pioneers used the soil itself as the material for their houses as well as for their schools. Hundreds of sod schools were built throughout the plains states, particularly in Texas, Oklahoma, Kansas, Nebraska and the Dakotas. A sod school could be built for the cost of rafters, window glass and frames, a cast-iron stove and paint for the blackboard.

Immigrant homesteaders built above-ground sod schools by using a special "grasshopper" plow to cut the sod, which they then laid in strips, sliced into blocks and stacked to make walls. The sod blocks were 2 to 4 inches high, 10 to 12 inches wide and 18 to 24 inches long and created exterior walls two feet thick. Soft mud was used for mortar, and the roof was braced with cedar pole rafters and piled brush with sod on top. As district finances improved, a frame roof with wooden rafters replaced the earthen ceilings. Most sod schools had dirt floors as well as a dirt roof, both of which were havens for rodents and reptiles, including rattlesnakes, which would occasionally drop from the ceiling. Although sod schools were relatively well insulated and were warm in winter and cool in summer, heavy rains often forced the children up on benches, out of reach of the water that had leaked

Sod school (c. 1880), District No. 60, Thomas County, Kans. The school's far right corner was damaged, possibly by cattle. (Kansas State Historical Society)

East School (c. 1905), District No. 15, Logan County, Colo., 1909. This dugout school made full use of berm building techniques. (M. Madilene Veverka, Library of Congress)

Dugout school (c. 1880), Thomas County, Kans. Although many dugout schools had only sod front walls, this school had a clapboard facade and four windows. (Kansas State Historical Society)

from the roof and turned the floor into a sea of mud.

Martha Bayne, a teacher in Russell, Lincoln and Osborne counties in Kansas for 10 years in the 1880s, taught at only three schools that had floors. Wood was just too scarce on the prairie, and even if the residents of the district could afford lumber, they still had to haul the boards many miles to the site. Fleas frequented dirt floors in the winter, and when spring thaws came, the sod school floors were often slick as grease.

Sod schoolhouses presented even worse problems than this. *Let Your Light Shine* (1965), compiled by the Pioneer Women Educators of Wyoming, includes an experience of Hannah Johnson, who arrived from Nebraska to teach in Daniel, Wyo., to find that her school had four walls but no roof. It was spring, and the ranchers were taking their cattle to the summer range, but they stopped their work to board the roof. However, the mail-order roofing paper did not arrive before a heavy rain. The rain splashed down between the boards as the teacher taught from under her umbrella and the children sat under their desks to work. A school built in 1886 in Scotts Bluff County, Neb., with walls of baled straw, a sod roof and a dirt floor, 16 feet long, 12 feet wide and 7 feet high, was devoured by cattle within two years. B. C. Jones taught her first school in Custer County, Neb., in a 14-by-28-foot dugout where the cornstalks that were burned as fuel were piled on the edge of the schoolhouse roof. Class was sometimes disturbed by the hogs that ran wild and got on the roof and into the corn.

Dugouts were another inventive type of school used on the prairie. Dugout schools were simple earth shelters that could be made in a day by excavating the side of a hill. The hill itself then formed the long walls and the rear of the shelter, and all that was needed to complete the structure was a pole and brush roof covered with sod and a sod front wall with a window to let in light. A plank door served as an entrance. Dugout schools were strictly temporary, and occasionally abandoned dugouts were pressed into service as schools.

On July 3, 1872, the first county superintendent in Washington County, Neb., visited a school in District No. 39 and reported, "School in a cave, rude, rough, but comfortable, furniture homemade and very temporary." Twenty-four years later and 500 miles north, in Logan County, N.D., a school board official described the dugout schools in the district: "Let us take a glance at our schoolhouses, or more appropriately, school caves. The greater number [of students] are being taught in Russian homes. These houses are what eastern people call caves or out-door cellars; being built of sod and covered with clay. They are heated with Russian ovens and have no ventilation except the door." What the school board official failed to note was that most such caves faced south and were built into slight rises in the land to provide shelter from the north wind; these dugouts are variants of the increasingly popular berm building construction.

Although earthen structures were remarkably well adapted to the plains, frame schools were often built as soon as money was available. Yet, in 1934, 45 years after the end of the frontier in the United States, a sod high school was built with some Works Progress Administration labor in the Sandhills region of Nebraska. Three years after the completion of the Empire State Building in 1931, dedicated ranchers volunteered to begin construction of this two-room sod school so that their children could get a high school degree close to home. Built of prairie sod with a sod roof supported by pole rafters, the building housed the classroom and living quarters for the teacher. Two toilets and a barn—all built of sod—made up the outbuildings for Lakeland Sod High School, and the rooms were heated by "prairie coal" (cow chips) gathered by students, teachers and parents and stacked to the eaves of the building each year before school began. Eleven students enrolled at first, and altogether 33 students attended Lakeland, with 11 receiving high school diplomas. Some students rode up to 10 miles to school; others lived with families, helping with the chores for their room and board, or lived at the school with the teacher. The school closed after the term ended in 1941, and only a roadside monument remains to tell the story of dedicated parents who wanted a high school education for their children during the hard times of the 1930s.

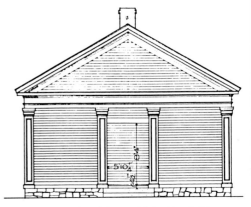

West Part School (pre-1837), Pittsfield, Mass. (Tito Cascieri, HABS)

### Frame Schoolhouses

The best way to prove community stability was to build a permanent school building—such as one made of 2-by-4s, clapboard siding and a shingled, gabled roof. Although the early wood frame schools were of mortise-and-tenon construction using post-and-beam techniques, by the last quarter of the 19th century frame schools were built with the balloon framing techniques still prevalent today. Wood siding patterns using horizontal boards included weatherboard, shiplap and clapboard siding; beveled siding, which is identical to clapboard except that the boards are longer, was used extensively. One-room frame schools of the late 19th century were similar in appearance. Variation came with each commuity's individual and modest adaptation of contemporary styles such as Gothic Revival, Queen Anne and Italianate.

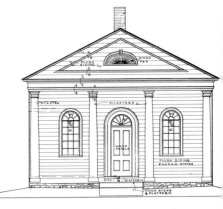

One Room School, Waverly, Pa. (Willard L. Remaley and Henry J. Condefer, HABS)

Because of the influence of educators such as Henry Barnard and Horace Mann, Massachusetts was one of the first states to have well-built frame schools by the early 19th century. The schoolhouse at Prescott in Hampshire County was built in 1813 with double entrances, clapboard siding, a detailed wooden cornice and the standard three windows facing east and west. The West Part School in Pittsfield, a village school built before 1837, featured a perfectly symmetrical, windowless south side with wooden pilasters in a hybrid Greek style with an abacus and echinus in a flat wooden capital. This was no simple country school: Only an architect would suggest wooden pilasters with Doric capitals as part of a design of a four-window, 1,100-square-foot school. The Wapping School, built in 1839 in Deerfield, also had square-cut pilasters on the corners and in the middle of the east and west walls. Floor plans for all the Massachusetts frame schools were nearly identical because they were built from plans supplied by county superintendents of schools.

A Pennsylvania school appropriately called One Room School carried Greek Revival patterns to their ultimate expression in wood. This school, at Waverly in Lackawanna County, had arched windows, a fanlight above the door and unfluted pilasters that rose to an unadorned capital, above which was a typical Tuscan order plain entablature that extended the length of the front. A smaller typanum inside the larger typanum formed by the gabled roof had an intricate fan arch with a detailed key block. The same fan style can be found on the front of the restored Thomas Filer Schoolhouse (c. 1820), now located at the Farmers' Museum in Cooperstown, N.Y.

By the late 1870s and increasingly by the 1880s and 1890s, frame one-room schools began appearing all over the West, becoming more functional as they moved west with the frontier. These buildings usually had a front entrance that faced south, a brick chimney or stovepipe at the north end of the building and a bank of three windows on the east and west sides. The window shutters, if any existed, were hung only on the north side of the window. Architectural plans were rarely used; a builder was simply given the required dimensions and asked to produce a school based on his practical knowledge of headers and stringers and gabled roofs. Such schools dotted the plains wherever homesteaders settled. Although some of the district officers may have added a vestibule or cloakroom to act as a buffer against the frigid prairie winds, frame schools were virtually identical in appearance.

In 1874 the Masons in Bannack, Mont., built a school with a bell tower to house both the one-room school and a Masonic lodge. The building, in contrast to familiar western frame schools, was an imposing two-story structure with 22-foot fluted pilasters, each rising to a classic Tuscan capital and a bracketed projecting cornice. The five windows on the front have hood molds with corbel stops, and the building itself has beveled siding. The west wall has four windows; the east wall, which extends 42 feet, originally had two windows; the only windows upstairs are at the north and south ends of the building. To go upstairs, one had to use an outside staircase along the east wall. The building must have been the pride of the mining camp; only a shell remains.

Two-story schools were extremely rare west of the Mississippi River. Two such schools that were built in different parts of the Midwest at different times bear a striking similarity. The Belvoir School, District No. 84, erected in 1877 in Douglas County, Kans., is quite similar to the Broken Bone School (1904) at Pleasant Lake, N.D. An architect must have drawn plans for this school design, which had an outside entrance to the top story and an interior staircase leading from the cloakroom. Records of the Belvoir School show that $18.75 was paid for the architect's plans—a huge sum, half the price of the outhouse that was constructed at the same time as the school. Both communities must have used similar architectural plans for their schools or had builders who came from the same part of the East and had constructed similar two-story, two-room schools.

## Stone Schoolhouses

In New England and the northern Midwest, many schools were constructed of sandstone, limestone, river rock or fieldstone taken from glacial deposits. Stone schools were common in New Jersey, where several have been preserved. Built by skilled craftsmen, using native masonry materials, schools generally had walls 18 inches thick, a stone foundation, deep-set windows and sills, stone lintels above the windows and door, and stone entrance steps. As the walls rose higher,

School and Masonic Temple (1874), Bannack, Mont. (James J. Thompson, HABS)

Clapboard school (c. 1885), District No. 4, Peach Valley, Colo. Few vernacular schoolhouses with a front porch and double entrances were built west of the Mississippi River. This school, with its double set of wooden stairs up the front porch, was an exception. (Andrew Gulliford)

the stone mason often chose smaller, lighter stones because the top of the walls could be thinner. The roof, door, window sash and sometimes the floor were often built from dimension lumber. A common architectural feature of one-room stone schools in the East is a single door set off-center into the long wall beside the windows. Few other stone, frame or brick schools had this type of fenestration.

Most stone schools have lost whatever name they originally had and are simply referred to as the Old Stone School. (Similarly, brick schools were known in the community as the Little Brick Schoolhouse.) Yet, despite this generic title, each school had subtle distinctions that set it apart from its neighbors. The Old Stone School House (1810) in Cumberland County, N.J., was the predecessor of all other school buildings in the county. Shutters and doors were uniquely constructed of 1¼-inch cedar slabs joined by dowels; no battens were used. The wood aged to a silver gray patina. As with most stone schools of the period, all shutters and doors were hung with massive hand-forged wrought-iron hinges. The instructor sat at a cedar desk and the students at long, narrow benches without backs.

The Stone School House (c. 1820) in Bedford, N.Y., was 28½ by 20½ feet complete with a stone well house. The cupola had a finial on top and, as at most schools, the bell tower was open. The walls of the Old Stone School (1835) in Bristol, Maine, were composed of huge rough stone blocks 4 and 5 feet long, 2 feet high and the standard 18 inches thick. The door in this school faced to the southeast, as did two windows. No windows faced the northeast.

In the upper Midwest, stone schools that were even more substantial were built by Old World masons. Not content to use rough stone, these craftsmen painstakingly squared each rough edge; the pride in workmanship is akin to that of the log builders who hewed the outer logs on wooden schoolhouses. The large Stone School (c. 1850), built from native buff sandstone near East Troy in Walworth County, Wis., was 51 feet 4 inches by 31 feet 5 inches. The school had the familiar 9-over-9 windows, but there were four windows on each side and two in the front, in perfect symmetry with the door. Perhaps the builder had seen other large schools or was familiar with formal architectural design elements, because he gave the perfectly proportioned school a main projecting cornice and a belfry cornice two-thirds the scale of the bracketed roofline cornice.

Kansas pioneers built their own vernacular stone schools using native limestone and sandstone after the Civil War. Seventeen stone schools were built in Douglas County, Kans., between 1862 and 1905. The walls of three of the schools were laid up by the same stonemason, Lewis Swanson, a Swedish immigrant from Minnesota; marks of a channel bar, a long grooved bar of rolled metal, and rock hammer are visible on the walls. The Blue Mound School, District No. 29, was begun in 1862 but required nearly three years to complete. Even the outhouse was constructed of stone. The school took the longest to build of any school in the county, but it also stayed in use the longest, for the district did not consolidate until 1949. The Baldwin School (1864), District No. 41, was built by a German stonemason, as was the Barber School (1871), District No. 82. The simple contract between

Stone School House (c. 1820), Bedford, N.Y. (E. P. Abbiati, HABS)

Old Stone School House (1810), Greenwich, Cumberland County, N.J. (Clement C. Cassell, HABS)

Old Stone School (1835), Bristol, Maine. As with many stone schools in New England and the Mid-Atlantic states, the door was on a side elevation rather than a gable end. (HABS)

Ruby Valley School (c. 1880), Ruby Valley, Nev. A folk vernacular stone school, the only evidence of formal architectural influence is the brick arches above the windows. (Andrew Gulliford)

the school district and the mason, Solomon B. Geery, dated October 23, 1871, reads:

> Article of agreement between School District No. 82 Douglas County Kansas of the first part and S. B. Geery of the second part. S. B. Geery of the second part agrees to furnish material in the wall of school house in District No. 82 the size being 24 x 36 to be 18 inch wall, and one partition wall in the foundation the same size. The foundation to be 18 in. in the ground and level to two ft. in the front, to be 12 ft. story, the jams of the windows to be flaired. The plastering to be done according to his bid, to build a good chimney flue of brick. Arches to be turned over the windows and front door with brick. Wall on the front and north side to be pointed up. The work to be done in good order for which we the Board of said District No. 82 Douglas County agree to pay the sum of ($600) Six Hundred Dollars.

In this case, the district hired a stonemason rather than use the labor of parents to build the school. No mention in the contract is made of roof, windows or doors; it must be assumed that the district completed these on its own or used another builder. In District No. 14, also in Douglas County, the community went ahead with its building plans for the Pleasant Valley School, despite the fact that the outcome of the Civil War was still in doubt, and completed its stone school in 1864, having outgrown a dugout school and then a log school. With the confidence of settlers committed to a new land, the residents also had 21 new desks of native walnut built.

As settlers poured into the Wasatch Valley of Utah, stone schools were erected, and wherever Mormon ranchers settled—in the farthest canyons of Utah, the high tablelands of Arizona and the broad, arid valleys of Nevada—they built schools using a readily available material, stone. The Ruby Valley School (c. 1880) nestles against the Ruby Mountains of central Nevada. The front door looks out across a wide and treeless valley, where there are low bushes and tamaracks but no oak or chestnut trees like those that shaded schoolyards back east. The schoolhouse the Mormon ranchers built, although no longer in use, remains a monument to their resolve.

### Brick Schoolhouses

Masons laid not only stone schools but also, wherever there was a source of brick, a little red schoolhouse—or a yellow, cream or brown one, depending on native clays. Brick vernacular schools, which often followed stone schools in a community, can be found throughout the United States, particularly in the Midwest, where they were built by the hundreds. The schools are both folk vernacular, made from brick baked in local kilns, perhaps even on the site, and mass vernacular, made of standard-sized brick. The majority of brick one-room schools built after the Civil War used mass vernacular construction materials and had hardwood wainscoting halfway up the wall inside the classroom. Because of their large numbers, sturdy construction and easy adaptability, brick schools remain plentiful—helping reinforce the popular conception of the little red schoolhouse.

School districts usually hired an expert mason to construct the walls. The buildings tended to follow two basic design tenets: (1) They were symmetrical from the front, with the door squarely in the middle (or, if they had two doors, the front view was always symmetrical); and (2) the door faced the adjacent local road, perhaps as a symbol of the building's access to anyone in the rural community.

Perhaps the oldest brick one-room school in the United States is the Quasset School (1798) near South Woodstock, Conn., which has been reerected on a new site. The brick was a local product, and the lintels, door sills, windows and foundation are cut granite. The school has a simple gabled roof and 9-over-9 windows, three on either side of the front door.

District No. 4 built a school in North Pepperell, Middlesex County, Mass., around 1805. As in eastern stone schools, the door was on a side with windows, near the corner of the 34-foot-long wall. But unlike other eastern schools, the school featured a wood-floored porch or piazza that provided an overhanging shelter above the door entrance; it was 3 feet 11 inches deep and ran the length of the wall. The porch and a bell tower were added about 1840.

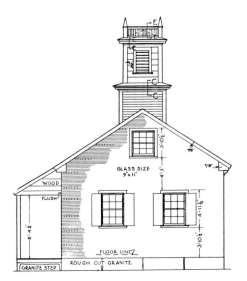

Brick school (c. 1805), District No. 4, North Pepperell, Mass. (Philip A. Martineau, HABS)

Brick schools were built also in New Jersey, taking their architectural cues from churches and meetinghouses. The Friends School in Rancocas, Burlington County, N.J., was built around 1807 and had the standard gabled roof, simple brick cornice and wooden lintels above the windows. The Friends School was virtually square; its exterior dimensions were 32 by 30 feet. As with other brick schools, its interior walls were plastered. The entrance faced due south, and three windows let in light from both east and west. The Brainerd School (c. 1810) in Mount Holly, N.J., was only 20 by 24 feet. Although it was a plain building, detailed work went into the door trim and windows, each of which had simple 9-over-9 lights and heavy frame shutters kept in place by well-crafted wrought-iron rattails. The school gave the appearance of being a small but impregnable brick fortress.

The Friends School (c. 1807), Rancocas, N.J. (Edwin Mason, HABS)

Generally, country schools were symmetrical from front to back and had the same trim all around. But President Grant's Schoolhouse (c. 1830) in Georgetown, Brown County, Ohio, has brick arches above the windows and two doors in the front only. This two-room brick school is 9 feet 6 inches from floor to ceiling and uses brick corbeling in lieu of a cornice. Each door has a transom above it, and lanterns were suspended over each entrance. The line of brick headers was the same for windows and doors. One room had an open flagstone fireplace, while the other had a brick chimney for a stove.

The variant in southern Colorado, New Mexico, Arizona, Texas and southern California was the folk vernacular adobe brick school made from local materials with 8-foot-high walls and gabled roofs. These Territorial-era schools were superceded by adobe Mission-style structures built in numerous southwestern communities by the Works Progress Administration during the 1930s. The WPA adobe schools featured flat roofs and simple facades with a Mission-style curvilinear gable over the front entrance. They were functional, rectangular boxes built with community labor and support. Dozens of such schools dotted New Mexico, which had 685 school districts at the end of World War II. Plans for the buildings can in some instances be traced to a pamphlet entitled "Designs and Specifications for New Mexico School Buildings," issued by the Territorial Department of Education in 1909. Drawings were by Johnston Brothers, school architects from Alma, Neb. In contrast to the few remaining adobe schools, which are from the first quarter of the 20th century, brick one-room schools from both the 19th century and early 20th century are plentiful and continue to reinforce the stereotype of the little red-brick schoolhouse.

## Inside the Schoolroom

"American popular education was at best a disorderly process, and any reforms that might reduce the disorder were to be regarded as desirable," observes Fred Schroeder. Nowhere was this truer than inside the country school. Schroeder describes a common early 19th-century interior in "The Little Red Schoolhouse":

> In the classroom, seating was on backless benches, and if desks were provided, they were likely to be no more than unplaned wood counters stretched across the width of the room, making movement around the classroom nearly impossible.
>
> Overcrowding was the pattern, ventilation almost nonexistent. In wintertime, the heating was inadequate or totally absent. There were no cloakrooms to hang and dry wet clothing. Floors were caked with mud and manure. It was common practice to crowd as many as sixty pupils into rooms of the size that Winslow Homer depicts. Overall, the usual district school was a dirty, crowded, fetid carton where school was held because the law required it.

The seating arrangement mistily pictured by Winslow Homer in *New England Country School* (1872) shows an interior typical of many of the earliest rural schools built in the United States, but in 1872 it was already out of date, replaced by reform-based specifications in many places. Schroeder describes Homer's classroom in further detail in "Educational Legacy: Rural One-Room Schoolhouses":

> Benches and tables are placed around the perimeter of the room, which has windows set at children's eye level. The benches do not have backs (except ones for infants, which do not have tables), the tables are too high for most children, the center of the room is empty (although it would have had a stove in wintertime) and the only furnishing is a blackboard. Nostalgic though Homer's painting may be, the furnishings were uncomfortable and the use of space was wasteful and devoid of instructional rationale. The arrangement was a reflection of the haphazard educational system of the early republic, when school terms were short, the curriculum was

*New England Country School* (1872), by Winslow Homer. (Addison Gallery of American Art, Phillips Academy, Andover, Mass.)

ungraded and children and adults dropped in and out of school as farm chores permitted, bringing with them whatever books and materials they happened to own.

The interior changes propounded by the 19th-century education reformers—placing desks in rows in the middle of the room, providing more light and air, elevating windows above eye level, allowing space for pictures and educational tools—had a central purpose: "to make easier the maintenance of comfort, of discipline, of efficient learning," concludes Schroeder. "But neither will the significance of these reforms escape modern critics of American education. The reforms are authoritarian in effect, sacrificing individuality for orderliness and convenience" ("The Little Red Schoolhouse"). Typical of the instructions for better schoolhouses was this prototype published in the *American Journal of Education* and suggested by the Colorado superintendent of public instruction, Horace M. Hale, in 1873 for use in Colorado schools:

> This house should be 28x40 on the ground, height of ceiling at least 15 feet. The school room will then be 28x32; the two wardrobes each 8x9; the entry 8x10. The partitions and walls will, of course, lessen these dimensions to the extent of their thickness. This house will accommodate fifty pupils. For a very small district the building may be 24x32. Teachers' platform 6x10, or 5x8, 8 or 10 inches high. Wainscoting should extend entirely around the room and entry. Black boards of liquid slating entirely around the school room in width *not less* than 4½ feet; 5 feet is still better. The uppermost foot and a half is very useful for permanent copies in writing and drawing; and for other uses. The windows should be so constructed that they may be let down from the top. The heating should be by furnace, or by a ventilating stove. John Grossius, 389 Main street, Cincinnati, manufactures a school stove for fifty dollars, which is economical and efficient; by it, pure air is taken from the outside, heated and introduced into the school room, thus affording complete ventilation. Even country districts can well afford this luxury. Indeed they cannot afford to do without it.

Interiors of one-room schools varied from district to district. The quality and quantity of furnishings depended on the district's parents and their financial commitment to education. Floors were generally hardwood, with the walls painted white or cream. Late 19th-century schools featured dark wainscoting approximately 4½ feet up from the floor or just beneath the windows. Windows consisted of simple sash without decorative millwork. The more elaborate hood molds were reserved for the building's exterior. Most schools had curtains, but few had window shades. Differences in climate were not reflected in schools' interiors except for the installation of much larger stoves in cold areas. Country schools had no insulation or only dead air space between the interior and the brick or clapboard walls. Like the buildings themselves, furnishings and interior appointments remained eclectic until the push for standardization and major rural school reforms.

Although the reforms were widely adopted by the late 19th century, country school interiors nonetheless continued to exhibit a certain rough character, as many teachers and pupils are quick to point out. C. Ross Bloomquist has clear memories of what the Birtsell School (c. 1900), District No. 3, in Foster County, N.D., looked like when he entered first grade in 1914:

> In spite of the windows on three sides of the interior, the schoolroom was dark and uninviting when school was not in session. The wood walls and ceiling painted a bluish gray were sometimes cleaned but never repainted during my years in

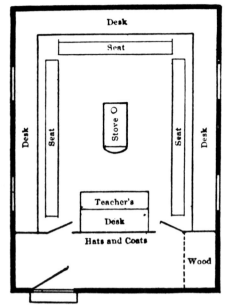

Floor plan by Ellwood P. Cubberly, 1914, showing furniture arrangement reflected in Homer's *New England Country School*. (*Rural Life and Education*)

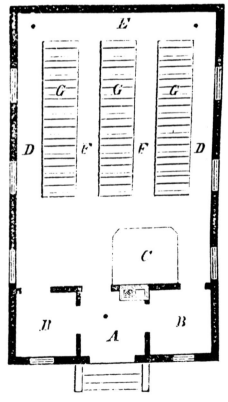

Floor plan showing seating arrangement propounded by education reformers in the 1870s. (*American Journal of Education*)

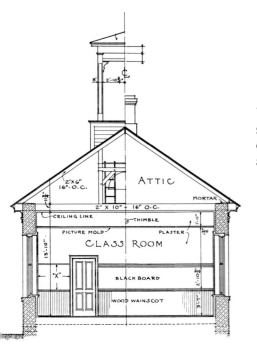

Mattock School (c. 1870), St. Paul, Minn. This section drawing shows a typical interior arrangement and finishes. (E. D. Corwin, HABS)

attendance. No permanent pictures relieved the monotony of the dull walls. The floor was dark and splintery. A six-inch high platform projected about five feet from the west wall. It stuck out a little farther in the center to give just enough space for the teacher's desk and the wastepaper basket.

In *Sod Walls: The Story of the Nebraska Sod House* (1968), Robert L. Welsch quotes Isabel Fodge Cornish, who tells about the new sod schoolhouse near Mason City, Neb., that was readied during the winter of 1884 for classes taught by the 15-year-old teacher in "short skirts and long braids":

The little, unpainted, rickety table and equally feeble chair had been salvaged from the unoccupied sod cabin of my grandmother, Mrs. Martha Mapes; the square, wood-burning stove had been lent by Reverend William Elliot, father of W. C. Elliot of Mason City; six wooden benches had been made to accommodate not only the six pupils but the people who would come there to attend church services or community affairs. At the training school we had been taught how to make a crude blackboard by applying a compound—chiefly of soot or lampblack—to a kind of building paper. When six feet of this had been put in place and a box of chalk purchased, the equipment was complete.

The home-made benches varied, as three had backs while three had none and the only boy, Ed Cooper, contended that he should occupy one of the most comfortable ones, so a compromise was necessary. As there were no desks, the writing lesson was a protracted one, each child in turn sitting on the teacher's chair at her table to laboriously write in his copybook.

The floor was dirt and during the cold winter of 1884 the teacher's feet were frosted. Later a quantity of straw was put on the floor which made it warmer but proved to be a breeding place for fleas. This was not conducive to quiet study but did afford the children some bodily activity.

The log school built in Madison County, Neb., in 1871 was described by a former student, Mrs. George Haight: "The first year we had no floor, but the second they sawed slabs and placed them round side down. Benches were made of slabs also with four sticks driven in for legs and unless we sat just so, down all would go which often happened. . . ." Olive Salladay, who taught in Park County, Colo., in 1927, summed up the appearance of her school this way:

After one look at the building, I was sure I had lost my mind. It was built of rough boards with double-boarded walls with tarpaper between the boards. We had a small box heater to heat the building which it didn't do in cold weather. When it was really cold we moved the desks up as close as we could to the stove.

Fred Schroeder, himself a former country school teacher, explains that his arrival at the Sunny Crest School (1894) in Manitowoc County, Wis., in 1952 was even then "a cultural shock, in spite of ample training at the 'county normal' " ("Educational Legacy: Rural One-Room Schoolhouses"):

Outwardly the Sunny Crest School was typically charming. Built of white clapboard with a plain, pretty bell tower and surrounded by elms and evergreens, it was situated on a rise of glacial moraine that it shared with a little Norwegian church and cemetery. The history of the construction of this Wisconsin school was also typical. The white building was the 1894 replacement of an 1879 red frame structure that had replaced the original log cabin; during the New Deal 1930s the schoolhouse had been provided with electricity but not with plumbing.

Inside, the Sunny Crest School was typical too. Ill-lighted by three widely separated windows on each side, the crowded room reeked of kerosene, oil-mopped floors, chalk dust, perspiration, damp wool and chlorine bleach that was poured into the pit of the attached privy at the rate of a gallon a day. . . .

The furniture arrangement of four rows of five desks per row reflected an advance in education dating from 1832; the fixed desks of oak and cast iron with tilting seats and book storage space were of a commercial design that was perfected before the Civil War. The widely separated windows indicated that the building was probably constructed prior to 1920; the fact that the teacher's desk was not on a platform-stage marked the school as being from the late 19th century, when such elevations were regarded as excessively authoritarian. A small table at the front of the room where pupils were summoned to recite the lessons of their grade level was the vestigal remains of the teaching method of colonial times.

The interiors of vernacular schoolhouses built from commercial, machine-made ("mass") materials might have such standard items as tongue-and-groove flooring, wainscoting, embossed metal ceilings, cast-iron desks, cabinets, shelving and slate blackboards. By the 1870s, when school plan books guided a growing number of schoolhouse designs, the manufacturers of school supplies had entered the education reform market by issuing their own plan books. Not only did these further the improvement and standardization of schools, they also increased the manufacturers' business. The availability of such mass-produced equipment as cast-iron and oak desks probably helped change the arrangement of classrooms as much as the entreaties of professional reformers.

Desks of all sizes were used because the ages of country school students ranged from five to 20 years. Five or six sizes of desks were available from furniture companies in New York, Chicago, Cleveland, Minneapolis and Richmond, Ind. These "patented" oak desks had ornamental ironwork on the sides, sometimes with a motto stamped into the grillwork along with the manufacturer's name and location. Each desk unit consisted of a stationary seat back and desk top and a wooden seat that folded. The back of one desk was the writing surface for the person sitting behind. Most desks had holes for inkwells. A few models could be purchased in different colors and types of wood. However, no desk could maintain its surface for long against the penknives of children eager to leave their initials. In "The Frontier Schoolhouse" (1974), Jonathan S. Minard discloses:

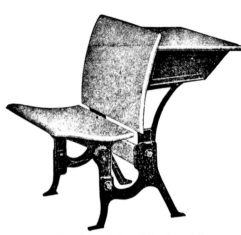

American Semi-Steel Combination Adjustable Desks with open-box tops. (Centennial School Supply Company, Denver)

> Those "clear stuff" pine desk tops were a great temptation to such of the boys who could boast the possession of a jack-knife, and afforded an opportunity for the gratification of a propensity which so distinguishes the American school-boy—result, in spite of all rules to the contrary, and a sharp lookout on the part of the teacher, those desks, after only a brief term of service, presented an incomprehensible maze of hieroglyphics.

Usually, girls sat on one side of the room and boys on the other. Children who misbehaved often would be asked to sit on the other side of the room and face the ridicule of their peers. In some schools, desks were bolted down. In others, such practices would have been unthinkable because they would have deprived the community of a place to hold its dances and box socials. The Junction School (1910), at what is now the Lyndon B. Johnson Historic Site near Johnson City, Tex., had desks fastened to the floor. During the period 1910–26, the students' desks were arranged in three rows facing the teacher's desk. The middle row was shorter because its front desk faced the potbellied stove. Boys sat in the east row and girls in the west row. The middle row contained the overflow of students from the other two rows.

Instructor's desk, Old Stone School House (1810), Greenwich, Cumberland County, N.J. (Clement C. Cassell, HABS)

Often, the only furnishings in the crude but expedient sod schools were benches for the students and a chair for the teacher. One other chair was usually in the room, in case the county superintendent should make his yearly visit. Desks came later and reflected a liberal attitude toward school expenditures on the part of a school board. In at least one Nevada mining camp, school children had the dubious distinction of sitting on empty dynamite kegs instead of at desks.

Teachers' desks varied from standard four-legged oak tables to elaborate desks with a top that lifted up to disclose secret drawers or slots for books. Some desks had small shelves that ran the length of the table top; here the teacher could put books and the class register as well as a small handbell, a wooden rule, or ferule, a few extra readers and a dictionary. The teacher's desk sat at the front of the room near the wall farthest from the door, often on a platform raised 6 to 8 inches above the rest of the floor, until this was later deemed too authoritarian. The platform gave the teacher several more inches on sprawling farm boys and provided a stage for plays, recitations and the ever-popular spelldowns. Both the raised wooden platforms and the schoolroom floors were often constructed of tongue-and-groove wooden flooring. They were maintained with a light coat of raw linseed oil, and even today many retired country schoolteachers can remember the pungent smell of the sweeping compound they used on the floor after the children had gone home.

Each country school also had its own potbellied stove, usually set in the middle of the room, with a long and poorly secured stove pipe meandering up from the stove and off at a 90-degree angle to a brick chimney. The stove sat on large cast-iron legs or on a heat-reflecting metal pad, the rationale being to extend the benefits of hot smoke throughout the room. In *These Happy Golden Years* (1953), Laura Ingalls Wilder describes the first winter she taught on the bitterly cold South Dakota prairies. The wind blew low and loud, and snow drifted through cracks in the walls. The county superintendent came to listen to the students' recitations, and Laura shuddered at what he might say. When he finally rose to go, he said, " 'Whatever else you do, keep your feet warm.' " From that day on, for the rest of the winter, the desks were placed very close to the red-hot stove, a practical move typical of schools in cold climates.

Stove size and type varied from school to school. Depending on the weather, the frugality of the school board and the availability of fuel, country schools were heated with wood, coal, cow chips and even twists of hay. Rarely did school board members plan ahead and stack the woodpile, so the wood was almost always unseasoned, hard to light and hard to burn. At the Junction School, the cast-iron box stove stood 2½ feet above the floor, in the middle of a sandbox, to help prevent fires from embers that might accidentally roll out onto the floor. By World War I, the most popular school stove was the huge Waterbury stove from Connecticut, with its gigantic circular sheet of embossed tin to reflect the heat and keep children from burning themselves on the stove's surface.

In a building without electricity and with no budget for kerosene, lighting presented a serious problem. Most schools, therefore, had

Boy loading coal stove, West Virginia. (National Archives).

windows on the east, and the blackboard was on the west. Some schools had windows on both sides, but by the 1890s education experts were arguing that light should come from from only one source and that it should fall over the left shoulder of pupils. No provision was made for left-handed students, and no thought was given to overcast days, when a minimal number of windows would mean minimal lighting. A few schools were outfitted with kerosene lamps, but they were to be used only in the evening or on special occasions. A few brave districts tackled the problem by putting windows on the north for a constant, even light, but the buildings were freezing cold in the winter.

Says Nora Mohberg, a retired teacher from Milnor, N.D.:

> The country schoolhouse was the most utilitarian building imaginable but in most instances it had one serious drawback. That was the cross-lighting that often injured the eyes of the students without being noticed at the time. If the windows were in the north and south walls, the damage was not so great. But windows on the east and west often created reflections that were injurious to the eyes of the students although no one really understood what was happening.

It is unfortunate that in so many of the schools in beautiful mountain valleys, windows were placed on only one side of the building. The pupils were forced to face the front of the classroom, where the morning light illuminated the blackboards while autumn's magnificent colors changed behind the students' backs. The problem with half-lighting, or cross-lighting, as first described by Henry Barnard in the 1840s, was never effectively solved until the 1940s with the almost universal introduction of electricity.

Many schools, even one-room buildings, had a cloakroom for the children's wraps. The hooks or nails were placed 3 to 4 feet off the ground. Usually a shelf for the children's lunches ran along the wall above the hooks, and a lower shelf held a wash basin, a cake of soap and a rough cotton towel.

A variety of blackboards could be found in country schools. At the Old Stone Schoolhouse (1784) in Newark, N.J., the blackboard is just that—planed pine boards that have been painted black. Other variations included slate boards (when the district could afford them), beaverboard that was painted black or canvas stretched over boards and painted. Erasers were made of rags, Brussels carpet strips or sheepskin glued to or tacked onto small blocks of wood. Country schools did not have the perfect cylinders of chalk now used in schools. Most teachers wrote with lumps of chalk called "crayons," while the students used slates and slate pencils. Some of the more expensive slates were double slates that folded together like a book and had red flannel and shoestring bindings. Most were single slates, however, and some carried the trademark "Germ-proof" on the wooden frame, developed to counteract the common practice of schoolchildren spitting on their slates and wiping them clean with their sleeves. No doubt the "germ-proof" slates were no more hygenic than their rivals, but the trademark may have helped sell more slates.

Few schools had flags until after 1900, when interest in Americanization increased. A monochrome portrait of George Washington usually graced the schoolroom and was hung 6 inches above the blackboard.

In most rural schools, a portrait of Abraham Lincoln joined Washington's, above and behind the teacher's desk. In the South, however, although Washington's portrait occupied the place of honor, Lincoln's portrait was not popular. At the Junction School, Robert E. Lee's portrait hung above the blackboard.

Clocks were also important, especially if the teacher had 30 students at different levels and more than 50 five-minute lessons to teach during the school day. The standard schoolroom clock had Roman numerals on a white face, a dark wood casing and a small glass window in the lower section; it stood two feet high. One ubiquitous brand of clock was called the Regulator and cost $6 around 1900.

Other commonplace objects in country schools included lunch pails (tin pails) or, more commonly, old lard pails, syrup pails or even tobacco buckets. The pails averaged 9 inches high and 6 inches in diameter with a close-fitting lid. Usually, these lunch pails sat on the cloakroom shelf. In winter, the lunches usually froze solid by lunchtime and had to be heated on top of the stove. One water bucket served everyone, and until the early 1900s most pupils shared the same tin dipper. Naturally, they also shared the same childhood diseases.

The interiors of country schools were serviceable if not always in line with the ideals of educators, parents, teachers or even students. But the ideal was clear, as expressed by the Nebraska state superintendent of schools in a 1871–72 report:

> The education of a child consists, not alone in what it learns from books, or from the precepts of parents and teachers, but every object upon which its eyes must constantly fall, silently but surely, imparts a lesson for its benefit or injury. The influence of a pleasant, well-lighted school room has much to do in softening the asperities of school life; and it is well worth the consideration of every friend of correct education.

## Standardization of Schoolhouses

Although 18th- and 19th-century schoolhouses were almost infinitely varied despite a basic similarity of form, later generations of students and teachers did not continue to experience the same variety in their schoolhouses. By the second decade of the 20th century, standardization of schools was well established. After a hiatus in the publishing of plan books during the Civil War, a new industry arose to promote progressive school design after the war through education journals and state publications. Passage of state laws aimed at unifying school conditions, as well as issuance of plan books and directives from state and federal education departments, helped carry out the process of standardization. By the mid-1920s, some county school superintendents awarded points to school districts for capital improvements, and if in a given year a school district did not make enough progress in remodeling its schoolhouse, the superintendent could threaten to close the school.

Yet, if standardization eliminated the traditional variety in local school architecture, it also established a common legacy that was experienced by most rural school children over the next 30 years. In North Dakota, from 1915 until the end of World War II, rural students

Jacknife School (c. 1920), Gem County, Idaho, 1939. This standard school, like most, had windows on one side only to prevent eye strain from cross-lighting. (Dorothea Lange, FSA)

shared the experience of a white frame one-room school within walking distance of the family farm. In Wyoming standardized elements such as good outdoor bathrooms, well sites, playground equipment, flag poles and additions to schoolhouses that prevented their relocation became the norm. Similar patterns were repeated throughout the country in answer to the cry for better buildings, schoolyards, playgrounds, libraries and heating systems. Standardization was designed to ensure that each rural school pupil have the opportunity to attend school under hygenic conditions, have sufficient books and supplies and learn from a qualified teacher.

School plans and plan books of the early 20th century were issued by state and federal educators, replacing the commercial guidelines so prevalent in the late 19th century. Model state schoolhouse designs were compiled in publications such as S. A. Challman's *The Rural School Plant* and bulletins from the U.S. Office of Education written by Fletcher B. Dresslar in 1914 and 1930. As state normal schools began to upgrade teaching requirements and education courses, college professors began to promote their own designs for rural schools. R. S. Parker, an education professor, recommended the design that was used for a Hays, Kans., model school (1917), which had two entrances, one from a porch and the other from the far side of a cooking room.

Plan books in the early 1900s called for built-in bookcases, mandatory cloakrooms and hipped roofs as visual expression of innovation in rural school construction. Ventilation was improved with air intakes from cellars, and the plans even included full basements designed for community use. By 1917 rural schools were supposed to have cloakrooms for girls and boys, sand tables for the small children and at least two closets. The teaching space was one room, but other conveniences such as a cooking range, a table for "domestic science" and interior chemical toilets were sometimes added.

By the 1920s the days of the vernacular schoolhouse were almost over, and contractors worked from architects' designs in the plan books. Such plans called for hipped roofs, Palladian porticos or porches and even dormers, creating a striking resemblance to bungalow houses of the same period. Windows were on one side of the room, close together to produce the effect of one large window, based on the common presumption that nerve disorders were traceable directly to eyestrain. Although northern light was better for its evenness, "the wholesome and disinfecting rays of the sun never enter a schoolroom with northern exposure," wrote S. A. Challman. For this reason, light was to come from the east or west. Cloakrooms were to be put along the front, according to Challman, "so as to allow for a pleasing facade." Window shades and window and door screens were recommended, and schools were to have furnaces or ventilating stoves instead of potbellied stoves. Better wells and outhouses were built. Oaken buckets and common dippers gave way to water dispensers or fountains. Schools began ambitious landscaping programs on Arbor Day and planted windbreaks on the northern plains. For the first time, rural schools had playground equipment such as swings, teeter-totters and merry-go-rounds. Fenced yards were constructed to keep the children

Standard school (c. 1920), Wheatland, Wyo. The bank of windows on one side and the hipped roof were common to standardized schools. (Andrew Gulliford)

194

Elevation drawing for a standardized Wisconsin rural school, 1917. (S. A. Challman, *The Rural School Plant*)

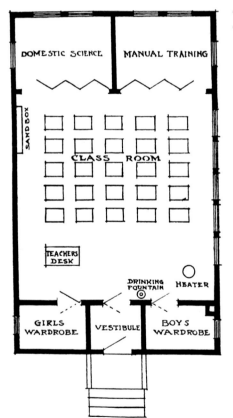

Floor plan for an Iowa model school, 1917. This plan called for separate areas for domestic science and manual training, as well as a sandbox for younger students. (S. A. Challman, *The Rural School Plant*)

in and the cattle out. The average cost of construction for these schoolhouses was $1,700.

The long history of country school construction in the United States ended essentially by the late 1920s. Rural one-room schools continued to be used widely well into the 1940s, and some were even constructed then. In 1949 the Teachers College of Columbia University published *Planning Rural Community School Buildings,* by Frank W. Cyr and Henry H. Linn. Some of the book's designs were used in the Catskill Mountains of New York to build one-room schools that were functional variations on the one-teacher vernacular schoolhouse, with small-paned windows and a houselike porch. Some of these designs could be called International Style, and, like their forebears, many owe kinship to residential architecture. But it was just a matter of time in most places until consolidation of schools eliminated the need for most country schools. The rectangular frame schools of the late 19th century gave way to yellow school buses (whose color was urged by Frank Cyr), which transported more and more rural children to town.

But the legacy of the one-room country schoolhouse lives on even today, not only in the old schools that are still being used to educate children in isolated rural areas. Modern classrooms in larger, urban elementary, intermediate and high schools are built to about the same dimensions used so successfully in country schools—the 30-by-40-foot rectangle recommended as early as 1831 by William Alcott. "The architectural variety of urban schools today," notes Fred Schroeder, "results from different schemes for arranging these rectangular spaces into rows, stacks or sprawls of specialized 'one-room schools'" ("Educational Legacy: Rural One-Room Schoolhouses"). He explains:

The interiors of large city schools developed from the basic one-room design in two directions. Elementary schools placed children of the same age in rooms where the teacher taught all subjects in much the same manner as in the rural school. High schools specialized by subject rather than by age, a pattern developed as early as 1840 in New England in Barnard's plan for Providence, R.I., where students were summoned from a large assembly hall to satellite rooms for recitation and instruction. By 1940 the arrangement had reversed and the last vestige of the large common-room was the high school "study hall," satellite to the complex of regular classrooms.

Schroeder points out that such urban specialization has brought many gains for American education, as well as permitting more architectural "style" for larger schools. But, he adds:

In spite of the improved efficiency of modern schools, American educators have attempted time and again to recoup the curricular integration, the personal attention to each pupil, the responsiveness to community values and the self-reliant resourcefulness of the best of country schools and teachers. . . .

It is a quarter of a century now since my cadet-teaching at the Sunny Crest School. I have taught in many sorts of schools since then, rural and urban alike. I have worked with students of all ages through postgraduate and I have visited scores of schools and colleges from coast to coast as a consultant in interdisciplinary humanities. But the farther I travel from that quaint and fragrant beginning, the closer is my affinity to the goals of the resourceful and idealistic rural teacher for whom no subject, course or age was separated from its neighbors, and with whom the school day became an invitation to circles of experience, widening outward from the common room so that child, nature, books and imagination were unified in an adventure of growing and learning.

The Birtsell School (c. 1900), District No. 3, in Foster County, N.D., was old even when I started in the first grade in the spring of 1914. The schoolhouse yard of somewhat more than an acre was virgin prairie not absolutely level since the northeast corner next to the quarter line collected water after a heavy rain or during the spring thaws. During vacation time many species of prairie flowers managed to grow and bloom in spite of the children's efforts to wear out the grasses and plants during playtime. . . .

Besides the schoolhouse, there were three other structures on the school grounds. The ramshackle barn near the south boundary had in years past stabled the horses of children who rode or drove to school. . . . In the distant past it had been painted red, but most of the color had long since weathered away. . . . We played in the barn occasionally on rainy days, but its main use was as a place to hide behind during recess and noontime hide-and-go-seek games. The two outhouses, boys' and girls', were situated along the west boundary of the schoolyard. . . .

The schoolhouse itself was a simple frame structure about 20 by 30 feet with a single gabled roof with a belfry at the east end. The windowless entry facing east also had a smaller gabled roof. The exterior had been painted white with red trim around the windows, eaves and corners. It was never repainted during my days there. Both the north and south sides had two windows placed symmetrically; the east wall had two flanking the entry. The west wall was blank except for the brick chimney protruding from the west gable.

C. Ross Bloomquist, 1980

opposite
Upper Cattle Creek School (c. 1900), Carbondale, Colo. The austere gabled-roof frame schoolhouse is enlivened by Carpenter Gothic woodwork in the porch. (Andrew Gulliford)

*above*
School, Marshall County, Iowa, 1939.
The farm setting was typical of the
Midwest. (Arthur Rothstein, FSA)

*right*
Rural school, Starke County, N.D.,
1942. The open space and unfenced environment were common to most country schools on the Great Plains. (John
Vachon, FSA)

*One looks as if it had been a wanderer in a strange land, without friends or home, and having set down at the forks of a road, by the side of the brook, to weep over its desolation, some benevolent individual had taken pity on it and fenced it in. Another is in the further corner of a cow pasture, and were it not for a door and window in front, and a beautiful woman and bright children within, would certainly be taken for a cow shed. . . these are country schools.*

B. N. Seymour, Superintendent, Alameda County, Calif., 1861

*right*
Mustang School (c. 1890), Huerfano County, Colo. The barn sheltered the students' horses. (Edwin L. Dodds)

*below*
One-room school, near Nathrop, Colo. The school bell would have reverberated for miles around. (Colorado Historical Society)

*right*
The School House (c. 1910), South Pass City, Wyo. Section shows the interior arrangement of this log school, which was moved in the 1920s and used until 1946. (John Uhlir, HABS)

*below*
One-room school (c. 1885), Caldwell County, Ky. The logs were notched in the half-dovetail cornering technique common to the Blue Ridge Mountains, and clapboards were added below the gabled roof. Gutters made from logs extended the length of the sides. (Kentucky Department of Education)

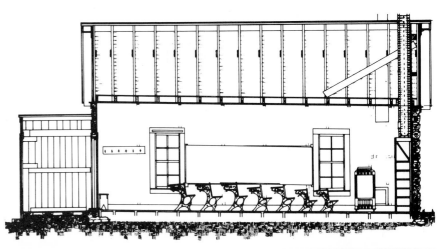

*above, left and right*
Little Greenbrier School and Church (1882), Elkmont, Tenn., 1936. The size of the logs and the workmanship, said a HABS architect, "mark this building as one of the finest log structures in the Great Smoky Mountains National Park." (HABS)

*right*
Brush arbor school, Live Oak County, Tex., 1887. Brush arbor schools were common throughout the Southwest, particularly in Texas and Oklahoma, as temporary quarters until a proper schoolhouse could be built. (Brack, Western History Collections, University of Oklahoma Library)

His school-house was a low building of one large room, rudely constructed of logs; the windows partly glazed, and partly patched with leaves of old copy-books. It was most ingeniously secured at vacant hours by a withe twisted in the handle of the door, and stakes set against the window-shutters; so that, though a thief might get in with perfect ease, he would find some embarrassment in getting out: an idea most probably borrowed by the architect, Yost Van Houten, from the mystery of an eel-pot.

Washington Irving, "The Legend of Sleepy Hollow," 1819–20

*right*
Sod school, District No. 15, Thomas County, Kans., c. 1885. Placement of the door in the gable end helped distinguish this schoolhouse from a house. (CSL)

*below*
Sod school, Custer County, Neb., c. 1889. A double layer of sod was added where the stovepipe pierced the roof, and a thin strip of wood was inserted under the eaves to keep the sod from sliding off during rains. (Solomon D. Butcher Collection, Nebraska State Historical Society)

*right*
School No. 3, District No. 37, North Dakota, c. 1890. Fallen sod on the far right reveals a wooden framework. The sod stacked around the base of the building may have helped insulate it. (North Dakota Institute for Regional Studies, North Dakota State University)

*below*
Sod school with hipped roof, Custer County, Neb., 1891. This county, which covered 2,552 square miles, in 1910 had 8,000 sod houses and, no doubt, dozens of sod schoolhouses. (Solomon D. Butcher Collection, Nebraska State Historical Society)

*above*
Republican School House (c. 1850), Ripon, Wis. The Republican Party was organized in this little white schoolhouse in 1854. (Clarence H. Lohfink, HABS)

*right, top*
School (c. 1870), Marshall County, Iowa, 1940. Pilasters and pedimented windows suggest influences from formal architectural styles. The building originally had two doors before the cloakroom was added, forming a single entrance. (Arthur Rothstein, FSA)

*right, below*
School (c. 1860), Coffee County, Ala., 1939. This clapboard school was built on a foundation of large, separately spaced stones. (Marion Post Wolcott, FSA)

*below*
Rural school (c. 1860), Gee's Bend, Ala., 1939. This one-room school with wood beveled siding resembled a corn crib more than a schoolhouse. (Marion Post Wolcott, FSA)

*It is situated on a slight elevation, and when seen from where we first observed it, appeared to be of sufficient size to accommodate quite a number of children, but, as we approached it, it grew "smaller by degrees" and not beautifully less. The teacher invited us to enter, and upon so doing we looked in astonishment. As well as I remember, the size of the building was ten feet by twelve in which were crowded twenty-one scholars, the teacher and myself. Some of the scholars were nearly full grown girls. There was but little room for necessary school furniture; there were no desks, no table, no windows; the door blew to with the wind while we were there, and the light [came] in through the cracks of the boards forming the sides. . . .*

California Superintendent of Schools, 1869

*right*
Frame school near Summerville, S.C., 1938. (Marion Post Wolcott, FSA)

*above*
Evans School (c. 1820), Gloucester, R.I. Federal and Greek Revival elements can be seen in the simple gabled roofline, flat lintels and arched fan in the gable. (Walter Nebiker, Rhode Island Historic Preservation Commission)

*right*
School, Daufuskie Island, S.C. This school for blacks included a porch to take advantage of southern breezes. (Daufuskie Island Historic District)

*above*
Whitehead School (c. 1860), North Carolina. This clapboard school, with its octagonal bell tower, received several additions. (North Carolina Division of Archives and History)

*left*
Dutch Flats School (c. 1915), Dutch Flats, Wyo. This schoolhouse appears to have been formed by two or three one-room buildings that were brought together and reroofed. (Wyoming State Archives, Museum and Historical Department)

*below*
Arroya School (c. 1915), Arroya, Colo. This two-room, architect-designed school featured hipped roofs, double entrances with separate porches and an arched bell tower. (Andrew Gulliford)

*right*
Clapboard school (c. 1890), near Mount Vernon, Ore. This shiplap school shows stylistic influences only in the bell tower and the brackets under the eaves. (Andrew Gulliford)

*above*
Willows School (1904), Custer County, Colo. This school epitomized the vernacular American rural schoolhouse in the pitch of the roof, placement of windows, door and chimney, and the lack of ornamentation. (Edwin L. Dodds)

*right*
Paradise Public School (c. 1900), Paradise Valley, Nev. This school was originally a one-room building, to which two gabled wings were added. Few rural schools had picket fences. (Nevada State Historical Society)

*right*
School (c. 1875), near Fort Bragg, Calif. Probably designed by an architect, this Gothic Revival school featured a round-arched lancet window in the attic and wooden buttresses. (HABS)

*below*
Mayer School (c. 1915), near Crawford, Colo. The roof of this plan-book school has a clipped gable, while the entrance combines a partly hipped roof and a straight gable. (Andrew Gulliford)

*right*
Unionville School (c. 1885), Unionville, Nev. Despite the isolated setting of this former mining town, the school was designed by an architect and resembled plans published in Kansas several years earlier. (Andrew Gulliford)

*top*
School, District No. 3, Heron, Mont., 1910. This four-room school shows Stick Style features. (E. J. Frazier, Library of Congress)

*above*
Fourth Ward School (c. 1880), Virginia City, Nev. Plans for this Second Empire–style school were included in Samuel F. Eveleth's *School-House Architecture* (1870). (Andrew Gulliford)

*right, top*
Cando High School (1894), Cando, N.D., 1902. An elaborate three-story structure with lancet and Palladian windows, this school represented the evolution of western rural schools from simple one-room structures. (State Historical Society of North Dakota)

*right*
Walhalla School (c. 1915), Walhalla, N.D. These two eight-room schoolhouses, which probably housed the upper and lower grades, were exact duplicates. (Library of Congress)

# Stone Schoolhouses

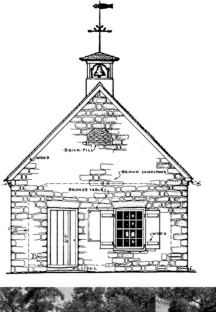

*left, top*
Stone School, near Trinidad, Colo. This vernacular stone school was typical of the place and period. (Andrew Gulliford)

*top*
Chancellor Avenue School (c. 1790), Newark N.J. A typical folk vernacular stone schoolhouse of the period, this received a decorative wrought-iron weather vane atop the bell tower. (Franklin Hart, HABS)

*above*
Rock School (1867), Fillmore, Utah. Built of locally quarried red sandstone with stone lintels above the windows and doorways, this school, like many others in the West, benefited from the talents of skilled frontier masons. (HABS)

*left*
Mattock School (c. 1870), St. Paul, Minn. The arched windows, distinctive bell tower and glass fanlight above the doorway suggest that this school was designed by an architect. (E. D. Corwin, HABS)

*above*
Cobblestone school (1819), District No. 5, Childs, N.Y. The Greek Revival style is evident in this school, which has a large bell tower and double entrances. Cobblestone buildings, rare in other areas of the country, are indigenous to this part of New York State. (Jack E. Boucher, HABS)

*right*
Westcliff School (1891), Custer County, Colo. This folk vernacular school featured quoins of different colored stone, arched brick window lintels and fishscale shingles in the clipped gable. The clapboard entrance is not original. (Edwin L. Dodds)

*right*
White Oaks School (c. 1890), Lincoln County, N.M. This four-room school was abandoned when the railroad bypassed the area. The two-story building included rough stone quoins, a hipped roof and an open bell tower. (White Oaks Historical Society)

*below*
Shumway School (c. 1900), Shumway, Ariz. This brick vernacular school was a type common in the Midwest but rare in the Southwest. (Andrew Gulliford)

*Do not imagine, in choosing a Building Committee, that a man, because he had built a barn once upon a time, that was capable of protecting cattle and their food from the weather, is qualified for building a school that shall best answer the purpose of instruction.*

Editor, *Farmer's Monthly Visitor*, 1853

*right*
Brick school (c. 1880), Utah. The arched brick lintels and the American bond masonry suggest that a skilled mason built this school. (Utah State Historical Society)

*below*
Old No. 2 School (1897), by Alfred N. Houghton. The drawing depicts the first public school in Alton, Ill., as it appeared in 1866. (Library of Congress)

*right*
Brick school (c. 1910), Minnesota. The influence of the Queen Anne style can be seen in the varied rooflines, mixture of materials and small windows in the gables. Eastlake-style millwork graced the porch. (Minnesota Historical Society)

## Brick Schoolhouses

*right*
District school (1898), Fairfield, Utah
An adaptation of the Romanesque Revival style, this buff-brick school featured assertive round arches. (HABS)

*below*
Gas Creek School (1883), District No. 20, near Buena Vista, Colo. Built from a plan book, this school had double entrances with canopies and an ornate bell tower. (A. E. Turner, U.S. Bureau of Reclamation)

*above*
Brainerd School (c. 1790), Mount Holly, N.J. This small school featured brick laid in Flemish bond and hand-hammered wrought-iron shutter hardware. (Raymond Tyrrell, HABS)

*above*
Ojo Sorco School (c. 1900), Ojo Sorco, N.M., 1943. This simple tin-roofed adobe school reflected local cultural and building traditions in materials and design. (John Collier, OWI)

*right*
Shawnee School (1919), Shawnee, Wyo. Built according to plans circulated by the county school superintendent, the stucco school's only deviation from specifications was the extra cloakroom, added as protection from winter winds. (Andrew Gulliford)

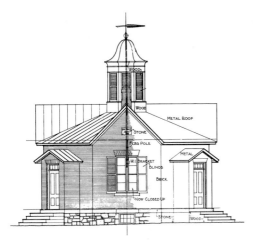

*above and right, top*
Octagonal school (1859), District No. 17, Skaneateles, N.Y. This brick octagonal schoolhouse boasted an octagonal cupola, a multigabled roof and a weather vane shaped like a quill pen. (Herbert A. Lawrence, HABS)

*right, bottom*
Octagonal school (1831), Cowgill's Corner, Del. One of the first public schools in Delaware, this school was built of stone imported into the county. The frame entrance was a later addition. (HABS)

*below*
Old Eight-Square Stone School (c. 1830), Fairview, N.J. This school had the standard hipped roof with rafters that rose from a hand-hewn plate. (Louis A. Zitzmann, HABS)

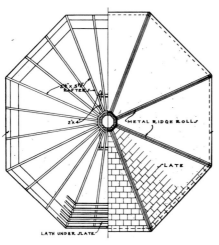

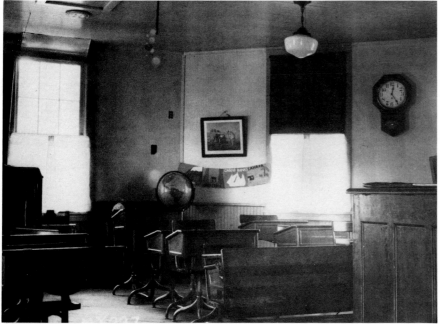

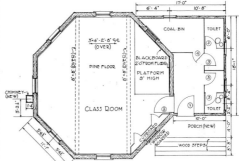

*left, below, bottom*
Octagonal school (1886), District No. 9, Marcellus, N.Y., 1936. This clapboard school was built of post-and-beam construction using vertical boards on a limestone foundation. The saltboxlike addition housed toilets and a coal bin. (Raymond L. Wheeler, HABS)

217

## Bell Towers

*right*
Cedar School (c. 1900, Troutdale, Ore.
The two rooms in this standardized
school were joined by an elaborate open
bell tower. (Oregon Historical Society)

*above*
School (c. 1905), Eagle, Colo. This
Queen Anne–style school had an
appropriately turreted and shingled bell
tower. (CSL)

*right*
Barclay School (c. 1905), Clover Valley,
Nev. An unusual hand-hammered copper bell tower topped the board-and-
batten school. (Dorothy Ritenour)

*below*
Twombley School (c. 1890) near Brush,
Colo., 1915. A forthright wooden bell
tower crowned this typical frame
schoolhouse. (Lewis W. Hine, Library of
Congress)

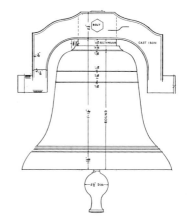

*above*
Bell from school (c. 1750), District No.
4, North Pepperell, Mass. (Philip A.
Martineau, HABS)

*left*
Antlers School (1887), Silt, Colo. An
enclosed tower was placed atop the
gabled roof of this two-room school.
(Andrew Gulliford)

*above*
Lida School (c. 1900), Esmeralda
County, Nev. Covered only by a tent,
this small frame school nonetheless had
an imposing tower for its bell. (Nevada
State Historical Society)

*left*
School (1882), Maysville, Colo. The bell
tower probably marks the front of the
original portion of this enlarged school.
(Edwin L. Dodds)

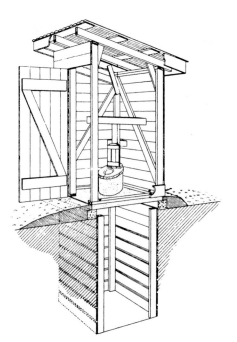

*above*
Outhouse plan recommended for Kansas schools by the state school superintendent, c. 1920.

*left*
School, Smithville, N.J. With its Greek Revival styling, this double outhouse was more elaborate than most. (Andrew Gulliford)

*left*
Colorado school outhouse. This typical structure had three walls, a door and a sloping roof. (Edwin L. Dodds)

*left*
Leadville, Colo., outhouse. Additional privacy for the occupants of this double privy was provided by the coal shed in between. (Edwin L. Dodds)

*left, below*
Smith Chemical Closet, 1915. During the standardization movement, this device could be purchased for $60. (Centennial School Supply Company, Denver)

*below*
Outhouse (1930s), Trinidad, Colo. This three-hole privy at a stone school helped accommodate adults at community events. (Andrew Gulliford)

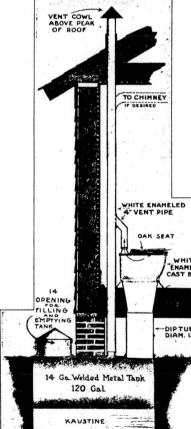

VENT COWL ABOVE PEAK OF ROOF

TO CHIMNEY IF DESIRED

WHITE ENAMELED 4" VENT PIPE

OAK SEAT

WHITE ENAMELED CAST BOWL

14 OPENING FOR FILLING AND EMPTYING TANK

DIP TUBE DIAM. 12"

14 Ga. Welded Metal Tank 120 Gal.

KAUSTINE

*left*
*The Noon Recess* (1873), by Winslow Homer. The benches and the furniture arrangement are typical of early rural schools. (*Harper's Weekly*, Library of Congress)

*below*
School (c. 1900), Sargent County, N.D. The centerpiece of this schoolroom, in addition to the large map, was a new Garland No. 18 nickel-plated stove produced by the Michigan Stove Company. (State Historical Society of North Dakota)

*A huge shiny black circular coal stove occupied a considerable portion of the north wall. I have never seen another quite like it. . . .*

*The pipe from the stove to the chimney came out only a few inches from the north wall. Protective metal plates shielded the pipe from the wall and ceiling. In a year the paint on the shields would become blistered by the hot gases radiating from the stovepipe. The shields failed to protect the walls one night in 1929. The walls caught fire, and the building burned.*

C. Ross Bloomquist, 1980

*above*
School, Fort Lupton, Colo., c. 1900. The round tub on top of the potbellied stove helped radiate additional heat. (Hazel Johnson Collection, Greeley, Colo.)

*right, top*
School, South Dakota, 1902. A pump organ was behind the teacher. Portraits of Washington, in an oval frame, and McKinley, assassinated a few months before this photograph was taken, hung above the blackboard. (South Dakota State Historical Society)

*right*
Kulm School (c. 1910), La Moure County, N.D. A large coal stove dominated this schoolroom, in which girls and boys sat on opposite sides. The window shades were drawn to eliminate glare. (State Historical Society of North Dakota)

*left*
School, Baker County, Ore., 1939. The archetypal schoolroom, this was furnished with portraits of Washington and Lincoln above the blackboard on either side of the stove pipe. (Dorothea Lange, FSA)

*below*
School for blacks, Heard County, Ga., 1941. Only crude furnishings were available for these students—rough-hewn benches (most rural schools had double or individual desks by the 1890s), a small stove, a blackboard made of two boards painted black and a teacher's chair in the corner. (Jack Delano, FSA)

*above*
Brookside School, Aberdeen, S.D., 1949. This schoolroom had both a bench and individual desks. Bookshelves under the windows provided additional storage space. (National Archives)

*right*
Churchill School (c. 1920), Brookfield, N.H., 1947. As late as the 1940s, one-room schools were still heated by wood and coal stoves. Two large stew pots, containing the students' lunch, were placed on top. (National Archives)

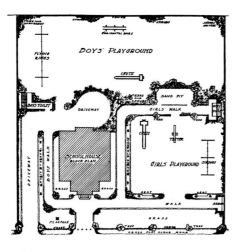

*above*
Oregon plan for rural school grounds, 1916. This elaborate model shows separate playgrounds for boys and girls, toilets at opposite sides of the lot line, a circular driveway and plentiful playground equipment, benches, trees and shrubs. (S. A. Challman, *The Rural School Plant*)

*right, top and middle*
Elevation drawing and floor plan of an Oregon one-room school. With designs such as this bungalow-style school with its library, the state superintendent hoped to ensure a type of school that would be "noted for its beauty of architecture and the utility of its floor plans." (S. A. Challman, *The Rural School Plant*)

*below and right, bottom*
Michigan model school, designed by Thomas E. White and Harry F. Weeks, Lansing, Mich. This plan combined double entrances and a gabled roof with a hipped roof and projecting wings. The boys and girls had separate cloakrooms and toilets. (S. A. Challman, *The Rural School Plant*)

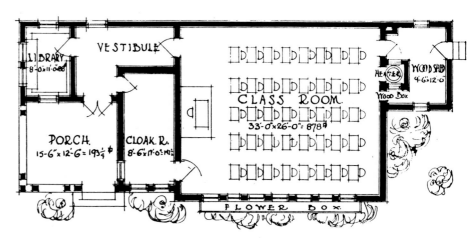

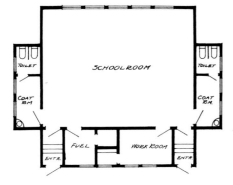

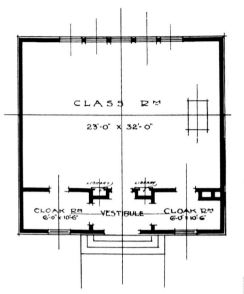

*above and right, top*
Oklahoma model school. This school was a 23-by-32-foot box with windows on the north and south only, a hipped roof, double doors, Carpenter Gothic entrance canopy and an eyebrow window in the attic. (S. A. Challman, *The Rural School Plant*)

*right*
A model rural school, designed by J. M. Felt and Company, Kansas City, Mo., and Mason City, Iowa, a bungalow-style building with a separate workroom. (S. A. Challman, *The Rural School Plant*)

*below and right, bottom*
New Mexico model one-room school, 1909. The design of this streamlined brick box predated by 20 years buildings constructed by the WPA during the 1930s. (S. A. Challman, *The Rural School Plant*)

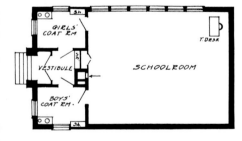

227

*left*
Standard school and teacherage, Ludlow, Colo. (Edwin L. Dodds)

*above*
Smith Sanitary Bubbler Drinking Fountain. This bubbler provided one solution for sanitary drinking water in rural schools without plumbing, but most schools used stoneware crocks with spigots and required each student to bring his or her own cup. (Centennial School Supply Company, Denver)

*left*
Consolidated school (c. 1925), District No. 87, Weld County, Colo. This two-story Prairie Style school housed six classrooms. (CSL)

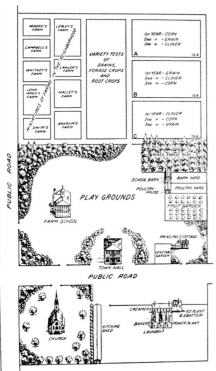

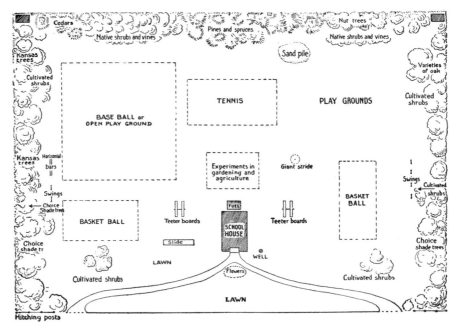

*above*
Diagram of a proposed country community center, 1912. The plan advocated consolidating all small schools in an area into one large farm school that would become the nucleus of a country community center, complete with a creamery, bakery, laundry, church and agricultural test plots. (Mabel Carney, *Country Life and the Country School*)

*right, top*
Big Rock School (c. 1930), Breathitt County, Ky., 1940. Under the direction of this county's school superintendent, one-room log and clapboard schools were replaced by stone schools such as this one. (Marion Post Wolcott, FSA)

*right*
Plan for a model school ground, with choice shade trees and cultivated shrubs, 1912. Few rural schools devoted the funds or time to ambitious landscaping projects recommended by state school superintendents. (Mabel Carney, *Country Life and the Country School*)

# COUNTRY SCHOOL PRESERVATION

# The New Three Rs:
# Restoration, Rehabilitation, Reuse

In 1916 there were 5,011 one-room schools in South Dakota. In 1981 a researcher conducting a schoolhouse survey in 21 southeastern counties of the same state found only 308 schoolhouses still intact and on their original sites, only 132 of which were in operation. As he was photographing and documenting one school, a large tractor-trailer arrived to haul the school to a neighboring farm. Today, South Dakota has only 87 one-teacher schools still in use.

A similar situation exists nationwide: Of the 200,000 one-room schools that were in operation at the start of the 20th century, perhaps only about 12,000 buildings remain. Of the approximately 830 one-teacher schools still in use in the United States, fewer than half are in original one-room buildings. Many of the existing buildings have been abandoned; others are in a state of disrepair. Their roofs are caving in, floorboards are rotting, foundations have crumbled, and bells have been stolen from bell towers.

Now, throughout the United States and Canada, movement is afoot to save and revitalize rural schools. Local historical societies, state park commissions, the National Park Service and numerous clubs and organizations are sponsoring preservation projects. The National Park Service has eight country schools under its aegis; two have already been meticulously restored. Country schools have become favorite projects for small historical societies with limited budgets and few if any full-time staff members. The same populist spirit that sustained the pioneers in building these schools now sustains their descendants as they seek to preserve them. Hundreds of schools also have been adapted for use as houses and second homes. Others have become community centers, day care centers, restaurants, offices, art galleries and exhibits at county fairs.

"Although the role of the schoolhouse has changed, it has not disappeared from the cultural landscape; it has merely taken on a number of different disguises," observes Dennis M. Richter in "The Changing Role of the Section Line Schoolhouse." A variety of options is available for country schools just as for all historic buildings worth preserving. These range from continued use as schools to adaptive use as houses, community centers and related purposes and to conversion for museum use, including development of living history programs that continue the schools' educational role. As with all preservation decisions, the guidance of a 19th-century Frenchman, A. N. Didron, serves as an accepted preservation principle even today: "It is better to preserve than to repair, better to repair than to restore, better to restore than to reconstruct."

## Planning for Preservation

Preservationists who seek to save a country school often first face the problem of trying to identify who owns the school. In many cases,

*opposite*
Eight Square School (1827), Dryden, N.Y. Open until 1941, this brick octagonal schoolhouse was later used by the town and donated to the DeWitt Historical Society in 1955. Now restored, it once again welcomes area students who temporarily relive old school days. (Skip Thorne)

ownership of abandoned schools has reverted to the heirs of the families who originally deeded the land for the school. Trying to find the rightful owners can be difficult. Because records on country schools have been dispersed following consolidation or redistricting, they may be filed in any number of places: the county clerk's office, the town government, the school district, local, county or state historical societies or other historical collections. These sources, as well as traditional methods used for title searches, may turn up the needed records.

A case in point is the Prill School (1876) near Rochester, Ind. The Prill School Museum Association leased the building from the farmer whose land it was on and initiated a restoration project in 1971 in preparation for the school's centennial in 1976. After the restoration project was under way, however, questions arose about ownership of the land. Unlike most abandoned schools, the Prill School did not revert to the Prill family or to the farmer who had bought the Prill estate. Apparently the school was still owned by Henry Township, and the trustees prepared to sell it at auction. Further investigation revealed that when Henry Township became a part of the Tippecanoe Valley School Corporation, all school property was deeded to the school corporation. The Prill School Museum Association later agreed to a 50-year lease maintaining the Prill School as "a museum for the benefit of the public." In 1982 the school was listed in the National Register of Historic Places.

Whether a school is to be stabilized, rehabilitated for a new use or restored as a schoolhouse museum, a number of basic preservation steps should be taken before work is started. The first is to determine whether the school has received any official recognition in the form of designation as a local, county, state or national landmark. Such designation gives public recognition to historic buildings, provides varying degrees of protection against demolition and alteration and can be useful in securing support for preservation. The state historic preservation office maintains records on which state buildings and historic districts are listed in the National Register of Historic Places and provides advice on how to nominate new listings. The official inventory of the nation's cultural resources worthy of preservation, the National Register includes sites, buildings, structures, districts and objects of local, state, regional and national significance. Listing brings recognition of historical importance as well as some protection from federally funded or licensed projects; it also confers eligibility for federal tax benefits (for buildings rehabilitated for income-producing purposes) and restoration funds when they are available. The nomination forms and files contain background historical information on the listings. Many states maintain their own separate state landmarks registers and related preservation programs. Local and state preservation organizations and state historical societies also have such information and can help answer preservation inquiries.

In addition, the school may have been documented as part of the statewide preservation survey or by a federal agency such as the Historic American Buildings Survey of the National Park Service, U.S. Department of the Interior. If so, both historical information on the school as well as photographs and sometimes measured drawings may be

Deserted frame school, near Canby, Minn. (Jeff Almen)

Jefferson Township School, District No. 6, New Haven, Ind., minus its bell tower, abandoned and vandalized. (Rod King)

available to aid in the research and restoration. In its 50 years of recording historic buildings throughout the United States, HABS has amassed documentation on many country schools—not only because of their contribution to American architecture but particularly to fulfill the agency's mandate of recording structures in danger of demolition. Many of the schools documented by HABS now exist only in its records.

Anyone contemplating the preservation of a historic country school will find it helpful to retain a qualified consultant to advise on potential uses or rehabilitation techniques. Feasibility studies of historic buildings usually include a structural analysis of the building, a design plan and cost estimates. It is essential that the consultant be knowledgeable about evaluating old buildings. Professional help can also be obtained to research the school's history and architecture, which will be necessary for historical interpretation programs.

If a campaign must be launched to save an endangered school, it is important to gain public support for preservation as well as to meet with all parties concerned to explore all options and seek possible solutions. The goal should be to offer solid reasons why and how the school should be saved and to avoid emotional arguments. Petition drives, letters to the editor and community meetings are useful for publicizing a preservation campaign and gaining support. Efforts can also be made to secure endorsements from prominent educators, historians, architects, planners and related preservationists—including former students and teachers. Regional offices of the National Trust for Historic Preservation are experienced in providing advice on such preservation efforts.

To help in swaying opinion, preservationists often prepare concise, factual statements of the issues involved before soliciting endorsements and media exposure. These may contain a short history of the building that includes date of construction; design and use over the years; reasons why the building should be preserved; suggestions of potential future use; identification of sources of support and opposition; and documentation such as photographs.

Sometimes the danger to country schools is less obvious than outright demolition or destruction through neglect. Sometimes the problem is simply to maintain the architectural integrity of the building. One such case involved the town hall in Webster, Minn., originally a simple brick schoolhouse built in 1924. The town board sought in 1980 to spend $27,000 to remodel it by reducing the windows in number and size, tearing out some walls and stuccoing parts of two sides of the building. Local preservationists obtained a temporary restraining order in Rice County District Court.

Residents claimed that the board's plan would destroy any historical value the school had, but what they were most concerned about was the appearance of the exterior after the proposed remodeling. Architect William Brodersen stated in his affadavit of May 1980:

Webster School (1924), Webster, Minn., now the town hall. (William Brodersen, Architectural Continuity, Inc.)

> When compared to buildings which have more detailed and ornate work, the building does not rate high in architectural achievement, but the building should not be judged insignificant because of its plainness. It is a good example of the frugality of a rural society which obviously had no money for "high enrichment."

That it is a product of a limited budget is a virtue, not a flaw. The brick building is well built with a good foundation and a straightforward roof. It is like the farmer with clean overalls—not fancy, but honest.

The building's greatest potential for service lies in developing its social-historical context. With respectful adaptive restoration it can be a significant tie with the families and community which made the building possible. Its heritage should not be hidden or destroyed. When it needs updating, such work should be carefully considered. Those charged with its care should make every effort to treat it kindly.

After a lengthy battle, no compromise has been reached. The school has a new roof and a new furnace, but its appearance remains much as it was when it was built.

One question that arises frequently in planning for the preservation of country schools is whether to move a school from its original site in order to save it. The rural schoolhouse was a community center shared by residents for miles around. Country schools defined the social life of rural areas and symbolized community pride in which residents from diverse ethnic and religious backgrounds could participate. Thus, relocating a school building destroys its historical context, because the site is an integral part of the school's history, just as with any historic building. When a school is moved from its original location, it loses not only the historical significance associated with its setting; it also invites loss of historic materials and possible damage to the structure itself. Accepted preservation policy throughout the country is to avoid moving any historic building unless this is a last resort—the only means of sparing it from destruction. Moving a building may result in loss of landmark designation as well, such as removal from the National Register of Historic Places.

On the other hand, some rural schools—at least in the Midwest and West—have a long history of mobility. In areas where schools were built of brick, stone or adobe, the schoolhouses remained rooted to the soil, but frame schools were frequently moved from place to place as the farming or mining population changed. A restored schoolhouse specifically designed to be moved was the Bairfield School (c. 1890), originally located near Clarendon, Tex., in Donley County. Built to serve the children of cowboys, ranchers and homesteaders, it had stone foundation supports only under the four corners of the building so that it could be easily moved as the student population shifted from ranch to ranch. Corner posts were sunk into the ground to keep the school from blowing off its underpinnings in a strong Texas wind. The school was used for both church and social activities, but the rural ranch population declined, and in 1937, when the last class was in session, it served only one student. Today, the white clapboard building is located at the Ranching Heritage Center, part of the museum at Texas Tech University in Lubbock, where corner posts continue to anchor the building.

Because country schools are often in isolated rural locations, vulnerable to vandalism, relocating a school to a museum site that has adequate security and regular maintenance may be the only option available for the building's preservation; local historical societies can proceed with restoration knowing that vandals will not undo their work. Many schools have been moved to create historical enclaves and villages throughout the United States, such as Old Sturbridge Village,

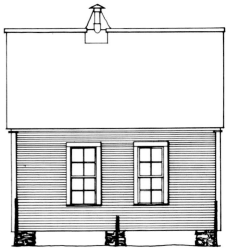

Bairfield School (c. 1890), Lubbock, Tex., part of the Ranching Heritage Center at Texas Tech University. (Elizabeth Sasser, HABS)

Granny Richardson Springs School (c. 1900), which was moved to the campus of Eastern Kentucky University, Richmond, Ky. (CSL)

Mass., Shelburne, Vt., Billie Village, Ind., and Knott's Berry Farm, Calif. Schools have also been moved to five museum sites in South Dakota as well as to Pioneer Village in Minden, Neb., South Park City in Fairplay, Colo., Heritage Hill Regional Park in Orange County, Calif., and History Village in Mount Pleasant, Iowa. Historic schools have been moved to the sites of county or state fairs and are staffed with retired teacher volunteers who during fair days teach children in a renovated classroom. Schools also have been relocated out of the path of roads and highways, and still others have been moved to provide more desirable settings for conversion to houses and other adaptive uses.

If a country school must be relocated, it should be moved intact, rather than dismantled and reassembled. Dismantling produces even greater potential loss of original fabric, and the building becomes essentially a reconstruction rather than a restoration. The school should be carefully photographed and documented on its original site before it is moved to aid in the reinstallation and interpretation. And, because country schools belong in the country, care should be taken to preserve open space at least around the building and recall its original setting; a new site similar in terrain and landscaping to the original should be sought or created. The restored school at Chadron State College, Chadron, Neb., stands alone on a hill, in a setting apart from other buildings, reminiscent of its original site in Dawes County, Neb.

Moving country schools may present great difficulties. Charles Patterson of the Howell Historical Society in Freehold, N.J., describes moving the Ardena School (c. 1860), a superb example of mid-19th-century architecture:

> In checking the only possible route to its present site—about 16 miles—we found 17 electric and telephone cables plus guy wires too low to permit the building to go under. We removed the roof and marked the hand-hewn rafters in order to have them replaced in the original positions. In a previous move the belfry and gingerbread had been torn off on both sides.

Craft shows and auctions helped pay for the new roof, and township engineers drew plans for the belfry from old photographs.

The roof of the Gore Creek Schoolhouse (1923) in Vail, Colo., did not have to be taken off, but the building had to be moved to make way for development. A professional moving firm relocated the school to Ford Park in October 1980. Four miles does not seem far to transport an old log school, but June Simonton, one of the founders of Save Our Schoolhouse (SOS), gives an idea of some problems involved:

> The route to the other side of the interstate was circuitous. Six skunks living under the schoolhouse relocated themselves without spraying anyone. The schoolhouse almost fell off the truck when it started down the steep hill. The fourth-grade teacher at the elementary school lined up his class on the bridge over the highway so they could cheer the passage of the Gore Creek Schoolhouse.

The four-mile journey took nine hours, but plans to move the school had begun a full two years before. Preservationists had argued with developers. Promises of money had been made and retracted. A woman with a claim to the building said that if she could not keep the school herself, she would burn it down. The cost of moving the school and placing it on a new foundation was originally estimated at $3,000; it

Ardena School (c. 1860), Freehold, N.J., relocated by the Howell Historical Society. (Andrew Gulliford)

Gore Creek Schoolhouse (1923), Vail, Colo., during its move to a new site. (Marika Christenson)

turned out to be $6,000. The Gore Valley Preservation Association took out a bank loan to pay the contractors. A nearby school district donated 25 school desks with filigreed cast-iron sides. Nine months later, 13 of the desks were stolen.

In 1982 a local craftsperson was hired to build a new entryway, windows, frames and chimney, install a stove and repair the sagging log walls to convert the school to a museum. Simonton states, "If you were to ask me why I did it, you wouldn't get a coherent answer. But I'm pleased with the new home and the new use for our little schoolhouse. And I hope it will bring pleasure to others for years to come."

Another western school recently relocated is the Grant Creek School (1907) now at Fort Missoula, Missoula, Mont. The building had served faithfully as a school until 1940, but later, while being used as a ranch building, the front porch had been removed and a double door installed. By 1976 the roof had caved in and the floor had deteriorated. The side and back walls were removed intact and set in place on a new foundation. Museum staff at Fort Missoula nailed the walls to the floor at the bottom and braced them at the top. With continued support from a chapter of Delta Kappa Gamma, the slow and expensive process of rehabilitation and restoration began. In 1976 donated funds provided the foundation, ceiling, joists, rafters and roofing. Additional funds were spent on lumber and mortar. Almost all the work was done by volunteers who donated many hours of time on afternoons and weekends. Restoration of the Grant Creek School was authenticated to the period 1910–15, thanks to facts gleaned from 50 oral history interviews with Grant Creek residents and former students and teachers. In a one-year period, about 1,000 schoolchildren enjoyed half-day sessions in the restored schoolhouse.

## Respectful Rehabilitation

Carefully researched standards for a variety of preservation options—from acquisition and stabilization to preservation, rehabilitation and restoration—have been developed and are increasingly being adopted nationwide. Such standards are useful to everyone involved with historic schoolhouses, whether in planning a museum or other new use or just in maintaining the historic character of the building if it continues to serve as a school. The goal is always to treat the building with the respect that its past deserves.

The most detailed and widely accepted standards have been developed by the U.S. Department of the Interior. The Secretary of the Interior's Standards, as they are known, distinguish among a variety of levels of preservation work that many people mistakenly use interchangeably. "Preservation," for example, is defined in the Secretary's Standards to include procedures that sustain the existing form and materials of a building or site, including stabilization and maintenance. "Rehabilitation" means returning a property to usefulness through repair or alteration while preserving significant features. "Restoration" involves accurately recovering the form and details of a property as it appeared at a particular time by removing later work or replacing missing earlier

Neldon-Roberts Schoolhouse (c. 1816–36), Montague, N.J. Located in the Delaware Water Gap National Recreation Area, the stone school has been restored by the National Park Service as a museum and community center. (National Park Service)

features. "Reconstruction," a process that is not recommended, relies on new materials to re-create the exact form and detail of a lost building.

Rehabilitation is the most prevalent treatment used today, one that allows efficient contemporary use of a historic building while preserving elements and details that are significant to its historical, architectural and cultural values. This definition assumes that at least some repair or alteration will have to take place to make the building suitable for modern use, but that this work will not damage or destroy the materials, features and finishes that are important in defining the building's historic character.

The 10 rehabilitation standards developed by the Interior Department are:

1.  Every reasonable effort shall be made to provide a compatible use for a property which requires minimal alteration of the building, structure or site and its environment, or to use a property for its originally intended purpose.

2.  The distinguishing original qualities or character of a building, structure, or site and its environment shall not be destroyed. The removal or alteration of any historic material or distinctive architectural features should be avoided when possible.

3.  All buildings, structures, and sites shall be recognized as products of their own time. Alterations that have no historical basis and which seek to create an earlier appearance shall be discouraged.

4.  Changes which may have taken place in the course of time are evidence of the history and development of a building, structure, or site and its environment. These changes may have acquired significance in their own right, and this significance shall be recognized and respected.

5.  Distinctive stylistic features or examples of skilled craftsmanship which characterize a building, structure, or site shall be treated with sensitivity.

6.  Deteriorated architectural features shall be repaired rather than replaced, wherever possible. In the event replacement is necessary, the new material should match the material being replaced in composition, design, color, texture, and other visual qualities. Repair or replacement of missing architectural features should be based on accurate duplications of features, substantiated by historic, physical, or pictorial evidence rather than on conjectural designs or the availability of different architectural elements from other buildings or structures.

7.  The surface cleaning of structures shall be undertaken with the gentlest means possible. Sandblasting and other cleaning methods that will damage the historic building materials shall not be undertaken.

8.  Every reasonable effort shall be made to protect and preserve archeological resources affected by, or adjacent to any project.

9.  Contemporary design for alterations and additions to existing properties shall not be discouraged when such alterations and additions do not destroy significant historical, architectural or cultural material, and such design is compatible with the size, scale, color, material, and character of the property, neighborhood or environment.

10.  Wherever possible, new additions or alterations to structures shall be done in such a manner that if such additions or alterations were to be removed in the future, the essential form and integrity of the structure would be unimpaired.

Restoration of the Neldon-Roberts Schoolhouse included rebuilding a stone cheek wall at the cellar entrance and repairing the interior plaster. (National Park Service)

These standards are used to evaluate work on properties listed in the National Register of Historic Places, buildings rehabilitated using federal tax credits, federal properties and related rehabilitations; in addition, numerous historic district and landmarks commissions and other preservationists have adopted them officially or informally to guide their own work.

Detailed guidelines also have been developed to supplement the department's comprehensive standards, addressing each level of work and all facets of a property—from the site to exterior and interior features, structural and mechanical systems, safety and building code requirements, additions, even archeological research and adjacent new construction. For each type of feature and activity, a sequence of work is recommended: first, identifying, retaining and preserving the materials and parts that are important in defining the building's historic character; second, protecting and maintaining the important features through such work as rust removal, caulking, limited paint removal, reapplication of protective coatings, cleaning of gutter systems or installation of fencing and other temporary protective measures; third, repairing where deterioration is present, including limited replacement of extensively deteriorated or missing parts with identical or compatible substitute materials if prototypes survive; fourth, replacing items that cannot be repaired if remaining physical evidence can be used. "Some exterior and interior alterations to the historic building are generally needed to assure its continued use," the standards add, "but it is most important that such alterations do not radically change, obscure, or destroy character-defining spaces, materials, features, or finishes." Alterations or additions applicable to country schools may include providing additional parking space, installing an entirely new mechanical system or removing site elements that are intrusive and thus detract from the overall historic character.

Exterior additions "should be avoided, if possible," the standards recommend, "and considered *only* after it is determined that those needs cannot be met by altering secondary, i.e., non character-defining interior spaces." In the case of the small, typically one-room country school, additions are seldom appropriate, particularly for schools restored as museums. The only exception might be the adaptation of a school for residential use, but even in this instance the first rehabilitation standard should be borne in mind: Find a compatible use that requires minimal alteration. If a schoolhouse is not big enough to be a home, it can be recycled in any number of other ways to save it, respectfully.

## Adaptive Use

Although the first solution often thought of for saving a country school is to convert it to a museum, exciting possibilities exist for other types of adaptive use. Because museum operations require a subsidy and continual fund raising, a more financially feasible option for saving schools and other historic buildings is often to recycle them for income-producing purposes. From banks to boutiques, community centers to churches and town halls, houses to summer houses, the sympathetic and economical uses for old schoolhouses are widely varied.

In a survey of old schools in south-central Wisconsin, Dennis M. Richter, a geographer at the University of Wisconsin-Whitewater, found that slightly more than half had been converted to permanent residences, and of these, 70 percent were brick structures. Richter also found that 18 percent of the schools, which were built between 1832 and 1938, had been abandoned but remained structurally sound. An additional 18 percent had been converted to community uses such as museums, 4–H clubhouses and grange halls. In "The Changing Role of the Section Line Schoolhouse," Richter wrote, "The majority of the schoolhouses that remain have been converted to residential use and will remain a part of the rural scene for the immediate future, and quite likely into the next century."

Because of their size and the fact that many one-room schools were built in picturesque rural locations, hundreds of schools have been converted to houses and summer homes. A one-room schoolhouse is, after all, a house in which teacher and students worked together in a familylike environment. Cynthia Parsons, a former schoolteacher and education editor of the *Christian Science Monitor*, lives in the clapboard Gassetts School (1874) near Chester, Vt., which she purchased in 1967 for $4,500. Parsons tells how the schoolhouse inspired her, even as a child:

> The nearest building to our 200-year-old farmhouse was a more-than-a-century-old one-room school. I was too old for it and had to ride the bus five miles into Galway and go to a four-room school. But my two younger brothers went there, and every New Year's Eve I climbed up on the roof and rang the bell with a crowbar at midnight.
>
> Then "progress" came. The school was closed, and some city people bought it. I rode my bike down in the summer and took them some homemade butter so that I could be invited in to see what the old school looked like.
>
> They were writers (they wrote detective stories for pulp magazines), and they were using the blackboard to put up their outline and story line. I thought of the horse story I was writing and kept in a cigar can at the back of the hay loft, and knew at last what "love at first sight" meant. I rode my bike home and reported to the family at the supper table that night what the city people had done and how. "When I grow up," I declared, "I'm going to write books and live in a one-room school."

Parsons made several early decisions in her adaptation of the schoolhouse:

> The blackboards would remain up. I would not lower the ceiling. The torn and fly-specked window shades would have to be replaced. I would retain the old hanging lamps and globes. I wouldn't partition the schoolroom. I would turn the boys' and girls' toilets into a single bathroom. I would put a circular staircase inside the hot-lunch preparation area and sleep in the loft.

The Gassetts School was built with only a crawl space under the foundation. As part of the Works Progress Administration effort during the 1930s, the schoolhouse was lifted off its foundation and a full cellar was installed, along with a wood-burning furnace in the basement and a new hardwood maple floor. Parsons replaced the wood-burning furnace with a forced hot-air oil furnace. A freestanding fireplace was installed where the original potbellied stove had once stood. "It was 15 years before I converted the old hot-lunch sink and drain to a full kitchen with cupboards, counters, an exhaust fan and lights," she said. A lilac bush, planted about 35 years ago on Arbor Day, sits in front of large windows that allow natural light into the room. A 75-year-

Gassetts School (1874), near Chester, Vt., converted to the home of Cynthia Parsons.

School (c. 1920), Loup Valley, Neb. Built from standardized plans, this school was adapted to house a Head Start program. (Andrew Gulliford)

Bodega Bay School (1873), Bodega Bay, Calif. This four-room Second Empire–style school was turned into a restaurant and art gallery. It also appeared in Hitchcock's *The Birds*. (Andrew Gulliford)

old elm that had long shaded the schoolyard had to be cut down, but its more than seven cords of wood kept the house warm for three winters.

In the true spirit of the one-room schoolhouse, Parsons welcomes neighborhood children to the school, lets them draw and write on the blackboard, fills school desks she has purchased with 19th-century spellers and readers and keeps a corner full of learning devices, including that newest of schoolhouse furnishings, a minicomputer.

After the Battlement School (1897) in Parachute, Colo., closed in the late 1940s, a small group of citizens tenaciously held on to the building in hope that some day it would be restored as the vital community center it had once been. Now a coalition of public and private groups using local, state and federal funding is preserving the 1,300-square-foot school, which will be restored to its 1928 appearance. Built of sandstone hand-quarried nearby, the school originally had one room, but an additional front room and a large cupola for the school bell were added in 1907. Long a landmark in the Colorado River Valley, the Battlement School is listed in the National Register of Historic Places.

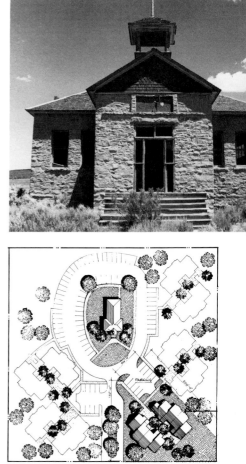

Restoration will return the school to one of its original functions as a community center. It will be used primarily by retired persons living in 40 apartment units on the four-acre schoolhouse site. The first phase of the project required $57,000 to shore up the foundation, tuck point the sandstone blocks, repair one seriously damaged 24-inch-thick wall, brace the floor and replace all windows, doors and cedar shingles. The roof was in danger of collapsing, requiring extensive buttressing in the attic. Funding for the first phase included a $30,000 grant from the Piton Foundation and $27,000 awarded by the Colorado Historical Society from a federal jobs bill.

In the second phase, the structure is to be furnished as an adult center with new wiring, plumbing and interior furnishings. Senior citizens in the area are seeking funds for the project's completion. Exxon Oil Corporation, which has extensive land holdings in the area, pledged a community service donation of the $2,500 utility tap, and Union Oil Corporation agreed to donate $4,000 worth of electrical and mechanical engineering. The area Agency on Aging, the county government and inmates from a nearby minimum security prison also will participate.

The Battlement Mesa Trust still owns the school and has signed a 99-year lease with Valley Senior Housing at $1 per year. The planned housing units will be built in a four-plex design with hipped roofs and exterior features that relate to the schoolhouse and the site. Funding for this innovative housing project, which will be the only senior citizen housing for a community of 2,000 persons, is expected from the Farmers Home Administration. Eight units should be completed by 1985. The project fulfills community goals and may be a model design in rural areas where retired persons need housing—and country schools require preservation.

In Norwalk, Conn., many people who once attended the Broad River Community Schoolhouse (1861) are now returning for sentimental reasons and opening accounts at this new branch of the Fairfield County Savings Bank (a comprehensive case study of the conversion

Battlement School (1897, 1907) Parachute, Colo. Now restored, the school will serve as the center of a new senior citizens housing development. (Andrew Gulliford; Chambliss Associates, Architects)

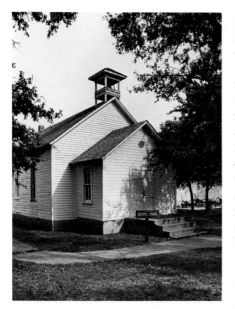

Rose Hill School (1895), Perry, Okla. In use until 1950, the school was moved from Noble County, Okla., to the grounds of the Cherokee Strip Museum. (Jim Argo)

follows this chapter). The bank hired Richard Bergmann Architects to return the school as much as possible to its original condition. The exterior now closely resembles the original, even down to the salmon color of the paint. All banking equipment and built-ins have been scaled down to correspond to the building's size, and a partial basement was excavated so that a furnace and air-handling unit could be installed in such a way that there were no signs on the exterior of contemporary alterations. Wainscoting that matches the original, a blackboard where former students are encouraged to write their names and photomurals of class photographs give customers an idea of how the interior used to look. The 1,100-square-foot building is at an important intersection, and patrons enjoy walking to the branch bank. Neither the architects nor the bank had any idea that the conversion would draw hundreds of visitors, many of whom came first to "look around" and then become customers.

## Schoolhouse Museums

For anyone rehabilitating a historic schoolhouse—for personal use or adaptive use—research into the building's past is a fascinating project that adds much to the understanding and enjoyment of the school. But for any group restoring a school for use as an educational museum, research becomes mandatory as a guide to both the restoration and the interpretation of the building's history. Research is the foundation on which an accurate restoration and meaningful education program can be built. As Fred Schroeder points out in "Schoolhouse Reading" (*History News,* 1981):

> Unfortunately, the historical interpretation is ordinarily nostalgic, and sometimes misinformed. An underlying problem is that these structures are so common and undistinguished that interpretation often goes no deeper than generalities. When we develop a program that begins with understanding the schoolhouse itself, however, it is possible to offer an interpretation that reflects at once the local uniqueness of the school and its place in the wider contexts of social and architectural history.

Understanding the schoolhouse itself is a prelude to restoring it properly. Among the materials that are likely to provide descriptions of what the school looked like are such documents as architectural plan books, if it is suspected that the building sprang from one; articles in education and architectural journals with drawings and floor plans; and catalogs showing school supplies, millwork, furnishings and hardware. Official district or state education documents, laws, reports, minutes and similar items also contain information on the appearance of local schools at various periods. Photographs and drawings often can be located in collections of libraries and historical societies as well as those belonging to local citizens and former teachers and students. For clearly vernacular schoolhouses, an examination of neighboring structures may provide clues as to the date, builders, materials and finishes of a school. The reminiscences of former students in particular can add in missing details especially about how the building looked or what its effect on the students was; the recollections of retired teachers will not extend so far back but may be more accurate.

A major decision involves determining the historical period on which to focus the restoration. Usually this is the date when the school first opened, but it might be the time of the school's greatest use, a period when irreversible changes were made in the building or a later date, perhaps the year in which classes ended. For example, many 19th-century rural schools were modernized during the 1930s. The question becomes whether to restore them to their original appearance or to a later period when the walls, ceilings and possibly even the foundation were altered. Where the physical evidence of evolutionary changes remains, it is possible to retain the changes as an opportunity to interpret the school's succeeding stages. Restoration architects, historians and other preservation professionals are available to assist with this research and decision making as well as to guide the actual restoration itself.

Cracking foundations, sagging exterior walls, crumbling brick and bulging boards are potential problems in school restorations. Additions such as porches, extra doors, paneling or false ceilings may have to be removed to achieve the correct appearance for the historical period chosen. Plumbing and wiring, as later additions not appropriate for the period, also may be taken out—or they may be added unobtrusively to provide the minimal amenities to allow contemporary use. The restoration research should include analysis of the original paint to determine proper exterior and interior colors; often the original colors lie buried under coats of paint applied over the years. If restoration cannot begin immediately, stabilization to prevent or slow deterioration is advisable, followed by mothballing until restoration work can proceed.

The decision to restore the Freeman School (1871) at Homestead National Monument near Beatrice, Neb., prompted a comprehensive historic structure report by the historic preservation team of the National Park Service. Built of brick fired in a local kiln, the solid 36-by-20-foot structure had 12-foot-high walls and 12-inch-thick brickwork. As early as 1874, however, problems with the foundation had been noted.

By 1972 stress from settling and mortar deterioration had produced a 9-inch crack in the east corner of the north wall of the building. Concrete patching had proved ineffective. On the west corner of the north wall, bricks had crumbled because the footings were of inadequate size and the foundation was not deep enough to prevent damage from freezing. After a heavy rain, 30 additional bricks fell out of the northwest corner, and on the northeast corner a major crack opened, 9 feet long and from ½ to 2½ inches wide. Only immediate repairs could save the schoolhouse.

As project supervisor for the repairs, Park Service engineer Renzo Riddo made certain that a new concrete foundation with metal reinforcement underneath the original stone foundation securely anchored the building's walls. A native of Venice, Riddo early learned the value of underpinning weak walls. Within a month, cracks in the walls had been repaired and the brick repointed, a new roof had been put on, and brick duplicating the original replaced brick that had been added in the 1940s. A concrete floor that was not historic and that was pushing the walls out was removed, and a hardwood floor, replicating the original flooring, was laid in its place. Work then began on the

Mountain Gap School (c. 1880), Leesburg, Va. Located near Oatlands, a National Trust property, the school was used until 1953, purchased by a former student, willed to Washington and Lee University and given to the National Trust in 1973. It is now open to schoolchildren. (National Trust for Historic Preservation)

interior, including restoration of the original plaster walls made of lime, coarse sand and horsehair. Woodwork ruined by rain penetrating the exterior brick walls was replaced. The interior was restored to its appearance in the late 1870s and early 1880s based on a historic structure report researched by Riddo and historian Lenard E. Brown. The school, which has an interpretive program, is open to visitors.

An 1832 school in District No. 10 has been restored by Historic Hildene in Manchester, Vt. Sidewalls had bulged far outward because of the unusual way in which the school was built: The structure had no vertical posts. Early school board members constructed the building by sandwiching sawn hemlock planks on top of one another, like boards stacked horizontally in a lumberyard. Narrow clapboards covered the outside walls.

Restoration contractor Peter Palmer says that the school "is a magnificent representative of a structural style that was tested and discarded." The building was, in essence, a log cabin made from 2-by-5-inch planks during a transitional period in 19th-century construction, after the use of post-and-beam framing and before the use of balloon framing. Although the original builders took a great deal of pride in their work, the school lacked lateral stability. Apparently, the walls had separated from an inside partition some time ago; newspapers from 1877 and 1878 were found stuffed into the cracks to stop the draft. To straighten out the bulge, Palmer and restoration architect John Haines devised an interesting technique: An entire structural framework was built on the inside of the building. Telephone poles 30 feet long were inserted through the empty window openings and then supported by blocks and timbers on the exterior of the building. A second set of telephone poles, 26 feet long, supported the top of the window heads. When all was in place, a set of heavy jacks mounted between the poles gradually lifted the whole schoolhouse by its window heads a foot or more off the foundation, which was then repaired with

Freeman School (1871), Homestead National Monument, near Beatrice, Neb., seen in a 1902 class photograph and readied for museum use. The plain facades are decorated only with vermiculated stone lintels above the door and windows. (National Park Service)

native fieldstone. Vertical timbers on the outside of the school linked by cables and turnbuckles gradually tightened together until the walls were plumb again and parallel.

Clapboards had been pulled off in areas where the underlying planks had rotted. "We saved every board of any kind that was possible," Palmer explained. "We cut out the decayed parts and replaced them with sound pieces, old but sound if possible, to retain the authentic fabric of the building." Where it was feasible, the school was repaired with square-cut nails of modern manufacture but resembling the originals of a century ago. In other structurally critical joints, 30-pound nails were used. The school is now replastered except for the cloakroom walls, which had always been exposed. Visitors to the school are surprised to see an interior wall made from horizontal planks.

Horizontal timbers were common in log structures such as the Fruita Schoolhouse (c. 1896) at Capitol Reef National Monument in Utah. In the early years, the building, which saw service as a meetinghouse for the Church of Jesus Christ of Latter-day Saints, stood near the Fremont River at the base of a huge sandstone cliff and talus slope. The school assumed its present appearance after being remodeled in 1914. The dozen or so families making up the Fruita community used it as a school until 1941. Lenard E. Brown suggested that the National Park Service refurnish the school as it was during the 1920s, and his recommendations are now being followed. Interpretive staff at Capitol Reef National Monument have conducted oral history interviews with former teachers and students, and a new volunteer program employing Daughters of the Utah Pioneers will help keep the one-room school open for visitors. A few of the volunteer interpreters attended the school, and they bring a special flavor to the interpretive program. The Fruita Schoolhouse is important because few of the original pioneer log schools remain. Most of those first generation one-room schools were razed or recycled years ago in communities where population growth demanded bigger and better school buildings.

Of the schools that have been moved to museum and university sites to serve as models of early schools and education techniques, the District No. 6 school (1875), now located on the Bowling Green State University campus in Bowling Green, Ohio, provides a case study in schoolhouse relocation and reconstitution. Beginning in 1969 William Jerome, president, and David Elsass, dean of education, sought to find a one-room school for the campus because they believed that "the preservation of the region's educational heritage will provide valuable authentic source materials for teachers, pupils and the public. . . ."

In 1972 a campaign was initiated to secure needed funds through donations. After two years the donations amounted to about $14,000 from cash contributions and subscriptions obtained in a way similar to a method of financing country schools a century ago. The Frank Linder family of Norwalk, Ohio, agreed to donate Huron County's old red-brick schoolhouse, which was located on their farm. Because of limited funds, Daniel Heisler, an education professor, and his three sons offered to donate hundreds of hours to dismantle the school and clean the bricks one by one.

The College of Education, Office of Development, Office of Alumni

District No. 6 school (1875), Bowling Green, Ohio, shown as it was being dismantled for relocation to Bowling Green State University. (Bowling Green State University)

Bowling Green State University's new Educational Memorabilia Center, reassembled on the campus. (Tom Cramer)

Teacher and class of the District No. 6 school, Norwalk, Ohio, in the 1920s. Historical photographs such as this are often used to guide the restoration and interpretation of historic schools. (Bowling Green State University)

Affairs and university administration all cooperated to promote and assist in preservation of the school. Interested donors received brochures on the schoolhouse and the education memorabilia center. A questionnaire sent to former students sought both general information on schoolhouse procedures and specific details to aid in furnishing the building—the color of the interior, height of the teacher's platform and use of window shades, light fixtures, instructional charts and framed pictures. An outline drawing of the school provided space to indicate placement of desks, benches, charts and the stove.

An advisory committee was formed from interested faculty, alumni, area educators and citizens. The committee members advised on the development of the center and its purposes, policies, plans and scope and served as regional representatives for inquiries about viewing the collection of first-edition textbooks and receiving donations. Despite the $14,000 in contributions, still more funds were required to keep the project from being abandoned. The planning committee even considered returning the donated funds and the schoolhouse.

But the schoolhouse had more friends than anyone knew. Arthur Wilkowski, then state representative from Toledo, gave his support to the project, introducing an amendment to a state lottery appropriations bill in the Ohio General Assembly. In 1974, after testimony by concerned Norwalk citizens to the finance committee of the Ohio House of Representatives, $50,000 from Ohio lottery funds was appropriated for the school. Because the school was to be rebuilt on state property, planners had to follow 52 steps required by the state for competitive bidding for any new construction. Estimates for the work soared to $90,000, including moving costs, but contributed labor and other savings reduced that amount to $65,000, the sum gleaned from state appropriations and increased donations.

The school had been remodeled in 1897; at that time the teacher's desk was moved from the front to a platform that extended across the back of the room. In 1917 electric lights were added and a new floor was installed. The school board purchased a new wood-burning stove and placed it in the center of the room instead of in the back corner.

With a hammer and chisel Heisler and his sons began taking apart the schoolhouse brick by brick, cleaning each brick of its old mortar as they went. While dismantling the schoolhouse, Heisler discovered the original floor, made of 1½-inch white ash; this was used to reconstruct the teacher's platform. The foundation stones were removed and numbered, for replacement in their exact positions. The most complicated job involved operating a hired crane to remove the 18-foot cupola that was supported not by the roof but by beams that ran to the foundation. Another serious obstacle, the stone steps in front of each door, had to be lifted with hydraulic jacks.

In the interior much of the wood had rotted because of a leaky roof, but the wainscoting and trim were in fair shape. Taking down the outside brick first, Heisler and his sons clipped the nails from behind the woodwork and removed the tongue-and-groove wainscoting. Stripped of five coats of paint by volunteers, the original white ash and walnut has now been varnished and reused although not repainted. The plaster walls, however, have been painted the original light cream color identified in the restoration process. Some wainscoting boards in the left front corner had been scorched because of frequent overheating from the stove. To preserve authenticity, the discoloration was not removed and the boards were repositioned in the same place.

Because of excessive deterioration of the materials, a new wood frame had to be built for the gabled roof and oak floor. Building code restrictions on a university campus required that one width of original bricks be used for the outside walls instead of the two-width technique, a 19th-century method of construction. By using only one width of bricks as a veneer, the school could be assembled with an original exterior surface. Foundation stones had been keyed together for additional strength, and the 100-year-old building did not have even a six-inch crack in the walls. Stone sills were reused, but wherever replacement parts were necessary, as in window frames, craftspeople replicated the originals including the accurate colors.

Bowling Green State University is not the only college with a restored one-room schoolhouse. Country schools have been moved to Northwest Missouri State College in Maryville, Mo., Eastern Kentucky University in Richmond, Ky., University of Tampa in Tampa, Fla., and Fort Hays State University in Hays, Kans., where 3,000 stones from the Plymouth Schoolhouse (1874) were marked, disassembled and transported to campus with volunteer labor and financial support from Phi Delta Kappa.

Organizations that plan to preserve and restore country schools as museums should spend as much time and consideration on the interior as on the exterior. Following a careful restoration of the exterior of the building, the sponsors or curator should try to replace or duplicate the original furnishings. The questionnaire for the brick school moved to Bowling Green State University asked visitors to fill out a "back-to-school exam" describing what they remembered about the school concerning placement of desks, books and other interior objects. Questionnaires might include questions about missing items. For example, the Bowling Green questionnaire requested information about the large exterior brass bell, stolen years ago; it has since been returned.

Each school had its own unique use of floor space, particularly for social events; therefore, the best way to authenticate the exact placement of objects is through extensive interviewing of former teachers and pupils. All purchased items were matters of record, which can be found in the minutes of school board meetings, if available.

Placement of desks is critical and depends on the number of students attending the school during the period represented in the restoration. Because desks often were built or bought at different times, they varied in type. Moreover, country school students ranged in age from 5 to 20 years, so desks of all sizes were needed. A curator might feel hesitant about mixing single and double desks, large and small desks and long recitation benches all in the same room, but many country schools had such eclectic furnishings. Unfortunately, schoolroom furnishings have become valuable as collectibles, so school preservationists must brace themselves for high prices if they want to purchase items.

In the cloakroom, suitable clothing can be left on coat hooks—heavy coats in winter and caps and sweaters in the spring and fall. Heather

Slater School (1918), Slater, Wyo. A clapboard plan-book school used until 1944, the building had built-in bookshelves and a table used as a portable sandbox for younger students. (Andrew Gulliford)

Charlestown School House (1838), District No. 2, Charlestown, R.I. Three rows of desks face the teacher's desk and stove, which is located at the front of this simple clapboard schoolhouse with double entrances. (Warren Jagger, Rhode Island Historic Preservation Commission)

Craigflower Schoolhouse (1855), Victoria, Vancouver Island, British Columbia. The large, two-story frame school differs architecturally from typical American country schools. (Andrew Gulliford)

Central School (c. 1900), Lusk, Wyo. Softball equipment hangs on the coat rack in this tiny log school museum as it might have originally. The school is part of the Niobrara County Museum. (Andrew Gulliford)

Huyck, a historian with the National Park Service, suggests in "Furnishing Plan for the Freeman School, Homestead National Monument" (1973), that in the cloakroom, "The towel should not be squarely placed, but rather carelessly left, as if a child has just thrown it down." Such effects can enhance the accuracy of the restoration.

Huyck also suggests that curtains should be made of white, lightweight dimity and should be half-length; they should not fit exactly, because most teachers brought curtains from the schools where they had previously taught. In the spring, flowers could be placed in a vase on the teacher's desk (students occasionally put dead frogs and snakes there, but visitors can be spared that sensation).

In refurnishing a school, it is important to avoid displaying too many objects. Care should be taken that all the objects are appropriate to the same period. An accurate restoration of a late 19th-century country school will not mix a 1920s clock with an 1870 wall map or 1880s slates with Big Chief tablets from the 1920s. A successful restoration is subtle, recalling the faint smell of chalk and the darkening of the room when the sun goes behind a cloud. A collection of appropriate textbooks will have more meaning than whole shelves full of used readers.

An exemplary restoration is the Craigflower Schoolhouse (1855), one of the earliest schools in British Columbia. Originally modeled after early 19th-century English national schools, the two-story wooden structure had a classroom downstairs with living quarters for the teacher upstairs. It was used until 1911, when it fell into disrepair. In 1927 it was leased by the Native Sons of British Columbia, Post No. 1, and the Native Daughters of British Columbia, Post No. 3, which restored the school as a museum that opened in 1931. The project was one of the earliest restorations of a historic building in the province. In 1974 the provincial government assumed ownership of the building, and today, after extensive research and further restoration work by the Heritage Conservation Branch, Ministry of Provincial Secretary and

Government Services, the Craigflower Schoolhouse again serves as an education, community and historic resource. On March 8, 1983, Queen Elizabeth II unveiled a plaque marking completion of the schoolhouse restoration and the 128th anniversary of the school.

Restoring the school to its 1855–60 appearance required removal of the front porch and a rear addition as well as extensive work on the interior. Rediscovering the original color scheme meant stripping the wainscoting and woodwork, which had been covered with gallons of battleship gray paint. According to John D. Adams, head of the interpretation section of the Heritage Conservation Branch, "The schoolroom previously was fitted out as a classroom cum relic room," not unlike dozens of American one-room school museums incorrectly stuffed with community bric-a-brac. The school desks from the period 1880–90 are now displayed in one of the second-floor rooms, and the schoolroom itself "is now furnished with reproduction benches and desks and arranged according to what we believe a National Society school would have been like," says Adams. He explains, "The room is to be used for school groups who may use everything in it. More traditional museum exhibits and dioramas using authentic period artifacts are on the second floor." Supporting materials for the extensive restoration verified that the Craigflower Schoolhouse served a predominantly Scottish community, whose teaching standards were high. From the beginning, classes were coeducational and included children from all social levels.

Monroe Schoolhouse (c. 1819), near Hamburg, N.J. The stone school typifies folk vernacular building traditions. (Conklin, Hardyston Heritage Society)

The Monroe Schoolhouse (c. 1819) in Hardyston Township near Hamburg, N.J., served continuously as a school until 1926 so it has been restored to its early 20th-century appearance. The school had suffered badly from the ravages of vandals. In 1977 it received a $60,000 grant for restoration through the U.S. Department of Housing and Urban Development. Although preservationists began with only a shell, enthusiasm ran high to recapture the school's appearance as carefully as possible.

One interesting facet of the project was the detailed archeological dig around the school site and beneath the school's floor. Under the floorboards, volunteers found pages from a Webster's dictionary with penmanship exercises and several pages of a student's notebook. They also discovered slate pencils, a Liberty-head nickel and mibs (handmade clay marbles). Another dig turned up an old slate and a whippletree, a pivoted crossbar from a wagon. Such excavations are rare at country school sites but should become standard practice for historical groups interested in collecting information for their school restoration.

The 20-by-25-foot Monroe Schoolhouse is the only school of hand-quarried stone in Sussex County, N.J., and one of the few vernacular stone schools in the East. Architect John Bruce Dodd re-created plans for the building based on old photographs and postcards showing a stone gable with a brick chimney resting on a stone shelf 7 feet above the floor. The walls, of hand-cut stone, have large stone lintels over the windows to support the masonry above. A fire must have occurred once in the small building, because it appears that a higher roof was built and the stonework raised an additional 1½ feet. At one time, the school was used as a county shop, and county maintenance crews replaced the front door with a large garage door; local stonemasons had to reconstruct the entire wall.

To be certain of fidelity to the original floor plan, Carrie Papa, director of the Monroe Schoolhouse Museum, recorded 26 oral histories given by local school graduates, collected in "Stones and Stories: An Oral History of the Old Monroe School" (1980), and learned a great deal about the school's interior as well as its role in the community. For example, a student who attended the school in 1912 provided many details of the interior:

> As you walked into the school, there were three rows of double seats and desks facing the door. The low seats and desks were first for the little kids. The seats gradually got larger until they reached the back of the room where the biggest ones were. They were plain wood with the seat and desk together, and there was a shelf underneath for books.
>
> The teacher's desk was just inside the door to the left. In the middle of the wall behind the teacher's desk was a big blackboard—there were blackboards on the sides, too. Above the front blackboard was a picture of George Washington. The flag was there, too. On the far side of the blackboard was a big Seth Thomas clock. I used to put my knee against the desk to hold one of those old willow rulers. Then I'd chew up a wad of paper, shoot it off the ruler and fasten it on the clock. But if we got too rowdy, Miss B. would send us out to cut down our own hickory stick. Then we got it.
>
> In the back of the room was this old flat-top, potbelly stove with a shield around it. We dried our mittens on the shield. In the winter that shield was covered with steaming mittens. And there was a big pot of water on the stove. About an hour before lunch, we put our little glass jars with homemade soup in that pot of water and then we had hot soup for lunch. Sometimes, Miss B. made cocoa, too.

"Descriptions of the school's interior and furnishings guided the restoration work," said Papa. "Memories provide a genuine interpretation of the exhibit." She adds, "Some of the Monroe families, with as many as three generations of students who attended the school, have donated books, diplomas, hand slates, games and pictures to the museum." More than 70 items were donated, including handmade wooden whistles (which the students used to distract teachers) and an embroidered pillow made by a student in 1902.

Like many school museums, the Monroe Schoolhouse could not have been opened without the assistance of a wide variety of local groups. The Hardyston Heritage Society, township officials, the Culverbrook Restoration Foundation, the Sussex County Historical Society and county, state and federal agencies all played important parts. Now, the school is a museum that offers living history sessions and is open to tourists and to the more than 4,000 annual student visitors in the northern New Jersey area. The school received a preservation award from the New Jersey Historical Society, and the Hardyston Heritage Society received a certificate of commendation from the American Association for State and Local History for the preservation of the school and the museum's interpretive and educational programs.

## Living History Programs

Although education has progressed beyond the mid-19th century, when students were content to write a good hand, speak a good piece and

Seneca Schoolhouse (1866), Seneca, Md. Another folk vernacular stone structure, this school was closed in 1910 but has been restored and opened for living history programs. (Historic Medley District)

know their times tables backwards and forwards, there remains a widespread desire to return to the days of the one-room country school. In "The Little Red Schoolhouse" (*Icons of America,* 1978), Fred Schroeder speaks of the "transcendent ideals" embodied in these schools:

> One of these ideals is expressed in Winslow Homer's paintings and in Frank Lloyd Wright's school: this is the idea of organic harmony of building, people and environment, and this is why Homer's rural-school paintings continue to appeal to us. In them, by means of the artist's unifying medium of sunlight, we see a rare sight: An institution serving people as individuals, within a non-compartmentalized community, and as sympathetic parts of an accessible natural environment.

Not only do adults feel this way. Children, too, love to experience what it must have been like to attend a one-room school. Yet, many children are put off by traditional museums. Rare objects on display are not suited to children's ways of learning through touch and movement. Even visiting museum villages and watching craftspeople reproduce brooms, tallow candles and homemade soap lacks the element of actually experiencing history and knowing from the inside out how things were a century or more ago.

The living history programs that have been developed at some country schools go beyond traditional museum experiences. They bring visitors right into the classroom and allow them to participate in the re-creation of a historic school day. Country schools make superb history-learning laboratories. Across the United States, a day spent at a restored country school is now an important part of many school curriculums. Children spend a day or half a day in period costume, eating pioneer lunches, learning lessons the old way and being respectful to the country school teacher.

School visitation programs are successful throughout the country. The Thomas Filer Schoolhouse (c. 1820) at the Farmers' Museum in Cooperstown, N.Y., boasts more than 10,000 student visitors annually. Students at the Cooperstown graduate program, State University of New York at Oneonta, have done extensive research on the building, the school's former teachers and early 19th-century education in New York State, culminating in the first accurate appraisal of the native fieldstone school since it was completely dismantled and rebuilt in 1944. Items such as the dunce cap and the blackboard were removed because they did not fit the 1840s time frame of the restoration (blackboards were not in common use in schools until after the Civil War). The one-room Old Stone Schoolhouse (1784), re-erected in 1938 in the Newark Museum garden, Newark, N.J., by the Works Progress Administration, is also popular; in 1981, 7,700 schoolchildren visited it. In Bronxville, N.Y., the Eastchester Historical Society has maintained the Marble School (1835) for more than 20 years, simulating an entire 1840s school day with spelling bees, oral reading and penmanship exercises and welcoming 2,000 children annually. Local kindergartners have their annual June picnic on the school grounds.

Summer living history programs also are popular. At Centennial Village in Island Grove Park, Greeley, Colo., the Lone Star School, built in 1920, sponsors one-week sessions for elementary school students throughout the summer. In June, July and August, retired teachers in Henry County, Iowa, manage the 1867 West Pleasant Lawn School.

Thomas Filer Schoolhouse (c. 1820), Cooperstown, N.Y., relocated to the Farmers' Museum and used for research and living history programs. (New York State Historical Association, Cooperstown)

Old Stone Schoolhouse (1784), Newark, N.J., now open to school groups as part of the Newark Museum. (Stephen Germany, Newark Museum)

In "The One-Room Schoolhouse Is Reborn," by Donna Heath (*National Retired Teachers Association Journal*, 1981), Esther Schmidt, who teaches for a week each summer at a one-room school in Pine City, Minn., says, " 'I've always had a strong feeling that community classrooms, as in the old rural schools, benefited children because they learned from one another. If they missed something, they heard it repeated often enough that they eventually caught on. . . . This is a golden opportunity to help preserve the history of rural schools. Before long the true experiences will be forgotten unless they are passed along from one generation to another.' "

A successful experience for children involves not just a visit to a well-restored facility but also previsit and postvisit activities. Many living history programs provide a teacher's guide that describes what students should bring, what they can expect and what the museum will provide. The Pioneer Classroom, a period room with historic furnishings at the Miller Park School in Omaha, Neb., provides a teacher's guide for the Omaha public schools; it includes brief notes on some of the items in the school—potbellied stove, metal woodbasket, recitation benches, teacher's desk, lunch shelves and half curtains (designed to let in light while discouraging daydreaming).

Previsit activities often include making puppets in period costumes or preparing drawings of period fashions; such projects help children decide on what clothing to wear when they visit the school. Typically, on such visits boys wear clothes one or two sizes too big, because country school children received hand-me-downs from older brothers and sisters. Shirts with collars and cuffs, bib overalls, patched dungarees and lightweight caps were standard. In the winter in colder areas, children came in wool socks and heavy boots; boys wore wool coats and caps with ear flaps. Visiting boys can wear socks outside their pants so they resemble knickers. Girls can wear dresses with petticoats, bloomers, long black or white stockings and a large ribbon or bow in their hair; scarves and sweaters complete their outfits. When visiting teachers also wear appropriate 19th-century attire, the visit to a one-room school has even more meaning.

Lunches for the schoolhouse visit should be prepared with historical accuracy; no soft drinks, canned foods, milk cartons, thermoses, plastic wrap or paper bags should be allowed. Country school students carried their lunches in a variety of tin containers or in baskets covered with a large piece of cloth knotted at the corners; the cloth was then made into a tablecloth to protect the desks. Traditional school lunches included cold sliced porridge, a hard boiled egg (when chickens were laying), a cold baked potato (if left over from dinner), a chunk of cheese, a piece of bread or bun, sandwiches spread with lard, bacon fat, molasses, syrup or jam, a cookie or a piece of cake and fruit (in season).

To ensure the validity of the experience, living history schools use textbooks from the proper period. (Naturally, most schools find it practical to use reproductions rather than allow children to handle original books, slates or quill pens.) Collecting 19th-century literature textbooks, which do not have colored illustrations or wide margins, makes for an interesting comparative study. Early geography books

A Morton County, N.D., schoolboy taking his lunch from a lard bucket, 1942. (John Vachon, FSA)

with outdated maps and outdated scientific theories promote lively discussion. At the Monroe Schoolhouse Museum and the Miller Park School, students are encouraged to make their own copybooks before their visit. Facsimiles of copybooks can be made by folding newsprint into a 9-by-12-inch booklet; these can be covered with brown paper (a paper sack will do) and stitched together at the spine.

Probably the most difficult task in preparing a living history interpretation is coordinating all the elements into a coherent span of historical time. The building itself, the furnishings, the textbooks, the costumes and the curriculum and methods of teaching are too often addressed separately, with the result that the program becomes a pastiche of things that were easy to research or for which resources were available.

One of the best living history programs at a restored country school is conducted at the Norlands School (1823), District No. 7, Livermore Falls, Maine. In June 1977 the Little Time Machine project of the Washburn-Norlands Foundation for elementary and secondary schools received state validation. This program was to serve as a demonstration project under the 1965 Elementary and Secondary Education Act for other school districts in Maine. Under the able direction of Billie Gammon, the Norlands School and the Washburn-Norlands Foundation have provided vitally needed and innovative educational services. Because of the success of this project, additional grants of up to $7,500 have been made available in Maine to local school systems interested in using the Norlands School living history model.

Norlands School (1823), Livermore Falls, Maine, the site of a living history program that serves as a model throughout the state. (Alice Brown, Washburn-Norlands Foundation)

In 1978 visitors to the Washburn-Norlands Foundation, including the Norlands School, totaled 15,290. One of the reasons people are so eager to visit is the meticulous attention Gammon has paid to presenting an 1840s interpretation of the school in every detail. Even the teachers must go through rigorous historical training. Each teacher is required to research, through letters, diaries, town records and state archives, the life and career of a person who taught at Norlands during the 1840s. He or she then assumes the name and personality of that 19th-century teacher, who, in effect, lives again. Reproductions of textbooks copyrighted before 1849 are required for all lessons. Students read from Salem Towne's *Readers* or from Colburn's *Intellectual Arithmetic* (1863) as they stand before the class and practice mental and written arithmetic.

Standard equipment includes a small blotter at each desk to absorb drips and spatters from pens and a brick or rock for sharpening slate pencils. Another necessity is a small rag for pupils to clean their slates, although most 19th-century students simply practiced their penmanship, spat on the slate, wiped it off with their shirt sleeves and began again. The only concession to the 20th century made at Norlands School is the substitution of washable blue ink for the old indelible ink, which came from ink powder or, more frequently, from the bark of swamp maples. The husks of butternuts were also used to produce a brown ink. These inks delighted children and horrified mothers because they permanently stained clothing and proved exceedingly difficult to remove from children's hands. At the Norlands School, outhouses are still in use.

Eight Square School (1827), Dryden, N.Y. Students now visit the school, which in its early days served as many as 70 pupils at a time; they sat in concentric rows of benches circling the room. Former students included town, county and school officials, the mother of a governor, a millionaire and the wife of a philanthropist. (Skip Thorne)

The Eight Square School was built for $550 to replace an 1815 clapboard school. The outhouses were added in 1928; electricity was not brought to the school until 1945, when it was a community center. (Skip Thorne)

Students come from all over Maine and even from neighboring states to participate in the Norlands School living history program. Because the children must ride school buses home, class sessions have been cut to a half day or even a few hours. Students also come on weekends. One child said, describing the Norlands School experience, "I liked the old school because there was no clock to watch the time go slow." The children's perception of the old discipline is fast and clear. "The schoolmaster told us what to do in the textbooks," another student related. "We were expected to behave at all times. I liked it."

Discipline also figures heavily in the living history experience in the Pioneer Classroom at Miller Park School. Children who visit are expected to behave the way they would in a pioneer classroom. For instance, when leaving their desks to go outside, students must always walk to the front of the room, turn left, turn left again, walk to the back of the room and out the door. When returning to their desks, students must proceed down the aisle that will allow them to enter the desk from the right side. The teacher calls each class forward to the recitation benches at the front of the room with the litany, "Turn, rise, pass." Those three words tell students to turn in their seats, rise and pass to the front of the room with books and minds ready for recitations.

Schoolhouse living history museums can teach students a great deal. As they experience firsthand what it used to be like to go to school, they gain new insights into childhood work and play and family and community life of earlier times. At the Old Stone Schoolhouse, students also learn about preserving and restoring historic structures like the schoolhouse itself and why historic buildings should be saved. The school becomes not only a mid-19th-century classroom but also a teaching laboratory for preservation techniques, with sessions on heating with wood, using natural light and building with stone. Students learn their lessons in the building while they learn about the building.

Interesting postvisit activities for students who have attended a living history classroom include recording oral histories from senior citizens who attended country schools and making an inventory of other historic local structures. Classes may want to compare the one-room school to their own classroom, analyzing the advantages and disadvantages through role playing or reenactments or applying recitations and memorization drills to their own arithmetic and spelling lessons. Students may also want to locate one-room schools and begin a pen-pal relationship with children who are currently attending one-room schools and who come to school on horseback, motorcycle, pick-up truck, snowmobile and, of course, on foot.

Living history programs in country schools allow children to experience history directly. The past becomes present, and children gain a deeper understanding of American history while also learning about themselves. Or, as Gammon said of the Norlands School, "The little one-room schoolhouse still stands at the crossroads. Its floor is worn; its desks are stained with ink. It is often cold and drafty and a mouse lives in the woodshed, but as long as the children come, expectant and eager, the little school will fulfill the purpose for which it was created more than 150 years ago."

# Growstown School
*Brunswick, Maine*
*1849*
*Living History Museum*
*Growstown School Living History Center*

*Client*

Bath-Brunswick Branch, American Association of University Women

*Architect*

All restoration decisions were made by a nonprofessional volunteer committee.

*History*

Built on one-fourth acre of donated land at a cost of $250, the school stands at the junction of two roads in a semirural area. The original plans called for the school "to have a good frame to be covered with sound boards . . . to have six windows 20 panes each . . . and to be painted two coats of lite straw color." Josiah and Osborne Melcher are credited with drawing up the plans. The school supposedly is built with pieces of wood salvaged from a school that previously stood on the same site and was torn down. In use as a school for 100 years, Growstown School is the only remaining one-room district schoolhouse of 26 that once existed in Brunswick. Among the few physical changes made were the addition of an ell for the outhouse and wiring for electricity. The school was closed in 1951.

Teacher Sara Sawyer with her pupils outside Growstown School, 1886.

*Description*

30 by 26 feet. Frame building with painted clapboards (light straw color), a gabled roof with natural cedar shingles, granite slab foundation, eight windows (12-over-8 lights), one 7-foot door with four lights above it, red brick chart chimney and granite slab doorstep. The building consists of one room with a partitioned woodshed off the small entryway. The walls are light cream-colored plaster above camel-colored, wide-board wainscoting. The room has a high white plastered cove ceiling with rounded corners, wooden blackboards and a wide pine floor. Two alcoves with metal hooks for coats are on either side of the room.

*Condition*

Neglect and weather hastened the decaying process after the school was closed; once it was boarded up, it became a neighborhood eyesore as well. By 1971 a town building inspector found that the granite slab foundation was in need of resetting, window sills were rotted and collapsed, the southeast wall was badly bowed out at the eaves, the southeast side of the roof was dangerously weak and sagging, cedar roof shingles were completely worn out, windows needed sash and glass replacement, the floor was sagging toward the outer walls and ceiling plaster and laths were falling. A neighborhood committee was formed in 1972 to make critical repairs to stabilize the building until complete restoration could take place; donations of money, labor and materials were obtained to reset the foundation, install a new cedar

Boys and girls line up separately to enter Growstown School for a living history session. (*Brunswick Times Record*)

Bell and stick in hand, the schoolmaster invites children to enter. (Millie Stewart)

shingled roof (boards beneath were replaced as necessary) and repair windows.

*Program Objectives*

The town has lost many of its historic buildings; thus, the primary aim of the project was to preserve the schoolhouse and see children return to it. The Bath-Brunswick Branch, AAUW, focused its attention on the school in 1981, almost 10 years after the initial stabilization work. Its objectives were (1) to restore the building; (2) to establish a living history program for use by area children, presenting a typical 1850s school day in an authentic setting; and (3) to ensure future use and care of the building for historical and education purposes.

*Planning and Research*

A committee of 10 AAUW members began in fall 1981 to raise funds; to solicit materials, labor, books and furnishings; and to begin historical research. A letter describing the project and its objectives was mailed to a select group, including former teachers and students of the school, people living near the school and preservation-minded residents in the area. Financial help, donation of materials for restoration, furnishings, books and labor were solicited. A raffle was held for an antique trunk refinished and filled with donated items from local merchants and handcrafted gifts from AAUW members. Chances were sold throughout the area to win the filled trunk. In addition, the AAUW chapter sold hand-stenciled tin lard pails with a schoolhouse design painted by AAUW members.

The town owns the building, and decisions about it are made by a board of five trustees, appointed by the town council. At present, the board consists of one town council member, one neighborhood resident and three AAUW members. The trustees present to the town council an annual report and a request for appropriations for maintenance expenditures.

Early photographs of the school were used as the basis for restoration. To date, no town records concerning the building have been located. The basic school structure had not changed between 1849 and 1981, with the exception of the added ell, which was subsequently removed. Other research materials for school furnishings and floor plans included (1) "State of Maine Annual Reports of the Superintendent of Common Schools 1859"; (2) *The School and the Schoolmaster*, Potter and Emerson (1842); (3) *New England Country School* (1872), painting by Winslow Homer; and (4) the Norlands School living history program in Livermore Falls, Maine.

The trustees decided that the building should remain a multipurpose building and that to remove the existing electricity would limit the building's use to only the 1853-period program planned. Future plans include a 1920s alternate program, and the light fixtures and stored desks will be authentic to that date. In the meantime, electricity allows for the safe use of the building in the evenings by other groups; oil lamps would present a fire hazard.

*Exterior Restoration*

1. The granite slab foundation was reset.

2. Rotted clapboards were replaced and repainted.

3. The roof was reshingled with cedar shingles.

4. Electrical wires were removed from the building and moved underground.

5. Windows (glass and sash) were repaired.

*Interior Work*

1. Rotted oak flooring was removed, and new floor joints, carrying timbers and a rough pine subfloor were installed.

2. Roof rafters were strengthened to support the weight of the new ceiling plaster.

3. A metal tie rod was attached between the outer walls to prevent them from bowing out.

4. Remnants of the original plaster ceiling were removed.

5. Ceiling laths were replaced and repaired.

6. Walls were repaired and patched with plaster.

7. The ceiling was plastered and painted white.

8. Loose paint only was scraped off the wide-board wainscoting; seven layers of paint were found.

9. Walls were painted cream, and the woodwork was painted a camel color; these colors corresponded to the bottom paint layers.

10. An eight-inch blanket of insulation with a plastic vapor barrier was placed under the subfloor to keep out cold and dampness from the earthen crawl space under the school.

11. A finished wide-board (11-inch) native Maine pine floor was laid over the subfloor with a felt paper layer in between.

12. The pine floor was sanded, stained with a puritan pine Minwax stain, and three coats of polyurethane finish were applied to protect the floor and make it easier to maintain.

13. Electrical service was removed from the building entrance and moved underground.

*Code Requirements*

1. The fire code required that the existing brick chimney be lined with tile and that a clean-out door, a small metal door cut into the chimney base for the removal of ashes and soot from inside the chimney, be put in before a permit could be issued to use a wood-burning stove.

2. The plumbing code allowed alternative toilets, so an exception was granted to use two 300-gallon concrete vault storage tanks beneath the outhouses.

*Site*

Two frame one-hole outhouses were built after the attached outhouse ell was removed because it was not a part of the original structure. No records of the originals could be found, so the outhouses were based on those of the Norlands School.

The restored classroom, furnished with the help of volunteers. (Millie Stewart)

The modern schoolmaster stokes the all-important stove. (Millie Stewart)

258

*Furnishings*

1. A reconditioned log-burning schoolhouse stove (purchased).
2. A brass bell previously used at the school (donated).
3. A schoolmaster's desk and stand (donated).
4. Seven double wooden desks (donated). These desks had been used at Miss Hinckley's School for Girls (1845) in Brunswick, Maine, according to records kept by Bowdoin College. This type of desk was mentioned in state records as being the most common for the time period of Growstown School. Fifteen double wooden desks made from a pattern based on the originals (labor donated by a vocational high school class; materials purchased).
5. Thirty small lap slates made from discarded blackboards (donated by a junior high industrial arts class).
6. A fire extinguisher, tin cups and quill pens (purchased).
7. Fifteen glass inkwells and 300 old school books (donated).

*Expenses*

|  |  |
|---|---|
| Cash items |  |
| Building repairs | $ 2,772 |
| Plastering | 1,500 |
| Paint and lumber supplies | 907 |
| Chimney work | 250 |
| Insulation | 675 |
| Finished floor | 2,850 |
| Stove, stove pipe | 485 |
| Noncash items |  |
| Items and materials donated | $ 4,095 |
| Labor of volunteers | 5,400 |

*Financing*

|  |  |
|---|---|
| AAUW Public Service Grant | $ 877 |
| Bath-Brunswick AAUW | 1,000 |
| Town of Brunswick | 2,771 |
| Prudential Insurance | 500 |
| Donations, fund raising (letter appeal, raffle, sales) | 4,000 |

The schoolmaster leads the class in blackboard exercises. (Millie Stewart)

# Broad River Community Schoolhouse

*Norwalk, Connecticut*
*1861*
*Adaptive Use*
*Fairfield County Savings Bank Branch*

*Client*
Fairfield County Savings Bank

*Architects*
Eli K. Street (1861); restoration and adaptive use design by Richard Bergmann Architects (1981).

*History*
The Broad River Community Schoolhouse, used as a school until 1924, is on its original foundation and site. The original plans and specifications were prepared for $5 by Eli K. Street, listed as a carpenter in the 1874 Norwalk directory. The lot, less than one-fourth acre, was purchased for $100; the costs of construction totalled $623.17. At a December 30, 1861, meeting, the school district board voted to hire George L. Finney as teacher, provided he could be hired on favorable terms and pass an examination; he was retained to teach for three months at wages not to exceed $20 per month. The first school session began in January 1862. For the next 62 years the building was used as a school, with as many as 48 students attending each term. Beginning in 1924, when a new town school was built, the city used the old schoolhouse as a community center, renamed the Broad River Community Club. Monthly meetings, social events and dances were held here. The schoolhouse was vacated in July 1980, at which time the city sold it to the Fairfield County Savings Bank. Designated a landmark by the Norwalk Historical Commission, the building is located at an important intersection and is accessible to both pedestrians and motorists.

*Description*
22 by 44 feet. Italianate-style frame building. Post-and-beam construction using corner posts with knee braces nailed together. Wall construction is frame filled in with brick.

*Condition*
The structure was basically sound when purchased by the bank. During the years it was used as a community center, it had remained relatively untouched, except for the interior, which was paneled with plywood sheets and a glued-on acoustic tile ceiling. The original exterior shutters had been removed years earlier and stored in the attic. As with any building more than 50 years old, the structural foundation sills had rotted and needed replacement. Floor joists were inadequate to support bank equipment. Roof rafters were inadequately framed by today's building code standards.

*Program Objectives*
When establishing a new branch, the Fairfield County Savings Bank tries first to find a building in the designated area to reuse; this is the

Elevation drawing made for the project shows the clapboarding, pedimented windows and doors, shutters and bracketed roof.

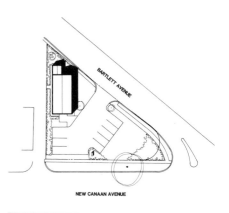

The site plan indicates the location of the school on the triangular lot and the added parking spaces.

bank's second adaptive use project for branch facilities. The bank's intention in preserving the schoolhouse was to help revitalize its older suburban neighborhood, which included small, rundown stores. Many elderly customers live in the neighborhood and can easily walk to this branch office.

The design goal was to retain the schoolhouse character inside and out and to provide a good balance of contemporary and traditional detail: (1) The exterior would be left intact, and the site would retain as much as possible the appearance of an 1860s schoolyard; (2) the structure was to be upgraded to meet new building code and structural requirements; (3) the bank's logo ("The Bank with a Heart") would be incorporated in the signage, but, to keep the historic fabric intact, there would be no signs on the building; and (4) the small interior was to be kept as spacious as possible but with indirect lighting.

*Planning and Research*

A brief history was compiled by Ralph Bloom, city-appointed historian for Norwalk, and Joan G. Robidoux, researcher. Several early exterior photographs that were found helped in identifying the original appearance of the schoolhouse. During removal of later materials, the structure was carefully analyzed. Paint scrapings of the exterior siding were examined under magnification in the architect's research shop and helped determine the original colors and the paint scheme. An 1889 black-and-white photograph, the earliest existing photograph, aided in determining color values and trim details. This photograph also was used to guide the exterior restoration, as were the Secretary of the Interior's Standards and Guidelines for preservation projects. Other information reviewed included *Preservation and Recycling of Buildings for Bank Use*, by Barbara Ann Cleary (Information Series, No. 18, National Trust for Historic Preservation, 1978).

*Exterior Restoration*

1. Exterior features were returned to their original 1861 appearance. Shutters and windows that had been removed over the years were replaced. An attached shed roof at the entrance was removed.

2. No contemporary alterations or additions were made on the exterior except for a free-standing contemporary sign, which is the only feature indicating the building's commercial use.

3. Floor joists and foundation sills were replaced with pressure-treated wood; stone foundations were repaired and repointed for sound, stable bearing.

4. Roof rafters were strengthened with new members, and the roofline was straightened.

5. Asphalt shingles, which were in poor condition, were removed and replaced with wood shingles, which, as indicated by photographs, were originally used on the roof.

6. New cedar clapboard siding was installed on fire-retardant gypsum sheathing to meet fire ordinances for public buildings.

7. Victorian-period colors were selected for the paint—salmon with sage green trim and forest green shutters; research indicated that these

Rehabilitated exterior with the new bank sign and parking lot.

colors, while perhaps not original, had been used during the period and closely matched the values in old photographs.

*Interior Work*

1. The floor was removed to excavate a crawl space and partial basement for a furnace and air-handling unit. A partial concrete slab was poured on grade to take additional weight from the vault and automatic teller unit.

2. A new HVAC (heating, ventilation and air-conditioning) system was installed.

3. A vault for daily deposits was installed.

4. Four teller stations, computerized and linked to the main terminal, were built in.

5. A lounge-kitchen for bank employees was created (there were few restaurants in the area).

6. Because adding a drive-in window would have extensively altered the building, a 24-hour automatic teller was installed in the vestibule, along with a glass front door for security purposes.

7. A storage room was added by enclosing some interior space.

8. Exposed light fixtures (not originals) were eliminated. To duplicate as much as possible the original unlighted space, indirect lighting was installed over teller stations.

9. R-11 insulation was added to inside walls and R-30 insulation in the attic; windows were reglazed and storm windows added.

10. New gypsum board was applied to walls and ceilings.

The schoolhouse as it looked before conversion to a bank, when it was used as a club. The small porch was added before 1913.

*Code Requirements*

1. Because the building was a frame structure, it had to be adapted to meet fire code regulations: Approved sheet rock was used on interior and exterior walls and under the roof and for extensive sheathing; smoke detectors were also installed. The bank had to obtain a zoning variance because the former schoolhouse was located on a 98 percent commercial lot. The variance, covering the remaining 2 percent, was granted on the conditions that lighting would not be reflected on the neighboring houses (residential neighbors are located to the rear and one side of the present bank), and that parking and planting plans would be presented to the zoning officer for approval. Low-brightness exterior site lighting (high-pressure sodium lighting) was selected to simulate the lighting level and warm glow that might have been used in the late 19th century.

3. A landscape screening plan was approved by the Norwalk zoning officer because neighbors had voiced concern about a large portion of the site becoming an asphalt parking lot.

4. The site was regraded to provide accessibility for the handicapped.

Renovation work done during the adaptation of the school as a bank.

*Site*

1. Utilities were placed underground to retain the appearance of an 1860s schoolyard.

2. Eight parking spaces were placed where the play area had been.

3. Screening and shrubs were required by the city's planning and zoning commission; creeping junipers fulfilled this requirement and kept the site flat and unencumbered. Three locust trees were planted between the building and parking lot for a softening effect.

4. A free-standing illuminated sign (5 by 2½ feet) with the bank's heart logo was installed 40 feet away from the building, so that the integrity of the building was not compromised.

*Furnishings*

1. All equipment and built-ins were scaled down to fit in the available space. The teller stations and manager's desk were custom designed to fit.

2. The bank's heart logo was incorporated into the design of the interior wall clock.

3. Red carpet and upholstery repeated the color of the heart logo, giving the bank's interior warmth and vitality.

4. Contemporary oak furniture and lighting provided the balance of contemporary design.

5. The appearance of an 1860s schoolhouse interior was retained by the installation of blackboards (where former students are encouraged to write their names), photo murals made from historic school photographs spanning the 62 years of the school's history, wainscoting that matches the original and white walls and ceilings.

6. The marble plaque inscribed "The Broad River Community Club" was reused as an inlay in the customer waiting area.

Group photograph outside the Broad River Schoolhouse, c. 1889. This was used to aid the exterior restoration. (Courtesy of Lockwood House Collection)

*Expenses*
Materials

| | |
|---|---|
| Lumber | In contractors' fees |
| Paint | $ 4,484 |
| Reglazing | 2,100 |
| Insulation | 1,260 |

Systems

| | |
|---|---|
| Total electric | $20,067 |
| HVAC system installed | 7,875 |
| Utility hook-ups | 3,700 |
| Plumbing | 6,134 |

Regulations

| | |
|---|---|
| Fire code regulations (approved sheet rock) | $ 3,145 |

Bank equipment

| | |
|---|---|
| Automatic teller unit | $ 31,755 |
| Vault | 23,106 |
| On-line terminals | 20,721 |
| Engineering | 17,625 |
| Countertops, drawers, etc. | 9,737 |
| Exterior sign | 2,425 |
| Lounge-kitchen (stove, sink, refrigerator unit) | 806 |
| Surveying | 546 |

| | |
|---|---|
| Paving | $17,625 |
| Landscaping | $13,254 |
| Contractors' fees | $99,774 |
| Architect's fees | $20,972 |
| Furnishings (furniture, carpeting, photo murals) | $13,989 |

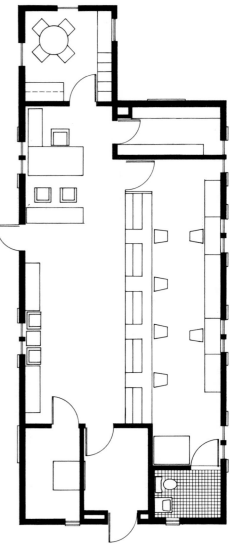

The floor plan illustrates how the bank facilities were fitted into the small schoolhouse space.

*Financing*
Entire cost ($350,000) paid by bank.

*Use*
Many customers in the neighborhood can easily walk to the bank. On opening day in 1981, the first customer, who lived only two blocks away, was a former student who is also pictured in a photo mural from a 1908 school photograph. Hundreds of families come to visit, and school groups come on field trips.

Illustrations courtesy of Richard Bergmann Architects

*right*
The original doorway, shutters and paint were re-created as part of the conversion.

*below*
Historical photographs and a blackboard help recall the school's past.

# Country Schools State by State

The following list of country schools represents the first effort to identify rural schools remaining in use as schools or as museums or community centers. It is necessarily preliminary in scope and reflects information available in mid-1984. Schools listed are predominantly original one-room public district schools in good condition. Not included in the list are those schools whose exterior has been altered or buildings that have been adaptively used for businesses, residences, stores and other purposes. The schools are listed by the nearest town or the county. The letter notations following each entry indicate the following: (NR) listing in the the National Register of Historic Places; (P) at least some work has been done to preserve the building (in some instances, indicates complete restoration); (C) community center; (LH) living history program; (M) museum; and (T) one-teacher school (although most of these latter are historic buildings, some are not). If no code is provided, present use of the school is unknown.

Information on the schools results from several years of research by Andrew Gulliford and two requests sent to state historic preservation offices in the fall of 1982 and in June 1984 for data on historic country schools. Because National Register listings and historic site information are not yet computerized by building type, each preservation office had to allocate staff time to review its state and National Register listings. Without the generous support of state historic preservation offices, this preliminary list would not have been possible.

Valuable assistance in helping identify and locate current one-teacher schools was provided by Bruce Barker, assistant professor of education, Texas Tech University; Ivan Muse, professor of education, Brigham Young University; and Ralph Smith, dean of education, Brigham Young University. Their chart of states with traditional one-teacher public schools in operation during the 1983–84 academic year appears at the end of the listings; states not listed reported no one-teacher schools in operation. Because of fluctuations in rural population, which affect the opening and closing of rural schools, there may be some discrepancies, depending on when each survey was taken, in the number of schools reflected in the chart and list.

Additions or changes to this list are welcome. Please contact Andrew Gulliford, *America's Country Schools*, c/o The Preservation Press, National Trust for Historic Preservation, 1785 Massachusetts Avenue, N.W., Washington, D.C. 20036.

## Alaska

*Anchorage,* Pioneer School House (NR)
*Birch Creek Village,* Birch Creek School (T)
*Chignik Lagoon,* Chignik Lagoon School (T)
*Chistochina,* Chistochina School (T)
*Clear,* Browns School (T)
*Edna Bay,* Edna Bay School (T)
*Egegik,* Egegik School (T)
*Hollis,* Hollis School (T)
*Hope,* Hope Elementary School (T)
*Igiugig,* Igiugig School (T)
*Ivanoff Bay,* Ivanoff Bay School (T)
*Kassan,* Kassan School (T)
*Ketchikan,* Smith Cove School, View Cove School (both T)
*Myers Chuck,* Myers Chuck School (T)
*Naknek,* South Naknek Elementary School (T)
*Nikolski,* Nikolski School (T)
*Oscarville,* Oscarville School (T)
*Paxson,* Paxson School (T)
*Pedro Bay,* Pedro Bay School (T)
*Petersburg,* Portage Bay School (T)
*Pilot Point,* Pilot Point School (T)
*Port Alexander,* Port Alexander School (T)
*Sitka,* Rowan Bay School (T)
*Skweetna,* Skweetna Elementary School (T)
*Stevens Village,* Stevens Village School (T)
*Telida,* Telida School (T)
*Tenakee Springs,* Tenakee Springs School (T)

## Arizona

*Blue,* Blue Elementary School, District No. 22 (T)
*Crown King,* Crown King Elementary School, District No. 41 (T)
*Douglas,* Apache Elementary School, District No. 42 (T)
*Hackberry,* Hackberry Elementary School, District No. 3 (T)
*Kirkland,* Walnut Grove Elementary School, District No. 7 (T)
*Littlefield,* Littlefield Elementary School, District No. 9 (T)
*Maricopa County,* Horse Mesa Accommodation School, District No. 509, Williams Air Force Base (T)
*Morristown,* Champie Elementary School, District No. 14 (T)
*Peach Springs,* Valentine Elementary School, District No. 22 (T)
*Salome,* Vicksburg Elementary School, District No. 3 (T)
*Shumway,* Shumway School (NR)

*Tubac,* Old Tubac Schoolhouse (NR)
*Winslow,* Chevelon Butte Elementary School, District No. 5 (T)

## Arkansas

*Alabam,* Alabam School (NR)
*Jacksonport,* Hickory Grove Church and School (NR)
*Larue,* Rocky Branch School
*Portia,* Portia School (NR)
*Prairie Grove,* Prairie Grove School, Prairie Grove Battlefield Park

## California

*Alderpoint,* Alice Jewett Elementary School (T)
*Amboy,* Amboy Elementary School (T)
*Arroyo Grande,* Santa Manuela School (P)
*Bear Valley,* Bear Valley Elementary School (T)
*Big Bear Lake,* Glen Martin Elementary School (T)
*Blue Lake,* Green Point Elementary School (T)
*Bodega,* Watson School (NR)
*Brooks,* Canon School (NR)
*Buena Park,* Iowa School, District No. 83, Knott's Berry Farm (P)
*Cambria,* Santa Rosa School
*Chinese Camp,* Chinese Camp Elementary School (T)
*Columbia,* Columbia Schoolhouse, Columbia State Historic Park (P)
*Corning,* Kirkwood Elementary School (T)
*Douglas Flat,* Douglas Flat School (NR)
*Dutch Flat,* Dutch Flat School (NR)
*Earlimart,* Allensworth Elementary School (T)
*Emigrant Gap,* Emigrant Gap Elementary School (T)
*Essex,* Essex Elementary School (T)
*Ferndale,* Grizzley Bluff School (NR)
*Flournoy,* Flournoy Union Elementary School (T)
*Hoopa,* Weitchpec Elementary School (T)
*Hornbrook,* Fall Creek Elementary School (T)
*King City,* Gloria School, Agriculture Museum at San Lorenzo Park (LH)
*Kneeland,* Kneeland Elementary School (T)
*Korbel,* Maple Creek Elementary School (T)
*Kyburz,* Silver Fork Elementary School (T)
*La Grange,* La Grange Elementary School (T)

*Livermore,* Harney School (T)
*Manchester,* Manchester Schoolhouse ((NR)
*Montague,* Bogus Elementary School, Little Shasta Elementary School (both T)
*Napa,* Capell Elementary School (T), Suscol Schoolhouse (NR), Wooden Valley Elementary School (T)
*Needles,* Chemehuevi Valley Elementary School (T)
*Paicines,* Panoche Elementary School (T)
*Paradise,* Centerville Schoolhouse (NR)
*Parkfield,* Parkfield Elementary School (T)
*Petaluma,* Laguna Joint Elementary School, Lincoln Elementary School (both T)
*Platina,* Platina Elementary School (T)
*Portola Valley,* Portola Valley School (NR)
*Ravendale,* Ravendale Elementary School (T)
*Sacramento,* Brighton School (NR)
*Salinas,* El Toro School (NR)
*San Benito,* Jefferson Elementary School (T)
*San Diego,* Mason Street School, Old Town San Diego State Park (P)
*San Luis Obispo,* Los Osos School (P)
*San Miguel,* Pleasant Valley School (T)
*San Rafael,* Dixie Schoolhouse (NR)
*Santa Paula,* Santa Clara Elementary School (T)
*Sawyers Bar,* Sawyers Bar Elementary School (T)
*Solvang,* Ballard Elementary School (T)
*Somerset,* Indian Diggings Elementary School (T)
*Stewart's Point,* Reservation Elementary School (T)
*Stockton,* Old Weber School (NR)
*Washington,* Malakoff Elementary School (T)
*Wawona,* Wawona Elementary School, Yosemite National Park (T)
*Whitehorn,* Etterburg Elementary School (T)
*Woody,* Blake Elementary School (T)

## Colorado

*Basalt,* Emma School (C)
*Boulder,* Guy Hill School (P)
*Brown's Park,* Old Ladore School (NR, C)
*Cortez,* Battlerock Elementary School (T)
*Crawford,* Mayer School (C)
*Dillon,* One-Room School, Summit Historical Museum (C, M)

*Drennan*, Drennan School (C)
*Florissant*, Standard School (C)
*Fort Collins*, Gleneyre Elementary School, Stove Prairie Elementary School (both T)
*Frisco*, Frisco Schoolhouse (NR, M)
*Glenwood Springs*, Canyon Creek School, District No. 32; Upper Cattle Creek School (both C)
*Greeley*, Lone Star School, Centennial Village (P)
*Gunnison*, Paragon Rural School, History Village Park (P)
*Gypsum*, Sweetwater School (C)
*Hahns Peak*, Hahns Peak School House (NR)
*Hartsel*, Hartsel Standard School (C)
*Lamar*, Alta Vista School (NR, T)
*Larkspur*, Spring Valley School (NR)
*Leadville*, District No. 11 School (P)
*Limon*, Pioneer Schoolhouse Museum (M)
*Littleton*, Littleton School, Littleton Historical Museum (LH)
*Marble*, Marble School (M)
*Maybell*, Brown's Park School (C, T)
*Meeker*, Strawberry Creek School (C)
*Morrison*, Morrison School House (NR)
*Norwood*, Basin Elementary School (T)
*Palmer Lake*, Glen Grove School (NR)
*Paonia*, Bowie School (R)
*Parachute*, Battlement School (NR, P, C), Morisiana School (C)
*Placerville*, Placerville School (C)
*Rifle*, Austin School, District No. 20, Rifle Creek Museum (M)
*Rio Blanco,* Rock School (T)
*Sedalia*, Indian Park School (NR)
*Snowmass Village,* Brush Creek School (C)
*Springfield*, Springfield Schoolhouse (NR)
*Steamboat Springs*, Moon Hill School (C)
*Sterling*, Stoney Buttes School, District No. 10 (M)
*Tructon*, Tructon School (C)
*Vail*, Gore Creek Schoolhouse, Ford Park (P)
*Wild Horse*, Wild Horse School (C)

## Connecticut

*Avon*, Avon School (M)
*Barkhamsted*, Barkhamsted Center School (M)
*Bloomfield*, Old Farm School House (Brick School) (NR, P); Southwest District School
*Bozrah*, Gilman One-Room School
*Canterbury*, District School
*Clinton*, Cow Hill School

*Coventry*, Second Congregational Academy (C)
*East Haddam*, Nathan Hale School
*Haddam*, Higganum School
*Ledyard*, Geer School (P, C), Lambtown School
*Norfolk*, Norfolk School (M)
*North Branford*, Red Schoolhouse (M)
*South Woodstock*, Quasset School (P)
*Washington*, Schoolhouse

## Delaware

*Cowgill's Corner*, Octagonal Schoolhouse (NR)

## District of Columbia

*Washington, D.C.*, Conduit Road Schoolhouse (P)

## Florida

*Bowling Green*, Duett Elementary School (T)
*Coconut Grove*, First Coconut Grove School
*Okeechobee*, Tantie School, District No. 14 (P)
*Tampa*, Old School House, University of Tampa (NR)

## Georgia

*Athens*, Chestnut Grove School
*Columbus*, Wynnton Male Academy
*Doraville*, Mechanicsville School
*Newnan*, Male Academy (M)
*Rome*, Berry Log School, Berry College (NR)

## Idaho

*Arbon*, Arbon Elementary School (T)
*Avery*, Avery Elementary School (T)
*Calder*, Calder Elementary School (T)
*Clarkia*, Clarkia School (T)
*Clayton*, Clayton School (T)
*Colburn*, Colburn Elementary School (T)
*Custer*, One-Room School (NR, M)
*Geneva*, Geneva School (T)
*Howe*, Howe Elementary School (T)
*May*, Patterson Elementary School (T)
*Mountain Home*, Prairie School (T)
*Moyie Springs*, Evergreen Elementary School (T)
*Nez Perce*, Big Butte Community School (C)
*Ola,* Ola Elementary School (T)
*Orofino*, Grangemont School (T)
*Peck*, Peck Elementary School (T)

*Rogerson*, Three Creek School (T)
*Senore*, Cavendish-Teakean Elementary School (T)
*Stanley*, Stanley Elementary School (T)
*Sweet*, Sweet Elementary School (T)
*Tendoy*, Tendoy School (T)
*Whitebird*, Whitebird School (T)
*Yellow Pine*, Yellow Pine School (T)

## Illinois

*Aledo*, Fairview Schoolhouse, Mercer County Historical Society Museum (M)
*Carterville*, Chamnestown Log Cabin School, Crab Orchard National Wildlife Refuge
*Geneseo*, Stone Street School, 1910 Farm
*Grove City*, Hemlock School
*La Salle County*, Aitken School
*Paris*, Pine Grove School, District No. 70 (NR, P)
*Princeton*, Colton School, Lovejoy Homestead Complex (P)
*Schuline*, Charter Oak School House (NR)
*Shipman*, Prairie Dell Schoolhouse
*Streamwood*, Hoosier Grove School
*West Chicago*, McAuley School (NR, T)

## Indiana

*Avilla*, One-Room School
*Bloomington*, Honey Creek School (P)
*Crown Point*, One-Room School
*Hammond*, Little Red Schoolhouse
*Home*, Goddard School
*Mecca*, One-Room School
*Noblesville*, Huxford School, Billie Creek Village, Connor Prairie Settlement (LH)
*Orland*, Collins School
*Rochester*, Prill School (NR, LH)
*Southport*, One-Room School
*Vandalia*, Vandalia Schoolhouse (P)

## Iowa

*Alexander*, Maysville Schoolhouse, Loomis Memorial Park (M)
*Allison*, Little Yellow Schoolhouse (M)
*Anamosa*, Antioch School, Grant Wood Memorial Park (M)
*Atlantic*, Schoolhouse Museum (M)
*Carroll*, Red Schoolhouse (M)
*Cedar Falls*, Old Bennington Township School, Black Hawk Park (M)
*Chariton*, Puckerbrush School
*Chickasaw County*, Jacksonville School, Adolph Munson Park (M)

*Clarinda*, Golden Rod School House (NR)
*Clarion*, Lake Township School, District No. 6 (M)
*Corning*, Icarian School (M)
*Creston*, Lincoln School, District No. 5 (M)
*Dakota City*, Willow School, Old Mill Farm (M)
*Davenport*, Gilruth School House (NR); One-Room School, Mississippi Valley fairgrounds (P); Walnut Grove School (M)
*Davis*, Old Center School (M)
*Decorah*, Locust School (NR)
*Denison*, Little Red Schoolhouse (M)
*Des Moines*, Old North Lincoln School, Heritage Village (P)
*Dubuque*, Humke School, Ham House Museum (M)
*Estherville*, Bolstead, Emmett County fairgrounds (M)
*Fairfield*, Peach Blossom School, Cedar District No. 6 (M)
*Farley*, Lincoln School (NR)
*Fort Dodge*, Border Plains School, Fort Museum (M)
*Greenfield*, Old Grand River School, District No. 3, Adair County fairgrounds (M)
*Grundy*, Herbert Quick Schoolhouse, Orion Park (M)
*Hampton*, Maysville Schoolhouse (NR)
*Henry County*, West Pleasant Lawn School (LH)
*Hopkinton*, One-Room Rural Schoolhouse, Historical Museum Complex (M)
*Independence*, Westburg School, District No. 7 (M)
*Indianola*, Mount Hope Schoolhouse (M)
*Jefferson*, Minnehan School, Greene County fairgrounds (M)
*Knoxville*, Pleasant Ridge School, Marion County Park (M)
*Lansing*, Lansing Stone School (NR)
*Le Claire*, Stone School (NR)
*Le Mars*, Steele School, Plymouth County Historical Complex (M)
*Lineville*, Little Red Schoolhouse (M), Pleasant Hill School (NR)
*Manchester*, Red School House (M)
*Maquoketa*, Bridgeport School (M)
*Marshalltown*, Wetherbee School, Susie Sower Historical House Site (M)
*Mediapolis*, Zion School (M)
*Milford*, Viola School, Meadow District No. 7 (M)
*Montrose*, Galland School (M)
*Mt. Pleasant*, One-Room School, History Village (LH)

*Mt. Vernon*, Abbe Creek School (M)
*Nevada*, Halley School (M)
*North English*, Gritter School (M)
*Northwood*, Swensrud School (M)
*Ogden*, Hickory Grove School, Don Williams Recreation Area (M)
*Orange City*, Orange City School (M)
*Oskaloosa*, Prine School, Nelson Homestead Pioneer Farm and Craft Museum (M)
*Peterson*, Rock Forest School, Heritage Area (M)
*Primghar*, One-Room Rural Schoolhouse, Heritage Park (M)
*Quimby*, Stiles Schoolhouse Museum (M)
*Riceville*, Saratoga School (Buresh School), District No. 4, Buresh Farms (M)
*Sigourney*, White Oak School, School District No. 5, Belva-Deer Park (M)
*Stanton*, One-Room Rural Schoolhouse (M)
*Tripoli*, Warren School, District No. 9, North Park (M)
*West Bend*, Carter School (M)
*West Union*, Pleasant Ridge School, Fayette County fairgrounds (M)
*Winterset*, North River Stone School House (NR)

## Kansas

*Beloit*, Honey Creek School, District No. 21 (LH)
*Clinton Lake*, Barber School (NR)
*Emporia*, One-Room School, Emporia State University (P)
*Fort Larned*, One-Room School (M)
*Frankfort*, Barrett School House (NR)
*Great Bend*, One-Room School, Barton County Historical Village (M)
*Hays*, One-Room School, Ellis County Historical Museum (M); Plymouth School, Fort Hays State University (P)
*Hillsboro*, One-Room School, Adobe House Museum (P)
*Kirwin*, District No. 1 School (LH)
*Lanesfield*, Lanesfield School (M)
*Larned*, Pawnee School, Santa Fe Trail Center, District No. 55 (P)
*Lindsborg*, One-Room School, McPherson County Museum (M)
*Marysville*, Bommer School (M)
*Oskaloosa*, One-Room School (P)
*Paxico*, Snokomo School (C, M)
*Rolla*, Dermont Elementary School (T)
*Sabetha*, Old Albany School House (NR)
*Selden*, Harmony School (P)

*Strong City*, Lower Fox Creek School (NR)
*Topeka*, Victor School, Ward-Meade House Museum (LH)
*Wakefield*, Sunny Slope School (M)
*Wamego*, Cottonwood School (C)
*Westmoreland*, Sales School (C)
*White Cloud*, White Cloud School (NR)

## Kentucky

*Banner*, Daniels Creek Elementary School (T)
*Greenup*, Claylick Buffalo School, Greenbo Lake State Resort Park
*Richmond*, Granny Richardson Springs School, Eastern Kentucky University (P)
*Salmons*, Salmons School (C)
*West Liberty*, Paint Creek Log School

## Louisiana

*Kentwood*, Tangipahoa Parish School (NR, M)

## Maine

*Alna*, Alna School (NR)
*Bingham*, C. E. Ball Franklin School, Caratuk School (both T)
*Brunswick*, Growstown School (LH)
*Caribou*, Sincock Elementary School (T)
*Cliff Island*, Cliff Island School (T)
*Cranberry Isles*, Longfellow School (T)
*Dixmont*, Louis I. Bussey School (NR)
*Frenchboro*, Frenchboro Elementary School (T)
*Georgetown*, Stone School House (NR)
*Isle au Haut*, Isle au Haut Rural School (T)
*Islesford*, Islesford Elementary School (T)
*Livermore Falls*, Norlands School, District No. 7 (LH)
*Long Island*, Long Island Elementary School (T)
*Monhegan Island*, Monhegan Island Elementary School (T)
*Newry*, Lower Sunday River School (NR)
*Rockland*, Matinicus Island Elementary School, District No. 65 (T)
*Wellington*, Wellington Elementary School (T)
*West Farmington*, Little Red Schoolhouse (NR, P)
*Wilson Mills*, Lincoln-Magalloway Elementary School (T)
*Winslow*, Brick School (NR)
*York*, Old Schoolhouse (NR)

## Maryland

*Clarksburg,* Clarksburg School (NR, C)
*Cumberland,* Union Grove School House (NR, C)
*Port Republic,* Port Republic One-Room School (P)
*Seneca,* Seneca Schoolhouse, Historic Medley District (LH)
*Tylerton,* Tylerton Elementary School (T)

## Massachusetts

*Brockton,* Little Red Schoolhouse (P)
*Deerfield,* Wapping School (P)
*Dennis,* West Schoolhouse (NR)
*Pittsfield,* Morewood School (P)
*West Springfield,* Little Red Schoolhouse, Storrowton Village, Eastern States Exposition Grounds (M)

## Michigan

*Alpena,* Green School, Jesse Besser Museum (P)
*Au Gres,* Whitney Township School, District No. 2, Arenac County Historical Society Museum (NR, M)
*Bad Axe,* Adams Elementary School, Becking School, Big Burning School, Rapson Elementary School (all T)
*Blissfield,* Victorsville School, Blissfield School Campus (M)
*Bridgeport,* Hess School (Bridgeport Spaulding Community School)
*Canton,* Canton Center School (M)
*Center Line,* Ellis School (T)
*Chassell,* Chassell New Elementary School (T)
*Copper Harbor,* Grant Township School (T)
*Dearborn,* Scotch Settlement School, Henry Ford Museum and Greenfield Village (M)
*Eagle Harbor,* Eagle Harbor Schoolhouse (NR)
*Edwardsburg,* Mason Schoolhouse, District No. 5 (C)
*Farmington Hills,* German School
*Grand Ledge,* Strange School (T)
*Harbor Beach,* Eccles Sigel School, District No. 4 (T)
*Hinchman,* Ferry Street School
*Ionia,* Benedict School (T)
*Jackson,* McCain School
*Lansing,* Old Gunnisonville School (M)
*Lawrence,* Barnes School
*Mulliken,* Loucks Elementary School (T)
*Nottawa,* Nottawa Stone School (NR)
*Oscoda,* Glennie Elementary School (T)
*Owosso,* Octagonal School (P)

*Pelkie,* Pelkie School House (M)
*Perry,* Lovejoy School (C)
*Pointe aux Pins,* Pines School (T)
*Port Hope,* Red School (T)
*Reese,* Hill District School (C)
*Shaftsburg,* Shaftsburg School (C)
*Skanee,* Arron Township School
*Spring Lake,* Little Red Schoolhouse (DeWitt Bicentennial One-Room School) (M)
*Temperance,* Banner Oak School (P)
*Three Rivers,* Lakeside School, District No. 2 (M)
*Troy,* Poppleton School (M)
*Vassar,* McKinley School (NR, M)
*Walled Lake,* Walled Lake School (M)
*White Cloud,* Birch Grove School (P)
*White Rock,* White Rock School Museum (M)
*Wyoming,* Lee Elementary School (T)

## Minnesota

*Ada,* One-Room School (P)
*Albert Lea,* One-Room School (P)
*Alexandria,* One-Room School (P)
*Almelund,* One-Room School (P)
*Angle Inlet,* Angle Inlet School (T)
*Annandale,* One-Room School (P)
*Apple Valley,* One-Room School (P)
*Artichoke,* District No. 13 School (P, C)
*Austin,* One-Room School (P)
*Bagley,* One-Room School (P)
*Becker,* One-Room School (P)
*Belview,* District No. 74 School (M)
*Bemidji,* One-Room School (P)
*Benson,* One-Room School (P)
*Bertha,* One-Room School (P)
*Brainerd,* One-Room School (P)
*Breckenridge,* One-Room School (P)
*Brooklyn Center,* One-Room School (P)
*Browns Valley,* One-Room School (P)
*Butterfield,* One-Room School (P)
*Cambridge,* West Riverside School (NR, LH)
*Coin,* Coin School (NR, P)
*Comstock,* One-Room School (P)
*Corcoran,* Burschville School (M)
*Crookston,* One-Room School (P)
*Currie,* Sunrise School, District No. 1 (P, C)
*Dalton,* One-Room School (P)
*Delano,* Franklin Township School (NR, P)
*Detroit Lakes,* One-Room School (P)
*Duluth,* One-Room School (P)
*Edina,* Cahill School (NR, LH)
*Elbow Lake,* Pleasant View School, District No. 7 (M)
*Ely,* One-Room School (P)
*Elysian,* Harty School (M)

*Esko,* One-Room School (P)
*Fairmont,* One-Room School (P)
*Falcon Heights,* Stoin School (LH)
*Faribault,* One-Room School (P)
*Franklin,* One-Room School (P)
*Glenwood,* Pleasant Hill School (M)
*Goodridge,* One-Room School (P)
*Grand Marais,* One-Room School (P)
*Grand Rapids,* One-Room School (P)
*Grandy,* One-Room School (P)
*Hanley Falls,* One-Room School (P)
*Hay Creek,* District No. 20 School (NR, M)
*Hay Lake,* One-Room School (P)
*Hendricks,* One-Room School (P)
*Homer,* Homer School (C)
*Howard Lake,* Welker School (M)
*Jackson,* One-Room School (P)
*Lake Bronson,* One-Room School (P)
*Lake Park,* One-Room School (P)
*Lake Shetek,* One-Room School (P)
*Le Sueur,* One-Room School (P)
*Lewiston,* One-Room School (P)
*Little Falls,* One-Room School (P)
*Long Lake,* District No. 50 School (M)
*Lonsdale,* Lonsdale Public School (C)
*Madison,* One-Room School (P)
*Mahnomen,* One-Room School (P)
*Marshall,* One-Room School (P)
*Melrose,* One-Room School (P)
*Moland,* One-Room School (C)
*Montevideo,* District No. 4 School (M)
*Moorhead,* Gunderson School, District No. 112 (C)
*Morris,* One-Room School (P)
*Morton,* One-Room School (P)
*Mountain Lake,* Mountain Lake School (M)
*New Scandia,* Hay Lake School (NR, M)
*New Ulm,* One-Room School (P)
*Osseo,* One-Room School (P)
*Owatonna,* District No. 14 School (M)
*Park Rapids,* One-Room School (P)
*Pelan,* One-Room School (P)
*Pine City,* District No. 69 School (M)
*Pipestone,* One-Room School (P)
*Preston,* O'Hara School (M)
*Princeton,* One-Room School (P)
*Ramsey,* District No. 28 School (NR, P)
*Redwood Falls,* One-Room School (P)
*Reeds Landing,* One-Room School (P)
*Renville,* One-Room School (P)
*Rochester,* One-Room School (P)
*Rollag,* One-Room School (P)
*Roseau,* One-Room School (P)
*Rowena,* District No. 8 School (NR, P, C)
*St. Charles,* Ganey School (M)
*St. Paul,* Mattock School (P)
*Sandstone,* One-Room School (P)
*Sauk Center,* One-Room School (P)

*Sauk Rapids*, One-Room School (P)
*Saum*, Saum School (NR, M)
*Shakopee*, Shakopee Parochial School (LH)
*Spencer Brook*, Isanti School, District No. 1 (NR, P)
*Stillwater*, One-Room School (P)
*Tamarac Wildlife Refuge*, One-Room School (P)
*Taylors Falls*, One-Room School (P)
*Thief River Falls*, Little Oak School, District No. 221 (M)
*Tyler*, One-Room School (P)
*Vasa*, One-Room School (P)
*Vesta*, One-Room School (P)
*Walker*, Log School (M)
*Warren*, Cook School (M)
*Waseca*, One-Room School (P)
*Wasioja*, One-Room School (P)
*Waterford*, Waterford School, District No. 72 (NR, C)
*Webster*, Webster School (C)
*Wells*, District No. 40 School (NR, C)
*Williams*, One-Room School (P)
*Willmar*, One-Room School (P)
*Winton*, One-Room School (P)
*Worthington*, One-Room School (P)
*Zumbrota*, District No. 30 School (M)

## Mississippi

*Richland*, Eureka Masonic College (Rob Morris Little Red Schoolhouse) (NR)

## Missouri

*Altenburg*, Concordia Log Cabin College (NR)
*Canton*, Lincoln School (NR)
*High Hill*, High Hill School (NR)
*Maryville*, Hickory Grove School, Northwest Missouri State College
*New Lebanon*, New Lebanon Cumberland Presbyterian Church and School (NR)
*Steelville*, Big Bend Rural School (NR)

## Montana

*Alzada*, Albion School, Alzada School, Ridge School (all T)
*Angela*, Sutherland School, Tree Coulee School (both T)
*Baker*, Fertile Prairie School (T)
*Belgrade*, Pass Creek School, Reese Creek School, Sedan School, Springhill School (all NR)
*Biddle*, Biddle School (T)
*Big Sandy*, Warrick School (T)
*Birney*, Birney School (T)

*Bozeman*, Cottonwood School (T), Lower Bridger School (NR), Malmborg School (NR, T), Pine Butte School (NR), Rea School (NR), Springhill School (T)
*Brady*, Knees School (T)
*Browning*, Croff Wren School (T)
*Brusett*, Blackfoot School, Pine Grove School (both T)
*Busby*, Big Bend Elementary School (T)
*Bynum*, Miller Colony School (T)
*Camp Crook*, Plainview School (T)
*Canyon Creek*, Trinity School (T)
*Carter*, Carter School (T)
*Chinook*, Cleveland School (T)
*Choteau*, New Rockport Colony School (T)
*Cooke City*, Cooke City School (T)
*Cut Bank*, Big Sky Hutterite Colony School, Glacier Hutterite School (both T)
*Decker*, Squirrel Creek Elementary School (T)
*Dodson*, Landusky School (T)
*Fallon*, Amo School (T)
*Floweree*, Benton Lake School (T)
*Gallatin Gateway*, Anderson School, Cottonwood School, Spanish Creek School (all NR)
*Gildford*, Gildford Colony School (T)
*Glasgow*, Faranuf School (T)
*Goldcreek*, Goldcreek School (T)
*Grassrange*, Ayers School (T)
*Great Falls*, Deep Creek School (T)
*Greenough*, Sunset School (T)
*Hammond*, Hammond School, Johnston School (both T)
*Hardin*, Blackwood-Halfway School, Big Horn County Historical Museum and Visitor Center
*Harlem*, North Harlem Colony School (T)
*Havre*, Davey School (T)
*Hilger*, Hilger School (T)
*Ismay*, Cottonwood School (T)
*Jordan*, Big Dry School, Cat Creek School, Kester School, Van Norman School (all T)
*Lambert*, Three Buttes School (T)
*Larslan*, Larslan School (T)
*Ledger*, Nickol School (T)
*Lewistown*, Brooks School, Cottonwood School, Deerfield Colony School, King Colony School, Spring Creek Colony School (all T)
*Lindsay*, Union School (T)
*Lloyd*, Ada School, Bear Paw Elementary School, Cow Island Trail Elementary School, Lone Tree Bench School (all T)
*Lodge Grass*, Corral Creek School (T)

*Lolo*, Powell School (T)
*Loring*, Loring Hutterite School (T)
*Malta*, Sun Prairie School, Tallow Creek School (both T)
*Manhattan*, Dry Creek School (NR)
*Marion*, Pleasant Valley School (T)
*Martinsdale*, Lennep School (T)
*Miles City*, Garland School, Hockett Basin School, Moon Creek School, Riverview School, Rock Springs School, S H School, S Y School, Trail Creek School, Twin Buttes School, Whitney Creek School (all T)
*Mill Iron*, Pine Hill School (T)
*Missoula*, Grant Creek School, Fort Missoula Historical Museum (P)
*Mosby*, Ross School (T)
*Nye*, Nye School (T)
*Otter*, Bear Creek School, Billup School (both T)
*Ovando*, Ovando School (T)
*Pendroy*, Pendroy School, Rockport Colony School (both T)
*Plains*, Camas Prairie School (T)
*Polaris*, Polaris Elementary School (T)
*Polson*, Valley View School (T)
*Poplar*, Mineral Bench School (T)
*Powderville*, Powderville School (T)
*Powerville*, Spring Creek School (T)
*Red Lodge*, Jackson Elementary School (T)
*Regina*, Second Creek School (T)
*Ringling*, Ringling School (T)
*Sand Springs*, Benzien School, Sand Springs School (both T)
*Springdale*, Springdale School (C, T)
*Swan Lake*, Salmon Prairie School (T)
*Trident*, Trident School (NR)
*Twodot*, Twodot School (T)
*Volborg*, Horkan Creek School, South Stacey School (both T)
*Wolf Creek*, Craig School (T)
*Wolf Point*, Prairie Elk School (T)
*Zortman*, Zortman School (T)

## Nebraska

*Adams County*, District No. 8 School (T)
*Antelope County*, Districts No. 15, No. 18½, No. 24, No. 35, No. 38, No. 97, No. 114 (all T)
*Arthur County*, Districts No. 1, No. 7, No. 12, No. 33 (all T)
*Auburn*, St. Deroin School (P)
*Aurora*, Old Country School, Plainsman Museum (M)
*Bassett*, One-Room School
*Boone County*, Districts No. 9, No. 13, No. 18, No. 20, No. 39, No. 60 (all T)

*Box Butte County*, Districts No. 16, No. 100, No. 124 (all T)

*Boyd County*, Districts No. 7, No. 40 (both T)

*Bridgeport*, Mud Springs School (NR)

*Broken Bow*, Goose Valley School, Tomahawk Park

*Brown County*, Districts No. 7, No. 13, No. 14, No. 17, No. 19, No. 50, No. 53, No. 65, No. 76 (all T)

*Buffalo County*, Districts No. 45, No. 52, No. 71, No. 80, No. 94 (all T)

*Burt County*, Districts No. 17, No. 21, No. 31, No. 37, No. 43, No. 48, No. 62 (all T)

*Butler County*, Districts No. 1, No. 3, No. 19, No. 24 (all T)

*Cambridge*, Sunny Hillside School, District No. 11

*Cass County*, Districts No. 12, No. 25, No. 30, No. 40, No. 58, No. 79, No. 81, No. 88, No. 96 (all T)

*Cedar County*, Districts No. 11, No. 28, No. 45 (all T)

*Chadron*, Evergreen School (C); Flag Butte School (C); One-Room School, Chadron State College (P)

*Cherry County*, Districts No. 4, No. 26, No. 31, No. 45, No. 61, No. 65, No. 71, No. 78, No. 83, No. 100, No. 101, No. 114, No. 117, No. 134, No. 143, No. 167, No. 170, No. 190 (all T)

*Cheyenne County*, Districts No. 14, No. 32, No. 75, No. 77 (all T)

*Clay County*, District No. 72 School (T)

*Colfax County*, Districts No. 1, No. 30, No. 56 (all T)

*Cuming County*, Districts No. 10, No. 14, No. 16, No. 17, No. 19, No. 21, No. 22, No. 31, No. 32, No. 33, No. 34, No. 40, No. 49, No. 72, No. 75 (all T)

*Custer County*, Districts No. 39, No. 96, No. 153, No. 169, No. 234, No 256 (all T)

*Dawes County*, Districts No. 41, No. 44, No. 47, No. 53, No. 69, No. 76, No. 84, No. 92 (all T)

*Dawson County*, Districts No. 12, No. 18, No. 19, No. 21, No. 32, No. 34, No. 44, No 47, No. 48 (all T)

*Dixon County*, Districts No. 4, No. 54, No. 59 (all T)

*Dodge County*, Districts No. 12, No. 24, No. 87 (all T)

*Edison*, District No. 102 School

*Fairbury*, School on the Oregon Trail (P)

*Franklin County*, District No. 9 School (T)

*Garden County*, Districts No. 23, No. 30, No. 33, No. 38 (all T)

*Garfield County*, Districts No. 5, No. 14, No. 21, No. 25 (all T)

*Gosper County*, Bethel District No. 4 School (T)

*Grand Island*, Gibbon School, Stuhr Museum (M)

*Grant County*, Districts No. 7, No. 9 (both T)

*Greeley County*, District No. 28 School (T)

*Hall County*, Districts No. 16, No. 24, No. 31, No. 37, No. 38, No. 51 (all T)

*Harrison*, District No. 7 School (P)

*Hitchcock County*, District No. 023 School (T)

*Holt County*, Districts No. 1, No. 3, No. 4, No. 6, No. 9, No. 10, No. 14, No. 17, No. 18, No. 22, No. 27, No. 35, No. 39, No. 49, No. 53, No. 60, No. 77, No. 81, No. 88, No. 90, No. 92, No. 146, No. 169, No. 205, No. 206, No. 210, No. 228, No. 231, No. 233, No. 238 (all T)

*Howard County*, Districts No. 14, No. 19, No. 21 (all T)

*Jefferson County*, Districts No. 1, No. 47, No. 69 (all T)

*Johnson County*, Districts No. 6, No. 19, No. 23, No. 41, No. 42 (all T)

*Keith County*, Districts No. 9, No. 14, No. 18, No. 22, No. 27 (all T)

*Keya Paha County*, Districts No. 1, No. 3, No. 17, No. 21, No. 49, No. 64, No. 76, No. 81 (all T)

*Lancaster County*, Districts No. 13, No. 38, No. 61, No. 69, No. 109, No. 158 (all T)

*Lewellen*, Ash Hollow School, Ash Hollow State Historical Park (P)

*Lexington*, Reed School, District No. 55

*Lincoln County*, Cunningham School, District No. 113, Nebraska State fairgrounds; Districts No. 31, No. 34, No. 36, No. 98, No. 104, No. 109 (all T)

*McPherson County*, Districts No. 7, No. 9, No. 26, No. 28, No. 69 (all T)

*Madison County*, Districts No. 3, No. 24, No. 34, No. 47, No. 88 (all T)

*Merrick County*, Districts No. 2, No. 15, No. 50 (all T)

*Minden*, Harold Warp School, Pioneer Village (M)

*Morrill County*, Districts No. 5, No. 44 (both T)

*Nance County*, Districts No. 2, No. 7, No. 11, No. 13, No. 18, No. 25, No. 28, No. 55 (all T)

*Nemaha County*, Districts No. 6, No. 18, No. 21, No. 32 (all T)

*Nuckolls County*, Districts No. 36, No. 52 (all T)

*Ogallala*, District No. 7 School (T)

*Osceola*, District No. 17 School, History Village (M)

*Otoe County*, Camp Creek School, District No. 54 (NR, T); Districts No. 1, No. 2, No. 11, No. 13, No. 17, No. 18, No. 20, No. 30, No. 31, No. 36, No. 37, No. 52, No. 53, No. 74, No. 78 (all T)

*Oxford*, Midway School, District No. 76, Harlan County Museum (M)

*Pierce County*, Districts No. 6, No. 36, No. 46, No. 55 (all T)

*Platte County*, Districts No. 17, No. 29, No. 40 (all T)

*Polk County*, District No. 28 School (T)

*Powell*, District No. 10 School (NR)

*Red Willow County*, Districts No. 004, No. 008, No. 031, No. 042 (all T)

*Rock County*, Districts No. 1, No. 55, No. 77 (all T)

*Saline County*, Districts No. 1, No. 11, No. 18, No. 25, No. 31, No. 57, No. 87, No. 88, No. 100 (all T)

*Sarpy County*, District No. 22 (T)

*Saunders County*, Districts No. 3, No. 5, No. 18, No. 19, No. 23, No. 24, No. 34, No. 36, No. 51, No. 54, No. 74, No. 75, No. 87, No. 91, No. 111, No. 115, No. 118 (all T)

*Seward County*, District No. 24 School (T)

*Sheridan County*, Districts No. 22, No. 27, No. 32, No. 35, No. 36, No. 43, No. 62, No. 64, No. 75, No. 78, No. 85, No. 88, No. 96, No. 100, No. 119, No. 122, No. 127, No. 131, No. 133, No. 141, No. 154 (all T)

*Sherman County*, Districts No. 2, No. 4, No. 14, No. 32, No. 73 (all T)

*Sioux County*, Districts No. 2, No. 6, No. 12, No. 14, No. 23, No. 43, No. 46, No. 48, No. 51, No. 65, No. 68, No. 73 (all T)

*Stanton County*, Districts No. 2, No. 10, No. 13, No. 14, No. 19, No. 28, No. 30, No. 31, No. 35, No. 36, No. 55, No. 81 (all T)

*Thurston County*, District No. 15 School (T)

*Valley County*, Districts No. 6, No. 19, No. 26, No. 29, No. 32, No. 56 (all T)

*Washington County*, District No. 31 School (T)

*Wayne County*, McCorkindale School, Wayne State College (P); Districts No. 5, No. 15, No. 33, No. 45, No. 47, No. 68, No. 76, No. 77 (all T)

*York County*, District No. 73 School (T)

## Nevada

*Denio*, Denio Elementary School (T)
*Duckwater*, Duckwater Elementary School (T)
*Elko*, Francis C. Kellar School (T)
*Fallon*, Harmon School (C)
*Goodsprings*, Goodsprings School (T)
*Jiggs*, Jiggs School, Mound Valley Elementary School (T)
*Mina*, Mina Elementary School (T)
*O'Neal*, O'Neal Elementary School (T)
*Orovada*, King's River Elementary School (T)
*Paradise Valley*, Montero School, Leonard Creek Ranch (T)
*Reno*, Glendale School (NR)
*Searchlight*, Searchlight School (T)
*Tuscarora*, Independence Valley Elementary School (T)
*Winnemucca*, Jackson Mountain Elementary School (T)
*Yerington*, East Walker School, Lyon County Museum (M)

## New Hampshire

*Alend*, Village School (T)
*Croydon*, Croydon School (T)
*Effingham*, Effingham Elementary School (T)
*Enfield*, Lockohaven Schoolhouse Museum (M)
*Hebron*, Village School (T)
*Landaff*, Landaff Blue School (T)
*Madison*, Madison School, District No. 1 (NR)
*Nelson*, Nelson Schoolhouse (NR)
*New Market*, Stone School (NR)
*Newport*, Little Red School House, District No. 7 (NR)
*Richmond*, Richmond School House, District No. 6 (NR)
*Stoddard*, Stoddard Central School (T)
*Waterville Valley*, Waterville Valley School (T)

## New Jersey

*Bridgeboro*, Schoolhouse (NR)
*Columbia*, Fairview School House (NR)
*Cranbury*, Old Cranbury School (NR)
*Florham Park*, Little Red Schoolhouse (NR)
*Freehold*, Ardena School, District No. 2 (NR)
*Hamburg*, Monroe Schoolhouse (NR, LH)
*Lyndhurst*, Little Red Schoolhouse (NR)
*Millville*, Centre Grove School, Wheaton Village (M)
*Morristown*, Flocktown School
*Newark*, Old Stone Schoolhouse (Lyons Farm Schoolhouse) (LH)

*Old Bridge*, Cedar Grove School (NR), Thomas Warne Museum School (M)
*Paramus*, Midland School
*Red Bank*, Union Schoolhouse (NR)
*Smithville*, Gravelly Run Schoolhouse, Pershing School (both M)
*Washington Valley*, Washington Valley Schoolhouse (NR)

## New Mexico

*Counselors*, Largo Canyon Elementary School (T)
*Garita*, Conchas Dam Elementary School (T)
*Jicarilla*, Jicarilla Schoolhouse, Lincoln National Forest
*Las Vegas*, Trementina Elementary School (T)
*Red River*, Red River Schoolhouse

## New York

*Burlington Flats*, The Flats School, District No. 3 (C)
*Cicero*, Stone Arabia School
*Cooperstown*, Center Valley School, District No. 13 (C); District No. 1 Schoolhouse, Old Schoolhouse Museum (M); Thomas Filer School, Farmers' Museum (M); Sand Hill School, District No. 8 (C); Whigs Corner School, District No. 6 (C)
*Corning*, Browntown Schoolhouse
*Dryden*, Eight Square School, District No. 5 (LH)
*East Campbell*, Red Schoolhouse, District No. 5
*Eastchester*, Marble School Museum (M)
*Essex*, Octagonal Schoolhouse (NR)
*Exeter Center*, Exeter Center School, District No. 2 (C)
*Garrattsville*, Garrattsville School, District No. 2 (C)
*Geneva*, Ansley School (LH)
*New City*, English Church and Schoolhouse (NR)
*North Greenbush*, North Greenbush Common School (T)
*Sagaponack*, Sagaponack Elementary School (T)
*Sheridan*, Sheridan School, District No. 3 (NR)
*Sodus*, Wallington Cobblestone School
*Wainscott*, Wainscott Elementary School (T)

## North Carolina

*Oaks*, Bingham School
*Salisbury*, Ebenezer Academy (M)

## North Dakota

*Amidon*, Conner School (T)
*Bismarck*, Manning School (T)
*Bowman*, Cottage Elementary School (T)
*Cartwright*, Horse Creek School (T)
*Cleveland*, Windsor School (T)
*Edgeley*, Edgeley Elementary School (T)
*Flasher*, Oak Coulee School (T)
*Grand Forks*, Blooming Township Hall and School, Myra Museum (M); Rye School, District No. 25 (T)
*Inkster*, Forest River Colony (T)
*McLeod*, Salund School (T)
*Mandan*, Sweet Briar School, District No. 1 (T)
*Medora*, Connell School, Myers School, Pelisser School, Snow School, Whitetail School (all T)
*Milnor*, Sundale Colony School (T)
*Minot*, Kottke Valley, District No. 4, McHenry County fairgrounds
*Pleasant Lake*, Broken Bone School (C)
*Rhame*, Mud Butte School (T)
*Rugby*, Juanita School and Silia School, Geographical Center of the United States Museum, Old Thresher's Museum (both M)
*Sidney*, Leland School, Plainview School, Squaw Gap School, Stevenson School (all T)
*Wahpeton*, Center School, District No. 4, Richland County Historical Museum (M)
*Wilton*, Grass Lake School, District No. 3 (T)

## Ohio

*Akron*, Old Stone School (LH)
*Archbold*, District No. 16 School, Sauder Farm and Craft Village (M)
*Ashland*, Anderson School House (NR)
*Berea*, Berea School, District No. 7 (NR)
*Bowling Green*, District No. 6 School, Bowling Green State University (M)
*Bryan*, Hay-Jay School (P)
*Chesterland*, Chester Township School, District No. 2 (NR, M); Ferry School, District No. 4 (C)
*Clairsville*, Great Western Schoolhouse (NR)
*Clarksville*, Pansy School, District No. 7 (NR)
*Claysville*, Claysville School (NR)
*Cleveland Heights*, East School, District No. 9 (NR)
*Defiance*, Cherry School, AuGlaize Village (M)
*Findlay*, Little Red School House (P)
*Georgetown*, President Grant's Schoolhouse (M)

*Greenville*, Beehive School (NR)
*Hamilton*, Hughes School (NR)
*Indian Hill*, Jefferson Schoolhouse (NR)
*Isle St. George*, North Bass Local School (T)
*Jeromesville*, Lakefort School (NR)
*Kelly's Island*, Kelly's Island Local School (T)
*Mayfield*, Old Center School (NR)
*Middleburg Heights*, Old District No. 10 Schoolhouse (NR)
*New Philadelphia*, Schoenbrunn Schoolhouse, Schoenbrunn Village (P)
*Norwich*, West Union School (NR)
*Sugar Grove*, Crawfis Institute (NR)
*Willoughby*, Little Red School House
*Willshire*, Willshire School (NR)
*Wintersville*, Bantam Ridge School (NR, M)

## Oklahoma

*Broken Bow*, Tiner School (NR, C)
*Henryetta*, Wilson School (NR)
*Kingfisher*, Gant Schoolhouse, Chisholm Trail Museum (M)
*McAlester*, Bugtussle School House (C)
*Marble City*, Dwight Mission School (NR)
*Perry*, Rose Hill School, Cherokee Strip Museum (M)
*Stillwater*, Stillwater School (NR, C)

## Oregon

*Agness*, Agness School, District No. 4 (T)
*Antelope*, Antelope School, District No. 50J (T)
*Ashwood*, Ashwood School, District No. 8 (T)
*Brogan*, Brogan School, District No. 1 (T)
*Burns*, Andrews School, District No. 29; Double O School, District No. 28 (both T)
*Burnt River*, Burnt River School (C)
*Clackamas*, Damascus School (NR)
*Enterprise*, Troy School, District No. 54 (T)
*Frenchglen*, Frenchglen School, District No. 16 (T)
*Jordan Valley*, Pleasant Valley Elementary School (T)
*Keating*, Keating School, District No. 5J (T)
*Lawen*, Lawen School (T)
*Mehama*, Mehama School (T)
*Olex*, Olex School (NR)
*Plush*, Plush School (T)

*Princeton*, Sodhouse School; Steens Mountain School, District No. 33 (both T)
*Riley*, Suntex School, District No. 10 (T)
*Shaniko*, Shaniko School (C)
*Stephens*, Calaphonia School (C)

## Pennsylvania

*Ardmore*, Old Dutch Schoolhouse
*Brockway*, Wray School (M)
*Chambersburg*, Old Brown's Mill School (NR)
*Coatesville*, Six-Sided Schoolhouse
*Haverford*, Federal School (NR, P)
*Lancaster*, Weavertown One-Room Schoolhouse (P)
*Landis Valley*, Maple Grove School, Pennsylvania Farm Museum (M)
*Lewistown*, Old Hoopes School (NR)
*Milford*, Schocopee School (P)
*Montandon*, Sodom Schoolhouse (NR, P)
*Mooresburg*, Mooresburg One-Room School (M)
*South Canaan*, Stone Jug School (NR)
*Strafford*, Eagle School
*Wayne*, Diamond Rock School (NR, P)
*West Chester*, Octagonal School, Birmingham Friends Meetinghouse (NR, P)
*Wrightstown*, Cedar Grove School (Wrightstown Octagonal School House)
*York*, Little Red Schoolhouse Museum

## Rhode Island

*Burrillville*, Joseph C. Sweeny School (P)
*Charlestown*, School House, District No. 2 (M)
*Coventry*, Read Schoolhouse (NR, M)
*East Providence*, District No. 6 Schoolhouse (NR)
*Exeter*, Hall School, Woody Hill School (both M)
*Middletown*, Paradise School (M)
*North Smithfield*, Forestdale School (M)
*Portsmouth*, Prudence Park School
*Potterville*, Potterville School (C)
*Richmond*, Bell School (M)
*West Greenwich*, Loutitt School (C)

## South Carolina

*Daufuskie Island*, Daufuskie Island School, District No. 109; Janie Hamilton School; May Field School; One-Room School (all NR)
*Frogmore*, Penn School (NR)

## South Dakota

*Agar*, East Cora School, Prairie View School (both T)
*Alexandria*, Millbrook Colony School (T)
*Batesland*, Oglala Community School, Porcupine School (both T)
*Beresford*, Brule School (T)
*Bison*, Union School (T)
*Buffalo*, Cox School, Govert School, Lincoln School, Ludlow School, Norbeck School (all T)
*Chamberlain*, America School, Cooper School, Lindley School, Ola School, Prairie Center School, Pukwana School, Roosevelt School (all T)
*Custer*, Cold Springs Schoolhouse, Black Hills National Forest (NR); Fairburn School (T), Spring Creek School (T)
*Delmont*, Delmont Junior High School, Greenwood Colony School (both T)
*Eureka*, Eureka Pioneer Museum School (M)
*Faith*, Cottonwood School (T)
*Faulkton*, Seneca School (T)
*Flandreau*, Jones School, District No. 60
*Fort Pierre*, Orton School, New Liberty School (both T)
*Frankfort*, Dieter School House, Fisher Grove State Park (P)
*Freeman*, Tschetter Colony School, Wolf Creek Colony School (both T)
*Gregory*, Gregory Schoolhouse
*Hettinger*, Ellingson School, Fredlund School, Sidney School, Swanson School (all T)
*Highmore*, Illinois School, Washington School (both T)
*Hill City*, Keystone School (T)
*Hot Springs*, Maitland School (T)
*Hoven*, Fayette School, Sanner School (both T)
*Huron*, Huron Colony School (T)
*Ipswich*, Rosette Colony School (T)
*Iroquois*, Pearl Creek Colony School (T)
*Kimball*, Lyons School, Maresh School, Pershing School (all T)
*Lead*, Nemo School (T)
*Lemmon*, Athboy School, Center School, Progress School (all T)
*Madison*, Prairie Village School (P)
*Menno*, Jamesville Colony School, Maxwell Colony School (both T)
*Miller*, Cedar School, Como School, Millerdale School (all T)
*Mission*, Happy Valley School, Klein School (both T)
*Mitchell*, Sanborn County Territorial School, Friends of the Middle Border Museum (M)

*Mobridge*, Klein Museum School (M)
*Newell*, Twilight School (T)
*Oelrichs*, Smithwick School (T)
*Parker*, Pioneer Museum School, Frontier Village (M)
*Parkston*, Washington School (T)
*Philip*, Alfalfa Valley School, Cheyenne School, Hart School, King School, Lincoln School, Old Trail School (all T), West River Museum School (M)
*Pierre*, Mentor School, Raber School (both T)
*Platte*, Carroll School, Castalia School, Cedar Grove School, Torrey Lake (all T)
*Rosholt*, White Rock Colony School (T)
*Sioux Falls*, Grinde School, District No. 52, W. H. Lyons Fairgrounds (LH)
*Sturgis*, Atall School, Elm Springs School, Fairpoint School, Hope School, Wetz School (all T)
*Tabor*, Fenanga-Hockey-Hilland School
*Tulare*, Spink Colony School (T)
*Tyndall*, Hutterische Colony School (T)
*Wall*, Big Foot School, North Creighton School, Pleasant Ridge School, Scenic School, Wasta School, White School (all T)
*Wessington Springs*, Fagerhaug School
*White River*, Big White School, Ringthunder School, Running Bird School (all T)
*Winner*, Beaver Creek School, Bijou School, Eden School, Greenwood School, King School, New Brunson School, N.W. Crystal Rose School, Pioneer Pocahontas School, Plainview School, Rielly School, Star Valley School, Weaver School (all T)
*Yankton*, Dakota Territorial Museum School (M)

## Tennessee

*Maryville*, Sam Houston School House (NR)

## Texas

*Austin*, Esperanza School (C)
*Carta Valley*, Carta Valley Independent School (T)
*Comfort*, Cypress Creek School (C)
*Dallas*, Renner School (P)
*Del Rio*, Juno Common School (T)
*East Bernard*, East Bernard School (C)
*Grason*, Cold Springs Log Cabin School (M)
*Kennard*, Rosenwald School (T)
*Kerrville*, Divide Common School (T)
*Leesville*, Leesville School House (NR)

*Lubbock*, Bairfield School, Ranching Heritage Center, Texas Tech University (M)
*Luckenbach*, Luckenbach School (C)
*Marathon*, Pioneer Schoolhouse (C)
*Mesquite*, Oates School (C)
*New Braunfels*, Church Hill School (C)
*San Angelo*, Fort Concho School (M)
*Sierra Blanca*, Allamoore Common School (T)

## Utah

*Antimony*, Antimony Elementary School (T)
*Boulder*, Boulder Elementary School (C)
*Cedar Valley*, Cedar Valley Elementary School (T)
*Garrison*, Garrison Elementary School (T)
*Grass Valley*, New Castle School (C)
*Ibapah*, Ibapah Elementary School (T)
*Park Valley*, Park Valley School
*Pleasant Grove*, Old Bell School (NR, M)

## Vermont

*Baltimore*, Baltimore School (T)
*Bartonsville*, Athens School (T)
*Belvidere*, Belvidere Central (T)
*Bennington*, Grandma Moses Schoolhouse, Bennington Museum (M)
*Brookline*, Brookline Union School (T)
*Castleton*, Hydeville School (NR)
*Goulds Mill*, Eureka Schoolhouse (NR)
*Granby*, Granby Central School (T)
*Granville*, Granville School (T)
*Guildhall*, Guildhall Elementary School (T)
*Lyndonville*, Squabble Hollow School (T)
*Manchester*, District No. 10 School (P)
*Norton*, Norton Village School (T)

## Virginia

*Leesburg*, Mountain Gap School, Oatlands (M)

## Washington

*Connell*, Star Elementary School (T)
*Curlew*, Curlew School (NR)
*Decatur Island*, Decatur Elementary School (T)
*Ellensburg*, Damman Elementary School (T)
*Hazelmere*, Hazelmere Elementary School (T)
*Leavenworth*, Winton Elementary School (T)

*Shaw Island*, Shaw Island Elementary School (Little Red Schoolhouse) (NR, T)
*Stehekin*, Stehekin Elementary School (T)
*Vernita*, Vernita Elementary School (T)
*Wilkeson*, Wilkeson School (NR)

## West Virginia

*Auburn*, Auburn School (T)
*Capon Springs*, Willow Chapel Schoolhouse
*Daybrook*, Fort Martin School
*Fairmont*, Snodgrass School, Fairmont State College (M)
*Fort New Salem*, Log Meeting Home and School
*Gassaway*, One-Room School, Chapel Community (C)
*Mount Heights*, Sarver School
*Telsa*, Windy Run School
*Volga*, Campbell School (P)

## Wisconsin

*Albion*, Sheepskin School (P)
*Berlin*, Clark School
*Brown Deer*, Little White Schoolhouse (P)
*Cameron*, Joliet School, Barron County Historical Museum (M)
*Cassville*, Stonefield School, Nelson Dewey State Park (P)
*Cooksville*, Cooksville Historic District Schoolhouse (NR)
*Dodgeville*, Old Rock School (NR)
*Eagle*, Ward Schoolhouse, District No. 3 (NR)
*Eau Claire*, Sunnyview School, Carson Park (M)
*Florence*, Fern School (NR)
*Fond du Lac*, Willow Lawn School, Historic Galloway House and Village (M)
*Franklin*, Whelan School, Legend Park (P)
*Fredonia*, Stoney Hill School (NR)
*Galesville*, One-Room School, Trempealeau County fairgrounds (M)
*Gotham*, Akey School (P)
*Janesville*, Frances Willard Schoolhouse (NR, M)
*La Crosse*, Glascow School, District No. 5 (C); Smith Valley School (NR)
*Ladysmith*, Little Red Schoolhouse, Rusk County fairgrounds (M)
*Lake Mills*, One-Room School, Lake Mills-Aztalan Historical Society Museum (M)
*Menomonee Falls*, Old Falls Village Schoolhouse (P)

*Monroe*, Green County Historical Museum and Little Red Schoolhouse (M)
*Prairie du Chien*, Old Rock School (NR)
*Red Springs*, Lutheran Indian Mission (NR)
*Ripon*, Little White (Republican) School House (NR)
*Saint Nazianz*, Old District School (P)
*Shawano*, One-Room School and Log Cabin (P)
*Sparta*, One-Room School
*Viroqua*, One-Room School
*Watertown*, First Kindergarten School (NR, M)
*Weyauwega*, Little Red Schoolhouse (P)

## Wyoming

*Alcova*, Lower Bates Creek School
*Arminto*, Arminto School (M)
*Arvada*, Arvada School (T)
*Atlantic City*, Atlantic City Elementary School (T)
*Bondurant*, Bondurant Elementary School (T)
*Buffalo*, Billy Creek Elementary School (T)
*Casper*, Freeland School (C), Red Creek Elementary School (T)
*Cheyenne*, One-Room School, Laramie County fairgrounds (M)
*Clearmont*, Hanging Woman Elementary School (T)
*Cody*, Irma Flats School (C), Valley School (NR)
*Crowheart*, Crowheart Elementary School (T)
*Douglas*, Dry Creek Elementary School, Moss Agate Elementary School, Ogallala Elementary School, Reynolds Elementary School, Wagonhound Elementary School, White Elementary School (all T)

*Gillette*, Cactus Elementary School (T)
*Glenrock*, Boxelder School (T)
*Green River*, Thomas Ranch Elementary School (T)
*Greybull*, Lower Shell Schoolhouse (NR, P, T)
*Hamilton Dome*, Hamilton Dome Elementary School (T)
*Horse Creek*, Ingleside Elementary School (T)
*Huntley*, Table Mountain Community Schoolhouse (C)
*Kaycee*, Willow Creek Elementary School (T)
*Laramie*, Valley View Elementary School (T)
*Lusk*, Central School (M)
*Newcastle*, Cheyenne River Elementary School, Seven Mile Elementary School (both T)
*Oshoto*, Nebraska Elementary School (T)
*Parkman*, Slack Elementary School (T)
*Riverton*, DelFelder Schoolhouse (NR), Gas Hills Elementary School (T)
*Rock River*, River Bridge Elementary School (T)
*Shawnee*, Shawnee School (C)
*Slater*, Slater School (P)
*South Pass City*, South Pass School (C)
*Storey*, Kearney School (T)
*Wheatland*, Cottonwood Elementary School, Palmer Elementary School (both T)

## Historic One-Room Schools of the National Park Service

*Beatrice, Neb.*, Freeman School, Homestead National Monument (M)
*Elkmont, Tenn.*, Little Greenbrier School and Church, Great Smoky Mountains National Park (M)
*Johnson City, Tex.*, Junction School, Lyndon B. Johnson National Historic Site (P)
*Montague, N.J.*, Neldon-Roberts Schoolhouse, Delaware Water Gap National Recreation Area (M, C)
*Peninsula, Ohio*, Everett Schoolhouse, Cuyahoga Valley National Recreation Area (P)
*Torrey, Utah*, Fruita Schoolhouse, Capitol Reef National Monument (M)
*West Branch, Iowa*, West Branch School, Herbert Hoover National Historic Site (P)

## One-Teacher Schools, 1983–84

| | |
|---|---|
| Alaska | 28 |
| Arizona | 12 |
| California | 41 |
| Colorado | 3 |
| Florida | 1 |
| Idaho | 23 |
| Kansas | 1 |
| Kentucky | 1 |
| Maine | 13 |
| Maryland | 1 |
| Michigan | 17 |
| Mississippi | 1 |
| Montana | 99 |
| Nebraska | 385 |
| Nevada | 12 |
| New Hampshire | 7 |
| New Mexico | 3 |
| New York | 3 |
| North Dakota | 25 |
| Ohio | 2 |
| Oregon | 15 |
| South Dakota | 87 |
| Texas | 4 |
| Utah | 3 |
| Vermont | 9 |
| Washington | 8 |
| West Virginia | 2 |
| Wyoming | 31 |

# Bibliography

## Country Schools in American Education

Agee, James. *Let Us Now Praise Famous Men*. New York: Houghton Mifflin, 1941.

American Association of School Administrators. *Schools in Small Communities*. Washington, D.C.: National Education Association, 1939.

American Country Life Association. *Standards of Living*. Proceedings of the 13th American Country Life Conference, Madison, Wis., October 7–10, 1930. Chicago: University of Chicago Press, 1931.

Bursch, Charles. "Survey of Schoolhousing Adequacy in California Elementary School Districts Not Administered by City Superintendents of Schools." Bulletin No. 5. Sacramento: State of California Department of Education, 1938.

Carney, Mabel. *Country Life and the Country School*. Chicago: Row, Peterson and Company, 1912.

Cremin, Lawrence A. *American Education: The National Experience, 1783–1876*. New York: Harper and Row, 1980.

———. *Traditions of American Education*. New York: Basic Books, 1977.

———. *The Transformation of the School: Progressivism in American Education*. New York: Vintage Books, Random House, 1964.

Cubberly, Ellwood P. *Rural Life and Education*. Cambridge: Riverside Press, Houghton Mifflin, 1914.

Foght, H. W. "Rural Education." Bulletin No. 7. Bureau of Education, U.S. Department of the Interior. Washington, D.C.: Government Printing Office, 1919.

Fuller, Wayne E. *The Old Country School*. Chicago: University of Chicago Press, 1982.

Gaumnitz, Walter H., and Blose, David T. "The One-Teacher School: Its Midcentury Status." Circular No. 318. Washington, D.C.: Government Printing Office, 1950.

Goodman, L. V., ed. *A Nation of Learners*. Washington, D.C.: Government Printing Office, 1976.

Hartford, Ellis Ford. *The Little White Schoolhouse*. Lexington: University Press of Kentucky, 1977.

Johnson, Clifton. *Old-Time Schools and School Books*. 1904. Reprint. New York: Dover, 1963.

Kaestle, Carl F. *Pillars of the Republic: Common Schools and American Society, 1780–1860*. New York: Hill and Wang, 1983.

Loeper, John J. *Going to School in 1776*. New York: Atheneum, 1980.

MacDonald, N. C. "A Square Deal for the Country Boy." Proceedings of the 25th Annual Session of the North Dakota Education Association, Fargo, N.D., November 1–3, 1911. Bismarck: North Dakota Department of Public Instruction, 1911.

Miley, Jess W. "Cracker Box Schools and Suitcase Teachers Are Depriving Country Children of the Education They Deserve." *Country Gentleman*, October 4, 1924.

Sargent, C. G. *The Rural and Village Schools of Colorado*. Fort Collins: Colorado Agricultural College, 1914.

Sher, Jonathan P., ed. *Education in Rural America: A Reassessment of Conventional Wisdom*. Boulder, Colo.: Westview Press, 1977.

Wilkinson, William A. *Rural School Management*. New York: Silver Burdett Company, 1917.

## The Four Rs: Reading, Writing, Arithmetic, Recitation

Arnold, Verda. *Our Yesterdays*. Maceline, Mo.: Pishel Yearbooks, Inc., 1970.

Arnow, Harriet Simpson. *Mountain Path*. 1936. Reprint. Berea, Ky.: Council of the Southern Mountains, 1963.

Burton, Warren. *The District School As It Was by One Who Went to It*. Boston: Carter, Hendee and Company, 1833.

Carpenter, Charles. *History of American Schoolbooks*. Philadelphia: University of Pennsylvania Press, 1963.

Colburn, Warren. *Intellectual Arithmetic.* New York: Hurd and Houghton, 1863.

Cubberly, Ellwood P. *Public Education in the United States.* Boston: Houghton Mifflin, 1934.

Cutter, Calvin. *Anatomy, Physiology and Hygiene.* Boston: Mussey, 1853.

Dilworth, Thomas. *Schoolmaster's Assistant.* 1743. 3rd ed. London: H. Kent, 1746.

Eggleston, Edward. *The Hoosier Schoolmaster.* 1871. Reprint. New York: Regents Publisher, 1974.

Eickoff, Rosa Lee. "A Selected Bibliography of Children's Books and Textbooks Used in Kansas Schools, 1875–1900." Unpublished manuscript, 1978. Fort Hays State University, Hays, Kans.

Elson, Ruth Miller. *Guardians of Tradition: American Schoolbooks of the Nineteenth Century.* Lincoln: University of Nebraska Press, 1964.

Finklestein, Barbara. "Pedagogy as Intrusion: Teaching Values in Popular Primary Schools in Nineteenth Century America." *History of Childhood Quarterly*, Winter 1975.

Ford, Paul Leicester. *The New England Primer.* 1760. Reprint. New York: Teachers College Press, Columbia University, 1962.

Goodrich, Samuel. *The Tales of Peter Parley About America.* 1828. Reprint. New York: Dover, 1974.

Greenwood, Isaac. *Arithmetic, Vulgar and Decimal.* Boston: S. Kneeland and T. Green for T. Hancock, 1729.

Haack, Paul, and Heller, George N. "Music, Education, and Community in Nineteenth Century Kansas, Euterpe, Tonnies, and the Academy on the Plains." Unpublished manuscript, 1981. Country School Legacy Collection, Kansas State Historical Society.

Johnson, Clifton. *Old-Time Schools and Schoolbooks.* 1904. Reprint. New York: Dover, 1963.

Lutes, Della. *Country Schoolma'am.* Boston: Little, Brown, 1941.

McGuffey, William Holmes. *McGuffey's Eclectic Readers.* 1836. Reprint. New York: American Book Company, 1921.

Martin, Almira, M. D. "Resolved that Reading and Writing and Other Subjects of Study Should Be Deferred Until the Third Grade," *Utah Educational Review.* January-February 1903.

May, Bill. Letter to author, September 13, 1980, and unpublished manuscript. Country School Legacy Collection, Western Historical Collections, University of Colorado, Boulder.

Morgan, Ruth, ed. *Memoirs of South Dakota Retired Teachers.* Stickney, S.D.: Argus Printers, 1976.

Nietz, John. *Old Textbooks.* Pittsburgh: University of Pittsburgh Press, 1961.

Palmer, A. N. *Palmer's Guide to Business Writing.* Cedar Rapids, Iowa: Western Penmanship Publishing Company, 1894.

Pike, Nicholas. *New and Complete System of Arithmetic.* Newburyport, Mass.: John Mycall, 1788.

Randall, S. S. *A Digest of the Common School System of the State of New York.* Albany: C. Van Benthuysen and Company, 1844.

Scott, William. *Lessons in Elocution.* 1785. Philadelphia: William Long, 1790.

Soltow, Lee, and Stevens, Edward. *The Rise of Literacy and the Common School in the United States.* Chicago: University of Chicago Press, 1981.

Spencer, Platt Rogers. *The Spencerian Key to Practical Penmanship.* New York: Ivison, Phinney, Blakeman and Company, 1866.

Towne, George, ed. *The Nebraska Teacher.* Lincoln: State Department of Education and State Teachers Association, 1906.

Towne, Salem. *The Child's First Reader.* 1848. Reprint. Livermore Falls, Maine: Washburn-Norlands Foundation, 1977.

———. *The Second Reader.* 1853. Reprint. Livermore Falls, Maine: Washburn-Norlands Foundation, 1978.

Webster, Noah. *The Elementary Spelling Book.* 1855. Reprint. New York: American Book Company, 1880.

Westerhoff, John H. *McGuffey and His Readers: Piety, Morality and Education in Nineteenth Century America.* Nashville: Abingdon Press, 1978.

Worcester, Samuel. *A Primer of the English Language for the Use of Families and Schools.* Boston: Jenks and Palmer, 1826.

## Teachers' Lives on the Western Frontier

Ainsworth Area Retired Teachers Association. *The Sway of the School Bell: Schools and Histories of Brown, Keya Paha, and Rock Counties Nebraska.* Ainsworth, Neb.: Bicentennial Committee, 1976.

Albany County (Wyoming) Cowbelles Club. *Cowbelles Ring Schoolbells: A Brief History of the Rural Schools of Albany County, Wyoming.* Cheyenne, Wyo.: Pioneer Printing Company, 1976.

Beecher, Catharine. *The Duty of American Women to Their Country.* New York: Harper and Brothers, 1845.

Birdick, Hetty. Letter to author, June 10, 1981. Country School Legacy Collection, Western Historical Collections, University of Colorado, Boulder.

Bourne, Eulalia. *Ranch Schoolteacher.* Tucson: University of Arizona Press, 1974.

Brown, Dee. *The Gentle Tamers: Women of the Old Wild West.* 1958. Reprint. Lincoln: University of Nebraska Press, 1981.

Colorado Retired Teachers. *From Inkwell to Ballpoint.* Denver: Colorado Education Association, 1976.

Conger, Robert L. Unpublished manuscript. Country School Legacy Collection, Kearney State College, Kearney, Neb.

Edwards, Elbert. *Maude Frazier: Nevadan.* Las Vegas: Southern Nevada Retired Teachers Association, n.d.

Embry, Jessie. "Schoolmarms of Utah: Separate and Unequal." Unpublished manuscript, 1980. Country School Legacy Collection, Utah State Historical Society.

Feidler, Marie Mynster, ed. *In Retrospect: Teaching in North Dakota. Recollections of Retired Teachers.* Grand Forks: North Dakota Retired Teachers Association, 1976.

Frandsen, Maude Linstrom. Letter to author, February 26, 1981, and unpublished manuscript. Country School Legacy Collection, Western Historical Collections, University of Colorado, Boulder.

Fromong, Terrence D. "The Development of Public Elementary and Secondary Education in Wyoming 1869–1917." Ph.D. diss., University of Wyoming, 1962.

Fuller, Wayne E. "Country Schoolteaching on the Sod-House Frontier." *Arizona and the West,* Summer 1975.

Grady, Frank. "Pioneer Life in Nebraska." WPA Writers Project, Series II, n.d. Special Collections, University Library, University of Nebraska–Omaha.

Hafner, Arabelle Lee. *100 Years on the Muddy.* Springville, Utah: Art City Publications, 1967.

Hanson, Frances, and Strayer, Elizabeth. *A History of Elk Mountain School, Carbon County, Wyo.* Waseca, Minn.: Walters Publishing Company, 1979.

Hockenberry, John Coulter. *The Rural School in the United States.* Westfield, Mass.: Massachusetts State Normal School, 1908.

Jeffrey, Julie Roy. *Frontier Women: The Trans-Mississippi West, 1840–1880.* New York: Hill and Wang, 1979.

Jevne, Louise. *Teachers and Pupils of Van Buren Township, Renville County, North Dakota 1902–1958.* Lansford, N.D.: Author, 1979.

Johnson, Hazel. "Snake in the Class!" *Senior Voice* (Greeley, Colo.), April 1981.

Kaufman, Polly Welts. "A Wider Field of Usefulness: Pioneer Women Teachers in the West, 1848–1854." *Journal of the West,* April 1982.

———. *Women Teachers on the Frontier.* New Haven, Conn.: Yale University Press, 1984.

Lucore, Lois. Unpublished manuscript. Country School Legacy Collection, Western Historical Collections, University of Colorado, Boulder.

Morgan, Ruth, ed. *Memoirs of South Dakota Retired Teachers.* Stickney, S.D.: Argus Printers, 1976.

Nater, Phoebe. *Koshapah.* New York: Vantage Press, 1972.

Neihardt, John G. *All Is But a Beginning: Youth Remembered 1881–1901.* New York: Harcourt Brace Jovanovich, 1972.

Porter, Kenneth Wiggins. "Catherine Emma Wiggins: Pupil and Teacher in Northwest Kansas, 1888–1895." *Kansas History,* Spring 1978.

Reiter, Joan Swallow. *The Women.* Alexandria, Va.: Time-Life Books, 1978.

Rodenberger, Lou. "Sand Tables and One-Eyed Cat: Experiences of Two Texas Schoolteachers." *West Texas Historical Association Yearbook.* Abilene, Tex.: Rupert Richardson Research Center for the Southwest, 1981.

Sandoz, Mari. *Winter Thunder*. Philadelphia: Westminster Press, 1954.

Schrimsher, Lila Gravatt, ed. "The Diary of Anna Webber, May-June 1881." *Kansas Historical Quarterly*, Autumn 1972.

Sikkink, J. A. Letter dated 1923. Country School Legacy Collection, University of South Dakota.

Staudy, Jeanette. Interview with Herbert Blakely, 1980. Country School Legacy Collection, University of South Dakota.

Steinbeck, John. *East of Eden*. New York: Viking Press, 1952.

Stratton, Joanna L. *Pioneer Women: Voices from the Kansas Frontier*. New York: Simon and Schuster, 1981.

Sugg, Redding S. *Motherteacher: The Feminization of American Education*. Charlottesville: University Press of Virginia, 1978.

Toyn, Rhea Paskett. Interview with Verna Richardson, October 21, 1973. Grouse Creek Oral History Project, Utah State Historical Society, Salt Lake City, Utah.

Twitchell, Neil C. Interview with Nancy Cummings, December 8, 1980. Country School Legacy Collection, Nevada Historical Society.

## Country Schools as Community Centers

Aldrich, Bess Streeter. *A Lantern in Her Hand*. New York: Grossett and Dunlap, 1928.

Arnold, Verda. *Our Yesterdays*. Maceline, Mo.: Pishel Yearbooks, Inc., 1970.

Ashworth, Walter V. Letter to author, January 12, 1982, and unpublished manuscript. Country School Legacy Collection, Western Historical Collections, University of Colorado, Boulder.

Baker, Bea. Interview with Robert Barthell, December 29, 1980. Pioneer Home, Thermopolis, Wyo. Country School Legacy Collection, Wyoming State Archives.

Barber, Marshall A. *The Schoolhouse at Prairie View*. Lawrence: University of Kansas Press, 1953.

Daniels, Goldie Piper. *Rural Schools and Schoolhouses of Douglas County, Kansas*. Baldwin City, Kans.: Telegraphics, 1978.

Darien, Margaret. Interview with author, November 12, 1980, Basalt, Colo. Country School Legacy Collection, Western Historical Collections, University of Colorado, Boulder.

Garland, Hamlin. *A Son of the Middle Border*. New York: Macmillan, 1917.

King, Peter. Interview with Robert Barthell, January 31, 1981, Thermopolis, Wyo. Country School Legacy Collection, Wyoming State Archives.

McNulty, John. Interview with author, April 28, 1981, Missouri Heights, Colo. Country School Legacy Collection, University of Colorado, Boulder.

Ogden, Roberta. Interview with Pat O'Neill, June 15, 1981, Debeque, Colo. Country School Legacy Collection, University of Colorado, Boulder.

Peterson-Wood, Helen. "Uncle Johnie, Honey Creek Correspondent, 1895–1903." *Kansas History: A Journal of the Central Plains,* Summer 1980.

Roosevelt, Theodore. *Outdoor Pastimes of an American Hunter*. New York: Charles Scribners' Sons, 1905.

Steinbeck, John. *East of Eden*. New York: Viking Press, 1952.

Stewart, Cora Wilson. *Moonlight Schools for the Emancipation of Adult Illiterates*. New York: E. P. Dutton, 1922.

Warburton, Lillian Grace Chadwick. Interview with Verna Richardson, October 17, 1975. Grouse Creek Oral History Project, Utah State Historical Society, Salt Lake City, Utah.

Zion, Lettie B. *Fairview: True Tales of a Country Schoolhouse*. Oceano, Calif.: Tower Press, 1981.

## Country Schools and the Assimilation Process

Agee, James. *Let Us Now Praise Famous Men*. New York: Houghton Mifflin, 1941.

Bassett, Laura, and Smith, Alice. *Helpful Hints for the Rural Teacher*. Valley City, N.D.: Bassett and Smith, 1924.

Bond, Horace Mann. "A Negro Looks at His South." In *The Negro Caravan*, edited by Sterling A. Brown, Arthur P. Davis and Ulysses Lee. New York: Dryden Press, 1941.

Bourne, Eulalia. *Nine Months Is a Year*. Tucson: University of Arizona Press, 1968.

Brown, Philip. "The Young Citizens League: Its Origins and Development in South Dakota to 1930." *Papers of the Thirteenth Annual Dakota History Conference*, edited by Herbert Blakely. Madison, S.D.: Dakota State College, 1982.

Bullock, Henry Allen. *A History of Negro Education in the South*. Cambridge, Mass.: Harvard University Press, 1967.

Carlson, Robert A. *The Quest for Conformity: Americanization Through Education*. New York: John Wiley and Sons, 1975.

Carney, Mabel. "Desirable Rural Adaptations in the Education of Negroes." *The Journal of Negro Education*, July 1936.

Chittick, Douglas. "A Recipe for Nationality Stew." In *Dakota Panorama*, edited by J. Leonard Jennewein and Jane Boorman. 3rd ed. Sioux Falls, S.D.: Brevet Press, 1973.

Davis, Philip, ed. *Immigration and Americanization*. New York: Ginn and Company, 1920.

DuBois, W. E. B. *The Souls of Black Folk*. Chicago: A. C. McClurg, 1903.

Ehrlich, Clara. "My Prairie Childhood." German-Russian Project, Colorado State University, 1962.

Favrot, Leo M. "How the Small Rural School Can More Adequately Serve Its Community." *The Journal of Negro Education*, July 1936.

Forten, Charlotte. "Life on the Sea Islands." In *The Negro Caravan*, edited by Sterling A. Brown, Arthur P. Davis and Ulysses Lee. New York: Dryden Press, 1941.

Goertz, Rueben. Interview with Randall Teeuwen, December 8, 1980, Greeley, Colo. Country School Legacy Collection, Western Historical Collections, University of Colorado, Boulder.

Hansen, Marcus Lee. *The Immigrant in American History*. Cambridge, Mass.: Harvard University Press, 1940.

Hartmann, Edward George. *The Movement to Americanize the Immigrant*. New York: Columbia University Press, 1948.

Henshaw, Beatrice. "... Like a Diamond in the Sky." *Chronicle: The Magazine of the Historical Society of Michigan*, Summer 1982.

Jones, Laurence C. "A Pictorial History of the Piney Woods Country Life School." Piney Woods, Miss.: Piney Woods School, 1951.

Lind, Mary. Interview with Randall Teeuwen, March 20, 1981, Windsor, Colo. Country School Legacy Collection, Western Historical Collections, University of Colorado, Boulder.

Luebke, Frederick C. "German Immigrants and Parochial Schools." *Issues in Christian Education*, Spring 1967.

————, ed. *Ethnicity on the Great Plains*. Lincoln: University of Nebraska Press, 1980.

Martin, Mattie M. Letter to author, April 10, 1981. Country School Legacy Collection, Western Historical Collections, University of Colorado, Boulder.

Martinez, Escolasticia Salazaar. Interview with Joanne Dodds, October 17, 1980. Country School Legacy Collection, Western History Research Room, Pueblo Library District, Pueblo, Colo.

Mohberg, Nora. *A Home for Agate*. Grafton, N.D.: Record Printer Publishers, 1966.

————. *The Straddlebug*. Grafton, N.D.: Record Printer Publishers, 1977.

Mollhagen, Harry. *In Reminiscence*. Lorraine, Kans.: Author, 1963.

Nielsen, Alfred C. *Life in an American Denmark*. Des Moines: Grand View College, 1962.

Painter, Nell Irvin. *Exodusters: Black Migration to Kansas After Reconstruction*. New York: Alfred A. Knopf, 1977.

Peterson, Carl H. Interview with Mrs. C. H. Ross. WPA Writers Project, Omaha Interview Series, n.d.

Rosengarten, Theodore. *All God's Dangers: The Life of Nate Shaw*. New York: Alfred A. Knopf, 1974.

Rylance, Daniel. "The Country School as an Historic Site and the Movement to Improve Rural Schools in North Dakota." Unpublished manuscript, 1980. Country School Legacy Collection, University of North Dakota.

Sallet, Richard. *Russian-German Settlements in the United States*. Translated by La Vern

Ripley and Armond Bauer. Fargo: North Dakota Institute for Regional Studies, 1974.

Schneider, Solomon. Interview with Randall Teeuwen, September 9, 1981, Fort Collins, Colo. Country School Legacy Collection, Western Historical Collections, University of Colorado, Boulder.

Scott, Irving E. *The Education of Black People in Florida.* Philadelphia: Dorrance and Company, 1974.

Seaman, Alberta E. "Stanley School, Big Piney District, 1926–27." Unpublished manuscript. Country School Legacy Collection, Wyoming State Archives.

Shunk, Harold. Interview with Caroline Hatton, Fall 1980. Country School Legacy Collection, University of South Dakota.

Smitter, Faith. "Needs of Rural Children and Youth in California." California State Department of Education *Bulletin*, July 1952.

Stipanovich, Joseph. *The South Slavs in Utah: A Social History.* San Francisco: RUE Research Associates, 1975.

Sturgis, Helen. Quoted in Anderson, Lars, "A History of Education in San Juan School District." Master's thesis, University of Utah, 1952.

Swaniga, Paul. Interview with author, January 30, 1981, Colorado Springs, Colo. Country School Legacy Collection, Western Historical Collections, University of Colorado, Boulder.

Taylor, L. N. "Our Colored Schools." *Kentucky Progress Magazine*, August 1932.

Teeuwen, Randall. "Frontier Education and the Americanization of Germans from Russia." Unpublished manuscript, 1981. Country School Legacy Collection, Western Historical Collections, University of Colorado, Boulder.

Thernstrom, Stephan, ed. *Harvard Encyclopedia of America Ethnic Groups.* Cambridge, Mass.: Harvard University Press, 1980.

Thorson, Playford V., and Sherman, William C. "Education and Ethnicity: A Study of German-Russians and Norwegians in North Dakota." Unpublished manuscript, 1981. Country School Legacy Collection, University of North Dakota.

Tilley, Laina Laitala. Oral History Collection, Immigration History Research Center, University of Minnesota.

Vouk, Valentine. Interview with Joe Stipanovitch, February 13, 1973. Utah Minorities Oral History Project, Price, Utah.

Washington, Aletha H. "The American Problem of Rural Education." *Journal of Negro Education*, July 1936.

Washington, Booker T. *Up from Slavery.* New York: Houghton Mifflin, 1901.

Watson, Mildred. Letter to author, April 2, 1981, and manuscript. Country School Legacy Collection, Western Historical Collections, University of Colorado, Boulder.

## Country Schools Today

Adams, Paul. Interview with author, November 15, 1980, Montello, Nev. Country School Legacy Collection, Western Historical Collections, University of Colorado, Boulder.

Barker, Roger, and Gump, Paul. *Big School, Small School.* Palo Alto, Calif.: Stanford University Press, 1972.

Bertilson, Anna, and Dinsmore, Jamie. Interview with author, November 16, 1980, Ruby Valley School, Arthur Route, Wells, Nev. Country School Legacy Collection, Western Historical Collections, University of Colorado, Boulder.

Bettelheim, Bruno, and Hall, Elizabeth. "Our Children Are Treated Like Idiots." *Psychology Today*, July 1981.

Campbell, Eugene J. Interview with author, April 8, 1980, Denver, Colo.

Carstensen, Cheryl. Interview with Caroline Hatton, Fall 1980, Alfalfa Valley School. Country School Legacy Collection, University of South Dakota.

Chrouser, Donna M. "A Rural Teaching Experience: Dream or Nightmare." *Small School Forum*, Spring 1980.

Cramer, Marian. "The Four R's: Reading, 'Riting, 'Rithmetic, Rural." *Papers of the Twelfth Annual Dakota History Conference*, edited by H. W. Blakely. Madison, S.D.: Dakota State College, 1981.

Creigh, Dorothy Weyer. Letter to author, October 10, 1980. Country School Legacy

Collection, Western Historical Collections, University of Colorado, Boulder.

Fantini, Mario. Telephone conversation with author, April 21, 1984.

Gjelten, Tom. "Consolidating Rural Schools—Is Bigger Better?" *Country Journal*, September 1980.

"Help! Teacher Can't Teach." *Time*, June 16, 1980.

Hostetler, John A. *Amish Society*. Baltimore: John Hopkins University Press, 1980.

Jones, Trent, and Stowers, Carlton. *Where the Rainbows Wait*. New York: Playboy Press, Simon and Schuster, 1978.

Kearns, Sandy. Interview with author, November 18, 1980, Leonard Creek Ranch, Black Rock Desert, Nev. Country School Legacy Collection, Western Historical Collections, University of Colorado, Boulder.

Lasure, Joyce. "Hey! Just Look at Us Now." *PURE (People United for Rural Education) Newsletter*, July-August 1979.

Lilley, Shirley. Interview with author, November 2, 1980, Harmony School, Albany County, Wyo. Country School Legacy Collection, Western Historical Collections, University of Colorado, Boulder.

Montero, Frenchy. Interview with author, November 17, 1980, Leonard Creek Ranch, Black Rock Desert, Nev. Country School Legacy Collection, Western Historical Collections, University of Colorado, Boulder.

Muse, Ivan. Interview with author, November 13, 1980, Brigham Young University, Provo, Utah. Country School Legacy Collection, Western Historical Collections, University of Colorado, Boulder.

Nachtigal, Paul M. *Improving Rural Schools*. Washington, D.C.: National Institute of Education, 1980.

————. *Rural Education: In Search of a Better Way*. Boulder, Colo.: Westview Press, 1982.

National Education Association. *One-Teacher Schools Today*. Research Monograph 1960–MI. Washington, D.C.: Author, June 1960.

"Nebraska's One-Room Schools." *Denver Post*, September 11, 1983.

Olsen, Brent W. "One-Room Schools in Washington State." In *Your Public Schools*. Seattle: State Superintendent of Public Instruction, August 1983.

"One-Room School Barely Surrenders to Time." *Rocky Mountain News*, May 11, 1981.

"The One-Room Schools." *Newsweek*, February 5, 1979.

Parks, Gail, ed. "Thank God for Country Schools: A Long Look at Rural Education." *PTA Today*, December 1979–January 1980.

*The Rural Schoolhouse*. Americana Series. Erie, Pa.: Hammermill Paper Company, 1974.

Sher, Jonathan P. "A Proposal to End Federal Neglect of Rural Schools." *Phi Delta Kappan*, December 1978.

————, ed. *Rural Education in Urbanized Nations: Issues and Innovations*. Westview Special Studies in Education. Boulder, Colo.: Westview Press, 1981.

Smith, Sally L. *No Easy Answers: The Learning Disabled Child*. New York: Bantam Books, 1981.

Vogeler, Dan. Interview with author, December 3, 1980, Brown's Park School, Greystone, Colo. Country School Legacy Collection, Western Historical Collections, University of Colorado, Boulder.

Zelter, Alan. "Population Sparsity and Geographic Isolation as It Relates to Staff Recruitment and Retention." *National Rural Project Newsletter*, Second Special Edition, December 1980.

Zimmerman, Donald H. Letter to author, January 3, 1984. Country School Legacy Collection, Western Historical Collections, University of Colorado, Boulder.

## Country School Architecture

Alcott, William A. *Essay on the Construction of School-Houses*. Boston: Hilliard, Gray, Little, and Wilkinson, and Richardson, Lord and Holbrook, 1832.

Barnard, Henry. *School Architecture: Or, Contributions to the Improvement of School-Houses in the United States*. 1838. Reprint. Classics in Education No. 42, edited by Jean and Robert McClintock. New York: Teachers College Press, Columbia University, 1970.

Bloomquist, C. Ross. Unpublished manuscript, 1980. Country School Legacy Collection, University of North Dakota.

Bohling, Beth S., and Bayley, Marc. *And Cattle Ate the School*. Lincoln: Nebraska State Education Association, 1967.

Burrowes, Thomas Henry, ed. *Pennsylvania School Architecture*. Harrisburg, Pa.: A. B. Hamilton, 1855.

California State Department of Education. *Twelve Small California Schools*. Sacramento: Superintendent of Public Instruction, 1969.

Challman, S. A. *The Rural School Plant for Rural Teachers and School Boards, Normal Schools, Teachers' Training Classes, Rural Extension Bureaus*. Milwaukee: Bruce Publishing Company, 1917.

Cyr, Frank W., and Linn, Henry H. *Planning Rural Community School Buildings*. New York: Teachers College Press, Columbia University, 1949.

Dick, Everett. *The Sod-House Frontier 1854–1890*. 1937. Reprint. Lincoln: University of Nebraska Press, 1979.

Dresslar, Fletcher B. *American Schoolhouses*. Washington, D.C.: Government Printing Office, 1911.

———. *A Rural Schoolhouse and Grounds*. Bulletin No. 12, U.S. Office of Education. Washington, D.C.: Government Printing Office, 1914.

Dresslar, Fletcher B., and Pruett, Haskell. *Rural Schoolhouses, School Grounds and Their Equipment*. Bulletin No. 21. U.S. Office of Education. Washington, D.C.: Government Printing Office, 1930.

Dwyer, Charles P. *The Economy of Church, Parsonage and School Architecture Adapted to Small Societies and Rural Districts*. Buffalo: Phinney Company, 1856.

Eveleth, Samuel F. *School-House Architecture*. 1870. Reprinted as *Victorian School-House Architecture*, with a new introduction by John Crosby Freeman. Watkins Glen, N.Y.: American Life Foundation, 1978.

Federal Writers Project. *Schools and Their Builders*. Mitchell, S.D.: Author, 1939.

Fowler, Orson Squire. *A Home for All; Or, the Gravel Wall, and Octagon Mode of Building*. 1848. Reprint. New York: Fowler and Wells, 1854.

Fuller, Wayne E. "Country Schoolteaching on the Sod-House Frontier." *Arizona and the West*, Summer 1975.

Haight, Mrs. George. "Deer Creek School of Early Days." Unpublished manuscript. Madison County Historical Society, Madison, Neb.

Heath, Kingston. "A Dying Heritage: One-Room Schools of Gallatin County, Montana." In *Perspectives in Vernacular Architecture*, edited by Camille Wells. Annapolis, Md.: Vernacular Architecture Forum, 1982.

Husband, Michael L. "The Recollections of a Schoolteacher in Disappointment Creek Valley." *Colorado Magazine*, Spring 1974.

Jackson, John Brinckerhoff. *Discovering the Vernacular Landscape*. New Haven, Conn.: Yale University Press, 1984.

Johonnot, James. *Country School-Houses*. New York: Ivison and Phinney, 1859.

———. *School-Houses*. New York: J. W. Schermerhorn, 1871.

Ley, Mary, and Bryan, Mike, eds. *Journey from Ignorant Ridge*. Austin, Tex.: Texas Congress of Parents and Teachers, 1976.

Lyman, Lucreti. Quoted in Anderson, Lars, "A History of Education in San Juan School District." Master's thesis, University of Utah, 1952.

Marsh, Alice. "Fifty Years Ago in Currie, Nevada." Country School Legacy Collection, Western Historical Collections, University of Colorado, Boulder.

Minard, Jonathan S. "The Frontier Schoolhouse." *New York State Tradition,* Winter 1974.

Mohberg, Nora. Interview with author, July 17, 1980, Wahpeton, N.D. Country School Legacy Film Interviews Collection, Western Historical Collections, University of Colorado, Boulder.

National Trust for Historic Preservation, Tony P. Wrenn, Elizabeth D. Mulloy. *America's Forgotten Architecture*. New York: Pantheon Books, 1976.

Nebraska State Superintendent of Schools. 1871–72 report. Lincoln: Journal Company, State Printers, 1872.

Parker, R. L. *Rural Schoolhouses and Their Equipment*. Fort Hays Normal School Bulletin, June 1916.

Pioneer Women Educators of Wyoming. *Let Your Light Shine*. Sheridan, Wyo.: Delta

Kappa Gamma, 1965.

Poppeliers, John C., S. Allen Chambers and Nancy B. Schwartz, Historic American Buildings Survey. *What Style Is It? A Guide to American Architecture*. 1977. 2nd ed. Washington, D.C.: Preservation Press, 1984.

Potter, Alonzo, and Emerson, George B. *The School and the Schoolmaster*. New York: Harper and Brothers, 1842.

Salladay, Olive. Unpublished manuscript. Country School Legacy Collection, Western Historical Collections, University of Colorado, Boulder.

Schroeder, Fred E. H. "Educational Legacy: Rural One-Room Schoolhouses." *Historic Preservation*, July-September 1977.

———. "The Little Red Schoolhouse." In *Icons of America*, edited by Ray Browne and Marshall Fishwick. Bowling Green, Ohio: Popular Press, Bowling Green State University, 1978.

———. "Schoolhouse Reading: What You Can Learn from Your Rural School." *History News*, April 1981.

Second Biennial Report of the Superintendent of Public Instruction of the Territory of Colorado for the Two Years Ending September 30, 1873. Denver: William N. Byers, 1874.

Sloane, Eric. *The Little Red Schoolhouse*. Garden City, N.Y.: Doubleday and Company, 1972.

Stilgoe, John R. *Common Landscape of America, 1580–1845*. New Haven, Conn.: Yale University Press, 1982.

Swaim, Doug, ed. *Carolina Dwelling. Toward Preservation of Place: In Celebration of the North Carolina Vernacular Landscape*. Raleigh, N. C.: North Carolina State University School of Design, 1978.

Territorial Department of Education. "Designs and Specifications for New Mexico School Buildings." Albuquerque, N.M.: Territorial Printer, 1909.

Twombly, Robert C. *Frank Lloyd Wright: An Interpretive Biography*. New York: Harper and Row, 1973.

Welsch, Roger L. *Sod Walls: The Story of the Nebraska Sod House*. Broken Bow, Neb.: Purcells, 1968.

Whiffen, Marcus. *American Architecture Since 1780: A Guide to the Styles*. Cambridge, Mass.: MIT Press, 1969.

Wilder, Laura Ingalls. *These Happy Golden Years*. New York: Harper and Row, 1953.

Wilson, Gordon. "Traditional Aspects of the One-Roomed School." *Kentucky Folklore Record*, January-March 1967.

## Country School Preservation

Adams, John D. "Furnishing Craigflower Schoolhouse c. 1855–58." Victoria, British Columbia: Ministry of Provisional Secretary and Government Services, Heritage Conservation Branch, 1982.

Bearss, Edwin C. "Historic Structure Report, Junction School, Lyndon B. Johnson National Historic Site, Texas." Denver: National Park Service, U.S. Department of the Interior, 1975.

Brown, Lenard E. "Furnishing Study, Fruita Schoolhouse, Capitol Reef National Monument." Denver: National Park Service, U.S. Department of the Interior, 1969.

Brown, Lenard E., and Riddo, Renzo. "Historic Structure Report, Freeman School, Homestead National Monument, Nebraska." Denver: National Park Service, U.S. Department of the Interior, 1973.

Curtis, John Obed. *Moving Historic Buildings*. Washington, D.C.: Technical Preservation Services, U.S. Department of the Interior, 1979.

Dufresne, Mildred. *Grant Creek and Its One-Room Schoolhouse*. Missoula, Mont.: Gateway Printing, 1981.

Educational Facilities Laboratories. *Surplus School Space: Options and Opportunities*. New York: Author, 1976.

Fiala, Holly H. *Surplus Schools*. Information Series, No. 32. National Trust for Historic Preservation. Washington, D.C.: Preservation Press, 1982.

Gammon, Billie. "Living History Techniques and Activities." Livermore Falls, Maine: Washburn-Norlands Foundation, 1979.

————. "Norlands Schoolhouse." Livermore Falls, Maine: Washburn-Norlands Foundation, 1978.

Heath, Donna. "The One-Room Schoolhouse Is Reborn." *National Retired Teachers Association Journal*, January-February 1981.

Huyck, Heather. "Furnishing Plan for the Freeman School, Homestead National Monument." Beatrice, Neb.: National Park Service, U.S. Department of the Interior, 1973.

International Centre for Conservation and International Centre Committee, Advisory Council on Historic Preservation. *Preservation and Conservation: Principles and Practices.* Washington, D.C.: Preservation Press, 1976.

Iwen, Duane. "The Pioneer Classroom at Miller Park School." Omaha: Omaha Public Schools, 1980.

Jasperse, Linda. "Guide Manual: Educational Memorabilia Center." 1978. Rev. ed. Bowling Green, Ohio: Bowling Green State University, 1980.

Newark Museum Education Department. "The 1784 Schoolhouse: A Teacher's Guide." Newark, N.J.: Newark Museum, 1982.

Palmer, Peter. Telephone conversation with author, June 12, 1984.

Papa, Carrie. "Stones and Stories: An Oral History of the Old Monroe School." Hamburg, N.J.: Hardyston Heritage Society, 1980.

Parsons, Cynthia. "Living in a 105–Year-Old Vermont One-Room School." Unpublished manuscript. Country School Legacy Collection, Western Historical Collections, University of Colorado, Boulder.

Patterson, Charles. Letter to author, August 28, 1978. Country School Legacy Collection, Western Historical Collections, University of Colorado, Boulder.

Prill School Museum Association. "Prill School." Fulton County Historical Society Quarterly, July 1977.

Richter, Dennis M. "The Changing Role of the Section Line Schoolhouse." Paper given at the 1983 Pioneer America Annual Meeting, Western Illinois University, Macomb, Ill., October 7–8, 1983.

Salay, David L. "Summary Report, 1975 Student Project. Research Report: The Schoolhouse." Cooperstown, N.Y.: New York State Historical Association, 1975.

Schlereth, Thomas J. *Historic Houses as Learning Laboratories: Seven Teaching Strategies.* Technical Leaflet No. 105. Nashville: American Association for State and Local History, 1978.

Schroeder, Fred E. H. "The Little Red Schoolhouse." In *Icons of America,* edited by Ray Browne and Marshall Fishwick. Bowling Green, Ohio: Popular Press, Bowling Green State University, 1978.

Simonton, June. Letter to author, July 12, 1982. Country School Legacy Collection, Western Historical Collections, University of Colorado, Boulder.

Spencer, Steven M., ed. "Restoration Work Begins on the Little Red Schoolhouse." *News from Historic Hildene* (Manchester, Vt.), Spring 1982.

Technical Preservation Services Branch, U.S. Department of the Interior. Preservation Briefs Series, Nos. 1–12. Washington, D.C.: Author, 1975 to present.

————. *Respectful Rehabilitation: Answers to Your Questions About Old Buildings.* National Trust for Historic Preservation. Washington, D.C.: Preservation Press, 1982.

————. *The Secretary of the Interior's Standards for Rehabilitation, with Guidelines for Rehabilitating Historic Buildings.* Rev. ed. Washington, D.C.: U.S. Government Printing Office, 1983.

Winser, Beatrice. "The Old Stone Schoolhouse." *The Museum* (Newark, N.J.), June 1939.

# Sources of Information

American Association for
State and Local History
708 Berry Road
Nashville, Tenn. 37204

American Association of
School Administrators
Small Schools Committee
1801 North Moore Street
Arlington, Va. 22209

American Council on
Rural Special Education
Western Washington University
Bellingham, Wash. 98225

Clearinghouse on Rural Education and
Small Schools
ERIC/CRESS
Box 3AP
New Mexico State University
Las Cruces, N.M. 88003

History of Education Society
School of Education
New York University
737 East Building
Washington Square
New York, N.Y. 10003

National Center for Small Schools
Texas Tech University
College of Education
Box 4560
Lubbock, Tex. 79409

National Register of Historic Places
National Park Service
U.S. Department of the Interior
Washington, D.C. 20240

National Retired Teachers' Association
1909 K Street, N.W.
Washington, D.C. 20049

National Trust for Historic Preservation
1785 Massachusetts Avenue, N.W.
Washington, D.C. 20036

*Regional Offices*

Northeast Regional Office
45 School Street
Boston, Mass. 02110

Mid-Atlantic Regional Office
Cliveden
6401 Germantown Avenue
Philadelphia, Pa. 19144

Southern Regional Office
456 King Street
Charleston, S.C. 29403

Midwest Regional Office
407 South Dearborn Street
Suite 710
Chicago, Ill. 60605

Mountains/Plains Regional Office
1407 Larimer Street
Suite 200
Denver, Colo. 80202

Texas/New Mexico Field Office
500 Main Street
Suite 606
Fort Worth, Tex. 76102

Western Regional Office
One Sutter Street
San Francisco, Calif. 94104

Park Historic Architecture Division
National Park Service
U.S. Department of the Interior
Washington, D.C. 20240

Pioneer America Society
Pennsylvania State University
American Studies and Folklore
Capitol Campus
Middletown, Pa. 17057

Preservation Assistance Division
National Park Service
U.S. Department of the Interior
Washington, D.C. 20240

PURE (People United for
Rural America)
RR1, Box 3S
Kamrar, Iowa 50123

Rural Education Association
Colorado State University
Fort Collins, Colo. 80523

Vernacular Architecture Forum
c/o Orlando Ridout V
47 Fleet Street
Annapolis, Md. 21401

# Index of Schools

# Other Books from The Preservation Press

*America's City Halls*
William L. Lebovich, Historic American Buildings Survey. A lavish pictorial survey with 500 photographs of 114 historically and architecturally significant city halls, this is the first book to focus on this unique building type. 224 pages, illustrated, bibliography, appendixes, indexes. $18.95 paperbound.

*Fabrics for Historic Buildings*
Jane C. Nylander. 3rd edition. A popular guide that gives practical advice on selecting and using reproductions of historic fabrics. A key feature is an illustrated catalog listing 550 reproduction fabrics. Also included are a glossary and list of manufacturers. 160 pages, illustrated, bibliography. $9.95 paperbound.

*Wallpapers for Historic Buildings*
Richard C. Nylander. This compact handbook shows not only how to select authentic reproductions of historic wallpapers, but also where to buy more than 350 recommended patterns. Arranged according to historical period, this catalog is the first to aid everyone who seeks an appropriate wall covering for an old or historic building. Included are a glossary, reading list and manufacturers' addresses. 128 pages, illustrated, bibliography, appendixes. $9.95 paperbound.

*Respectful Rehabilitation: Answers to Your Questions About Old Buildings*
Technical Preservation Services, U.S. Department of the Interior. This book answers 150 questions property owners and residents ask about rehabilitating old houses and other historic buildings. The answers are based on the Secretary of the Interior's Standards for Rehabilitation, which are reprinted in full. Includes an extensive reading list, sources of information, photographs and 100 drawings. 192 pages, illustrated, bibliography, glossary, appendixes. $9.95 paperbound.

*What Style Is It? A Guide to American Architecture*
John Poppeliers, S. Allen Chambers, Nancy B. Schwartz, Historic American Buildings Survey. One of the most popular concise guides to American architectural styles, this has just been published in a new format designed for easy identification of buildings at home or on the road. Individual chapters on 22 of the most important styles provide a concise look at the history and appearance of each style. 112 pages, illustrated, glossary, bibliography. $6.95 paperbound.

To order Preservation Press books, send total of book prices (less 10 percent discount for National Trust members), plus $2.50 postage and handling, to: Preservation Bookshop, 1600 H Street, N.W., Washington, D.C. 20006. Residents of California, Massachusetts, New York and South Carolina please add applicable sales tax.